The Reformed Pastor

The Reformed Pastor

RICHARD BAXTER

EDITED BY WILLIAM BROWN

The Banner of Truth Trust

THE BANNER OF TRUTH TRUST
3 Murrayfield Road, Edinburgh EH12 6EL
P.O. Box 621, Carlisle, Pennsylvania 17013, USA

*

First published 1656
This abridged edition first published 1829
Fifth edition of abridgement published 1862
The Banner of Truth Trust edition reprinted
from the 1862 edition, 1974
Reprinted 1979
Reprinted 1983

ISBN 0 85151 191 0

*

Printed in Great Britain by
Hazell Watson & Viney Ltd,
Aylesbury, Bucks

THE REFORMED PASTOR

is *a most extraordinary* performance, and should be read by every young minister, before he takes a people under his stated care; and, I think, the practical part of it reviewed every three or four years; for nothing would have a greater tendency to awaken the spirit of a minister to that zeal in his work, for want of which many good men are but shadows of what (by the blessing of God) they might be, if the maxims and measures laid down in that *incomparable* Treatise were strenuously pursued.

Philip Doddridge

INTRODUCTION

Introduction

James I. Packer

'BAXTER, Richard, gentleman; born 12 November 1615, at Rowton, Salop; educated at Donnington Free School, Wroxeter, and privately; ordained deacon by Bishop of Worcester, Advent 1638; head of Richard Foley's School, Dudley, 1639; curate of Bridgnorth, 1639–40; lecturer (curate) of Kidderminster, 1641–42; army chaplain at Coventry, 1642–45, and with Whalley's regiment (New Model Army), 1645–47; vicar of Kidderminster, 1647–61; at Savoy Conference, 1661; lived privately in or near London, 1662–91 (Moorfields, 1662–63, Acton 1663–69, Totteridge 1669–73, Bloomsbury 1673–85, Finsbury 1686–91); married Margaret Charlton (1636–81), 1662; imprisoned for one week at Clerkenwell, 1669, for 21 months at Southwark, 1685–86; died 8 December 1691; author of *The Saints' Everlasting Rest* (1650), *The Reformed Pastor* (1656), *A Call to the Unconverted* (1658), *A Christian Directory* (1673), and 131 other items printed in his lifetime, also of *Reliquiae Baxterianae* (autobiography, ed M. Sylvester, 1696), five other posthumous books and many unpublished treatises; special interests, pastoral care, Christian unity; hobbies, medicine, science, history.' Thus in *Who's Who* style we present Richard Baxter, the most outstanding pastor, evangelist and writer on practical and devotional themes that Puritanism produced.

Baxter was a big man, big enough to have big faults and make big errors. A brilliant cross-bencher, widely learned, with an astounding capacity for instant analysis, argument and appeal, he could run rings round anyone in debate, yet he could not always use his great gifts in the best way. In theology, for instance, he devised an eclectic middle route between the Reformed, Arminian and Roman doctrines of grace: interpreting the kingdom of God in

10

INTRODUCTION

terms of contemporary political ideas, he explained Christ's death
as an act of universal redemption (penal and vicarious, but not
substitutionary), in virtue of which God has made a new law
offering pardon and amnesty to the penitent. Repentance and
faith, being obedience to this law, are the believer's personal saving
righteousness. Baxter, a Puritan conservative, saw this quaint
legalistic construction as focusing both the essential Puritan and
New Testament gospel and also common ground about grace
which the warring Trinitarian theologies of his day actually
occupied. Others, however, saw that 'Baxterianism' (or 'Neo-
nomianism', as it was called because of the 'new law' idea at its
heart) altered the content of the Puritan gospel,[1] while its 'political
method', if taken seriously, was objectionably rationalistic. Time
proved them right; the fruit of the seeds which Baxter sowed was
neonomian Moderatism in Scotland and moralistic Unitarianism in
England.[2]

Again, Baxter was a poor performer in public life. Though always
respected for his godliness and pastoral prowess, and always
seeking doctrinal and ecclesiastical peace, his combative, judg-
mental, pedagogic way of proceeding with his peers made failure
a foregone conclusion every time. Though he was for more than
twenty years the nonconformists' chief spokesman, and though the
comprehensivist ideal which he championed was statesmanlike,[3]

[1] On this, see J. I. Packer, 'The Doctrine of Justification in Development and
Decline among the Puritans', *By Schisms Rent Asunder* (1969 Puritan
Conference Report), London, 1970, pp 25–28; C. F. Allison, *The Rise of
Moralism*, London, 1966, pp 154 ff; William N. Kerr, 'Baxter and Baxterianism', *The Encyclopaedia of Christianity*, Vol I, Wilmington, 1964, pp 599 ff.
In his *Vindication of the Protestant Doctrine concerning Justification*, 1692,
Robert Traill singles out as basic flaws in Baxter's scheme, first, its failure to
come to terms with Christ's representative headship as set forth in Rom.
5.12 ff; second, its unreality, inasmuch as sinners find relief for their troubled
consciences not by looking to their faith and telling themselves it is their
saving righteousness, but by looking to the cross. John Macleod's comment
on Baxter's view is perfect: 'There might be said to be in this line of things
a zeal for good works and a jealousy lest Justification by faith only should
make void the law. It looked as if in the last resort Paul must be saved from
himself . . .' (*Scottish Theology*, Edinburgh, 1943, p 139).
[2] cf Macleod, *op cit*, p 111; Hywel Jones, 'The Death of Presbyterianism',
By Schisms Rent Asunder, p 37.
[3] On Baxter's ecclesiastical ideals, see Irvonwy Morgan, *The Nonconformity of
Richard Baxter*, London, 1946; A. Harold Wood, *Church Unity without
Uniformity*, London, 1963.

Baxter can hardly be called a statesman himself. Granting that his habit of total and immediate outspokenness ('plain dealing') in all matters concerning his ministry was conscientious and not just compensation for an inferiority complex (in fact, it was probably a bit of both), his lifelong inability to see that among equals a triumphalist manner is counter-productive was a strange blind spot. That (for instance) in 1669 he went to the great John Owen to be 'a seeker of peace' between Presbyterians and Independents, though Owen and he had in the past crossed swords theologically and politically, was typical and admirable; that on meeting Owen 'I told him that I must deal freely with him, that when I thought of what he had done formerly, I was much afraid lest one that had been so great a breaker would not be made an instrument of healing', though he was glad to see that in Owen's last book he gave up 'two of the worst of the principles of popularity', was also typical, though perhaps less admirable; that he was afterwards surprised, disappointed and hurt that Owen, while professing good will, took no action is surely remarkable.[4] Whether different behaviour or absence on Baxter's part could have altered the wretched run of events between Restoration (1660) and Toleration (1689) is doubtful, for passion, interest and distrust ran very high; the fact remains, however, that Baxter's interventions regularly deepened division, as when in 1690 he published *The Scripture Gospel Defended* to stop Crisp's sermons from causing trouble and thereby wrecked the 'Happy Union' between Presbyterians and Independents almost before it had begun.[5]

As a pastor, however, Baxter was incomparable, and it is in this capacity that he concerns us now.

His achievement at Kidderminster was amazing. England had not before seen a ministry like it. The town contained about 800 homes and 2000 people. They were 'an ignorant, rude and revelling people' when Baxter arrived, but this changed dramatically. 'When I first entered on my labours I took special notice of every one that was humbled, reformed or converted; but when I had laboured long,

---

[4] *Reliquiae Baxterianae (RB)*, Part III, *pp* 61 *ff*.
[5] *cf* Peter Toon, *The Emergence of Hyper-Calvinism in English Non-conformity 1689–1765*, London, 1967, Chapter 3; *Puritans and Calvinism*, Swengel, Pa., 1973, Chapter 6.

it pleased God that the converts were so many, that I could not afford time for such particular observations . . . families and considerable numbers at once . . . came in and grew up I scarce knew how.'[6] 'The congregation was usually full [the church held up to 1000], so that we were fain to build five galleries. . . . On the Lord's-days . . . you might hear an hundred families singing psalms and repeating sermons as you passed through the streets . . . when I came thither first there was about one family in a street that worshipped God and called on his name, and when I came away there were some streets where there was not past one family in the side of a street that did not so; and that did not by professing serious godliness, give us hope of their sincerity.'[7] Later Baxter could write: 'though I have now been absent from them about six years, and they have been assaulted with pulpit-calumnies, and slanders, with threatenings and imprisonments, with enticing words, and seducing reasonings, they yet stand fast and keep their integrity; many of them are gone to God, and some are removed, and some now in prison, and most still at home; but not one, that I hear of, are fallen off, or forsake their uprightness.'[8] When in December 1743, George Whitefield visited Kidderminster he wrote to a friend: 'I was greatly refreshed to find what a sweet savour of good Mr Baxter's doctrine, works and discipline remained to this day.'[9]

A schoolmaster by instinct, Baxter usually called himself his people's teacher, and teaching was to his mind the minister's main task. In his sermons (one each Sunday and Thursday, lasting an hour) he taught basic Christianity. 'The thing which I daily opened to them, and with greatest importunity laboured to imprint upon their minds, was the great fundamental principles of Christianity contained in their baptismal covenant, even a right knowledge, and belief of, and subjection and love to, God the Father, the Son, and the Holy Ghost, and love to all men, and concord with the church and one another. . . . The opening of the true and profitable method of the Creed (or doctrine of faith), the Lord's Prayer (or matter of our desires), and the Ten Command-

---

[6] *RB*, Part I, *p* 21.
[7] *p* 84 *f*.
[8] *p* 86.
[9] *Works*, London, 1771, II.47.

ments (or law of practice), which afford matter to add to the knowledge of most professors of religion, ⟨takes⟩ a long time. And when that is done they must be led on . . . but not so as to leave the weak behind; and so as shall still be truly subservient to the great points of faith, hope and love, holiness and unity, which must be still [i.e., always, constantly] inculcated, as the beginning and end of all.'[10] Such was Baxter's teaching programme in the pulpit. In addition, he held a weekly pastor's forum for discussion and prayer;[11] he distributed Bibles and Christian books (one-fifteenth of each edition of his own books came to him free in lieu of royalties for him to give away); and he taught individuals through personal counselling and catechizing. Christians, he urged, should regularly come to their pastor with their problems, and let him check their spiritual health,[12] and ministers should regularly catechize their entire congregations.[13] To upgrade the practice of personal catechizing from a preliminary discipline for children to a permanent ingredient in pastoral care for all ages was Baxter's main contribution to the development of Puritan ideals for the ministry; and it was his concern for catechizing that brought *The Reformed Pastor* to birth.

The members of the Worcestershire Association, the clerical fraternity of which Baxter was the moving spirit, had committed themselves to adopt the policy of systematic parochial catechizing, on Baxter's plan. They fixed a day of fasting and prayer, to seek God's blessing on the undertaking, and asked Baxter to preach. When the day came, however, Baxter was too ill to go; so he published the material he had prepared, a massive exposition and application of Acts 20.28. Because of his forthrightness in rebuking and exhorting his fellow-ministers, he called it *Gildas Salvianus*, after two writers of the fifth and sixth centuries who also had not been mealy-mouthed about sin. But on the title-page of the first

---

[10] *RB*, Part I, p 93 f.
[11] 'Every Thursday evening my neighbours met at my house, and there one of them repeated the sermon, and afterwards they proposed what doubts any of them had about the sermon, or any other case of conscience, and I resolved their doubts: and last of all I caused sometimes one, and sometimes another of them to pray' (*RB*, Part I, p 83).
[12] See below, pp 86 ff, 170 ff.
[13] Baxter describes his own practice in detail in pp 162 ff below.

edition[14] it is the word 'REFORMED' in the sub-title that stands out, being printed in bigger and bolder type than anything else, and this is surely how Baxter wanted it. By 'reformed' he means, not Calvinistic in doctrine, but renewed in practice. 'If God would but reform the ministry,' Baxter wrote, 'and set them on their duties zealously and faithfully, the people would certainly be reformed. All churches either rise or fall as the ministry doth rise or fall (not in riches or worldly grandeur) but in knowledge, zeal and ability for their work.'[15] It was the 'rise' of the ministry in this sense that Baxter sought.

The Reformed Pastor was, and is, dynamite, and it made its mark at once. 'O man greatly beloved!' wrote Thomas Wadsworth to Baxter in the month following publication, 'The Lord hath revealed his secret things to you, for which many a thousand souls in England, shall rise up and bless God for you.'[16] An anonymous undated letter in the Baxter correspondence says: 'Mr Baxter's Gildas Salvianus was extraordinary, for which book I am obliged to bless God and thank Mr Baxter and wish with all my heart all young ministers on their entrance to the ministry would diligently and frequently peruse it.'[17] Oliver Heywood's diary records: 'Some three or four years ago having a fit of sickness I read over Mr Baxter's Gildas Salvianus or Reformed Pastor and was so convinced and awakened therewith that I resolved, if I recovered, to set upon the work of personal instruction. . . . I set upon the work on the Tuesday after June 23, 1661, going from house to house. . . .'[18] 'I have very great cause to be thankful to God for the success of that book, as hoping many thousand souls are the better for it,' Baxter wrote about 1665, 'in that it prevailed with many ministers to set upon that work which I there exhort them to. Even from beyond the seas, I have had letters of request, to direct them. . . .'[19]

[14] Reproduced opposite *p* 51 of J. T. Wilkinson's edition of *The Reformed Pastor* (London, 1939).
[15] *RB*, Part I, *p* 115.
[16] See Wilkinson, *op cit*, *p* 27. I am indebted to Wilkinson's Introductory Essay for most of the citations which follow.
[17] *op cit*, *p* 30
[18] *The Rev Oliver Heywood, B.A.: His Autobiographies*, ed J. Horsfall Turner, Brighouse, 1882, I.177.
[19] *RB*, Part I, *p* 115.

Baxter died, but his book lived on. Testimonies from the eighteenth century make fascinating reading. John Wesley's father Samuel, once a nonconformist, wrote: 'I wish I had the *Gildas Salvianus* again: Directions to the Clergy for the management of their people, which I lost when my house was last burnt. . . . He (Baxter) had a strange pathos and fire. . . .'[20] John himself told the Methodist Conference: 'Every travelling preacher must instruct them from house to house. . . . Can we find a better method of doing this than Mr Baxter's? If not, let us adopt it without delay. His whole tract entitled *Gildas Salvianus*, is well worth a capable perusal.' On another occasion he challenged his preachers: 'Who visits the people on Mr Baxter's method?'[21] Charles Wesley and William Grimshaw of Haworth conversing together agreed that preachers should 'visit from house to house, after Mr Baxter's manner."[22] Philip Doddridge's commendation is quoted elsewhere.[23]

From those days to ours *The Reformed Pastor* has held its place as a classic. On 19 August 1810, Francis Asbury, the Methodist apostle of America, wrote in his diary: 'O what a prize: Baxter's *Reformed Pastor* fell into my hands this morning.'[24] John Angell James, minister of Carr's Lane, Birmingham, and author of *An Earnest Ministry the Want of the Times* (what a Baxterish sentiment!), wrote in 1859, a few hours before he died: 'I have made, next to the Bible, Baxter's *Reformed Pastor* my rule as regards the object of my ministry. It were well if that volume were often read by all our pastors.'[25] James himself often read it on Saturday evenings, to prepare himself for Sunday, and Spurgeon used frequently to have his wife read it to him on Sunday evenings, when the day's preaching was done.[26] To Methodist, Congregationalist and Baptist praise, Anglican can be added. The first printing of William Brown's edition of the work, here reprinted, came out in 1830 with a preface from Daniel Wilson of Islington,

[20] Cited from Wilkinson, *p* 38.
[21] Cited from Wilkinson, *pp* 39 f.
[22] Thomas Jackson, *Life of Charles Wesley*, London, 1841, Vol II, *pp* 119 f.
[23] See *p* 5.
[24] Cited from Wilkinson, *p* 42.
[25] Cited from Wilkinson, *p* 44.
[26] *C. H. Spurgeon: The Early Years*, London 1962, *p* 417.

declaring *The Reformed Pastor* to be 'one of the best of Baxter's invaluable treatises. In the whole compass of divinity, there is scarcely anything superior to it, in close, pathetic appeals to the conscience of the minister of Christ, upon the primary duties of his office.' And in 1925 the then Bishop of Durham (H. Hensley Henson) declared: '*The Reformed Pastor* is the best manual of the clergyman's duty in the language, because it leaves on the reader's mind an ineffaceable impression of the sublimity and awfulness of spiritual ministry.'[27]

Has Baxter's book a ministry to ministers today? Three qualities which mark it justify the answer 'yes'. The first is its *energy*. What has been said of Luther's *Bondage of the Will* can also be said of *The Reformed Pastor*: its words have hands and feet. Sylvester says that Baxter had a piercing eye; certainly he had piercing words. He wrote as he spoke, and his words were, not emotional, since they came from the head, but passionate, for they came from the heart as well as the head. His book blazes with white-hot zeal, evangelistic fervour, and eagerness to convince. 'Richard Baxter is the most forceful of writers,' said Spurgeon; 'if you want to know the art of pleading, read . . . his *Reformed Pastor*.'[28] As *The Saints' Everlasting Rest* is the supreme transcript of Baxter's heart as a Christian, so *The Reformed Pastor* is the supreme transcript of his heart as a minister. And what comes from Baxter's passionate heart has energy and evocative power, and can still go to the heart across a three-centuries gap.

Then, second, the book has *reality*. It is honest and straight. It is often said, quite fairly, that any Christian who seriously thinks that without Christ men are lost, and who seriously loves his neighbour, will not be able to rest for the thought that all around him people are going to hell, but will lay himself out unstintingly to convert others as his prime task in life; and any Christian who fails so to live undermines the credibility of his faith, for if he cannot himself take it seriously as a guide for living, why should anyone else? Nowhere is this inconsistency more forcefully exposed than in *The Reformed Pastor*: for here we meet a passionate love and a terribly honest, earnest, straightforward Christian,

---

[27] Cited from Wilkinson, *p* 47.
[28] Cited from Wilkinson, *p* 45.

thinking and talking about the lost with perfect realism, insisting that we must be content to accept any degree of discomfort, poverty, overwork, and loss of material good, if only souls might be saved, and setting us a marvellously vivid example in his own person of what this may involve.

When one knows one is going to be hanged, said Dr Johnson, it concentrates the mind wonderfully; and when, like Baxter from the time of his majority, one lives with one foot in the grave, it imparts an overwhelming clarity both to one's sense of proportion (what matters, and what does not), and also to one's perception of what is and is not consistent with what one professes to believe. 'O sirs,' cries the vicar of Kidderminster to his ministerial brethren, 'surely if you had all conversed with neighbour Death as oft as I have done, and as often received the sentence in yourselves, you would have an unquiet conscience, if not a reformed life, as to your ministerial diligence and fidelity: and you would have something within you that would frequently ask you such questions as these: "Is this all thy compassion for lost sinners? Wilt thou do no more to seek and to save them? . . . Shall they die and be in hell before thou wilt speak to them one serious word to prevent it? shall they there curse thee for ever that thou didst no more in time to save them?" Such cries of conscience are daily ringing in my ears, though, the Lord knows, I have too little obeyed them. . . . How can you choose, when you are laying a corpse in the grave, but think with yourselves, "Here lieth the body; but where is the soul? and what have I done for it, before it departed? It was part of my charge; what account can I give of it?" O sirs, is it a small matter to you to answer such questions as these? It may seem so now, but the hour is coming when it will not seem so. . . .'[29] Nobody can say that Baxter was not real; and who will question our need of such reality today, and in the ministry most of all?

Third, the book is a model of *rationality*. Baxter is utterly thorough in working out means to his end. Like Whitefield and Spurgeon, he knew that men are blind, deaf and dead in sin, and only God can convert them; but, again like Whitefield and Spurgeon, he knew too that God works through means, and that rational men must be approached in rational fashion, and that grace

[29] See below, *p* 194 *f.*

enters by the understanding, and that unless all the evangelist does makes for credibility his message is not likely to be used much to convince. So Baxter insisted that ministers must preach of eternal issues as men who feel what they say, and are as earnest as matters of life and death require; that they must practise church discipline, to show they are serious in saying that God will not accept sin; and that they must do 'personal work', and deal with individuals one by one, because preaching alone often fails to bring things home to ordinary people. Baxter was very frank on this. 'Let them that have taken most pains in public, examine their people, and try whether many of them are not nearly as ignorant and careless as if they had never heard the gospel. For my part, I study to speak as plainly and movingly as I can . . . and yet I frequently meet with those that have been my hearers eight or ten years, who know not whether Christ be God or man, and wonder when I tell them the history of his birth and life and death as if they had never heard it before. . . . But most of them have an ungrounded trust in Christ, hoping that he will pardon, justify and save them, while the world hath their hearts, and they live to the flesh. And this trust they take for justifying faith. I have found by experience, that some ignorant persons, who have been so long unprofitable hearers, have got more knowledge and remorse in half an hour's close discourse, than they did from ten years' public preaching. I know that preaching the gospel publicly is the most excellent means, because we speak to many at once. But it is usually far more effectual to preach it privately to a particular sinner. . . .'[30] Therefore personal catechizing and counselling, over and above preaching, is every minister's duty: for this is the most rational course, the best means to the desired end. So it was in Baxter's day. Is it not so now?

The Reformed Pastor faces the modern minister with at least these questions. (1) Do I believe the gospel Baxter believed (and Whitefield, and Spurgeon, and Paul)? (2) Do I then share Baxter's view of the vital necessity of conversion? (3) Am I then as real as I should be in letting this view of things shape my life and work? (4) Am I as rational as I should be in choosing means to the end I desire, and am charged to seek? Have I set myself, as Baxter set

[30] See below, *p* 186 *f.*

himself, to find the best way of creating situations in which I can talk to my people personally, on a regular basis, about their spiritual lives? How to do this today would have to be worked out in terms of present circumstances, which are very different from those Baxter knew and describes;[31] but Baxter's question to us is, should we not be attempting this, as a practice constantly necessary? If he convinces us that we should, it will not be beyond us to find a method of doing it that suits our situation; where there's a will, there's a way! So now we had better close this introduction, and leave Baxter to speak for himself.

[31] See below, *p* 173 *ff*, *cf pp* 221–246.

PREFACE

Preface
William Brown

OF this work as published by the Author, the following was the title: *'Gildas Salvianus:* The Reformed Pastor, showing the nature of the Pastoral work; especially in Private Instruction and Catechizing; with an open CONFESSION of our too open SINS: Prepared for a Day of Humiliation kept at Worcester, December 4, 1655, by the Ministers of that County, who subscribed the Agreement for Catechizing and Personal Instruction at their entrance upon that work, By their unworthy fellow Servant, *Richard Baxter,* Teacher of the Church at Kederminster.'

Of the excellence of this work, it is scarcely possible to speak in too high terms. It is not a directory relative to the various parts of the ministerial office, and in this respect it may, by some, be considered as defective; but, for powerful, pathetic, pungent, heart-piercing address, we know of no work on the pastoral office to be compared with it. Could we suppose it to be read by an angel, or by some other being possessed of an unfallen nature, the reasonings and expostulations of our author would be felt to be altogether irresistible; and hard must be the heart of that minister, who can read it without being moved, melted, and overwhelmed, under a sense of his own shortcomings; hard must be his heart, if he be not roused to greater faithfulness, diligence, and activity in winning souls to Christ. It is a work worthy of being printed in letters of gold: it deserves, at least, to be engraven on the heart of every minister.

But, with all its excellencies, the 'REFORMED PASTOR', as originally published by our author, labours under considerable defects, especially as regards its usefulness in the present day.

With the view of remedying the imperfections of the original work, the Rev Samuel Palmer, of Hackney, published, in 1766, an Abridgement of it; but though it was scarcely possible to present the work in any form, without furnishing powerful and impressive appeals to the consciences of ministers, he essentially failed in presenting it in an improved form. In fact, the work in its original state was, with all its faults, greatly to be preferred to Palmer's abridgement of it: if the latter was freed from some of its defects, it also lost much of its excellence. We may often, with advantage, throw out extraneous matter from the writings of Baxter; but there are few men's works which less admit of abridgement. This sacrifices their fulness and richness of illustration, enervates their energy, and evaporates their power and pathos.

The work which is now presented to the public, is not, strictly speaking, an abridgement. Though considerably less than the original, it has been reduced in size, chiefly by the omission of extraneous and controversial matter, which, however useful it might be when the work was originally published, is for the most part inapplicable to the circumstances of the present age. I have also in some instances changed the order of particular parts. The 'Motives to the Oversight of the Flock,' which our author had placed in his Application, I have introduced in that part of the discourse to which they refer, just as we have 'Motives to the Over-sight of Ourselves,' in the preceding part of the treatise. Some of the particulars which he has under the head of Motives, I have introduced in other parts of the body of the discourse, to which they appeared more naturally to belong. But though I have used some freedom in the way of transposition, I have been anxious not to sacrifice the force and fulness of our author's illustrations to mere logical arrangement. Many of the same topics, for instance, are still retained in the Application, which had occurred in the body of the discourse, and are there touched with a master's hand, but which would have lost much of their appropriateness and energy, had I separated them from that particular connection in which they stand, and introduced them in a different part of the work. I have also corrected the language of our author; but I have been solicitous not to modernize it. Though to adopt the phraseology and forms of speech employed by the writers of that age, would be a piece of silly affectation in an author of the present day, yet there is something simple, venerable, and impressive in it, as used by the writers themselves.

While, however, I have made these changes from the original, I trust I have not injured, but on the contrary, improved the work; that the spirit of its great author is so much preserved, that those who are most familiar with his writings would scarcely be sensible of the alterations I have made, had I not stated them in this place.

Before I conclude, I cannot help suggesting to the friends of religion, that they could not perhaps do more good at less expense, than by presenting copies of this work to the ministers of Christ throughout the country. There is no class of the community on whom the prosperity of the church of Christ so much depends as on its ministers. If their zeal and activity languish, the interests of religion are likely to languish in proportion; while, on the other hand, whatever is calculated to stimulate their zeal and activity, is likely to promote, in a proportional degree, the interests of religion. They are the chief instruments through whom good is to be effected in any country. How important, then, must it be to stir them up to holy zeal and activity in the cause of the Redeemer! A tract given to a poor man may be the means of his conversion; but a work such as this, presented to a minister, may, through his increased faithfulness and energy, prove the conversion of multitudes. Ministers themselves are not perhaps sufficiently disposed to purchase works of this kind: they are more ready to purchase books which will *assist* them, than such as will *stimulate* them in their work. If, therefore, any plan could be devised for presenting a copy of it to every minister of the various denominations throughout the United Kingdom, what incalculable good might be effected! There are many individuals to whom it would be no great burden to purchase twenty, fifty, or a hundred copies of such a work as this, and to send it to ministers in different parts of the country; or several individuals might unite together for this purpose. I can scarcely conceive any way in which they would be likely to be more useful.

To the different Missionary Societies, I trust I may be allowed to make a similar suggestion. To furnish every missionary, or at least every Missionary Station, with a copy of the REFORMED PASTOR, would, I doubt not, be a powerful mean of promoting the grand object of Christian Missions. Sure I am of this, there is no work so much calculated to stimulate a missionary to holy zeal and activity in his evangelistic labours.

Edinburgh
12 *March* 1829

Contents

CHAPTER II

The oversight of the flock   87

Section 1

The nature of this oversight   87

THIS OVERSIGHT EXTENDS TO ALL THE FLOCK

Section 2

The manner of this oversight   111

THE MINISTERIAL WORK MUST BE CARRIED ON

Section 3

The motives to this oversight   124

CHAPTER III

Application   133

Section 1

The use of humiliation   133

Section 2

The duty of personal catechizing and instructing
the flock particularly recommended

PART I: MOTIVES TO THIS DUTY

ARTICLE I

Motives from the benefits of the work

ARTICLE I

ARTICLE 2

DEDICATION

Dedication

To my reverend and dearly-beloved brethren, the faithful ministers of Christ, in Britain and Ireland, Grace and Peace in Jesus Christ be increased.

REVEREND BRETHREN,

The subject of this treatise so nearly concerneth yourselves, and the churches committed to your care, that it emboldeneth me to this address, notwithstanding the imperfections in the manner of handling it, and the consciousness of my great unworthiness to be your monitor.

Before I come to my principal errand, I shall give you an account of the reasons of the following work, and of the freedom of speech I have used, which to some may be displeasing.

When the Lord had awakened his ministers in the county of Worcestershire, and some neighbouring parts, to a sense of their duty in the work of catechizing, and private instruction of all in their parishes who would not obstinately refuse their help, and when they had subscribed an agreement, containing their resolutions for the future performance of it, they judged it unmeet to enter upon the work, without a solemn humbling of their souls before the Lord, for their long neglect of so great and necessary a duty; and, therefore, they agreed to meet together at Worcester, December 4, 1655, and there to join in humiliation and in earnest prayer to God, for the pardon of our neglects, and for his special assistance in the work which we had undertaken, and for the success of it with the people whom we had engaged to instruct; at which time, among others, I was desired by them to preach. In compliance with their wishes, I prepared the following Discourse; which, though it proved longer than could be delivered in one or two sermons, yet I intended to have entered upon it at that time, and to have delivered that which was most pertinent to the occasion, and to have reserved the rest to another season. But, before the meeting, by the increase of my ordinary pain and weakness, I was disabled from going thither; to recompense which unwilling omission, I easily yielded to the request of divers of the brethren, forthwith to publish the things which I had prepared, that they might read that which they could not hear.

If it be objected, that I should not have spoken so plainly and sharply against the sins of the ministry, or that I should not have published it to the view of the world; or, at least, that I should have done it in another tongue, and not in the ears of the vulgar; especially, at such a time, when Quakers and Papists are endeavouring to bring the ministry into contempt, and the people are too prone to hearken to their suggestions – I confess I thought the objection very considerable; but that it prevailed not to alter my resolution, is to be ascribed, among others, to the following reasons:

1. It was a proposed solemn humiliation that we agreed on, and that this was prepared and intended for. And how should we be humbled without a plain confession of our sin?

2. It was principally our own sins that the confession did concern; and who can be offended with us for confessing our own sins, and taking the blame and shame to ourselves, which our consciences told us we ought to do?

3. Having necessarily prepared it in the English tongue, I had no spare time to translate it into Latin.

4. When the sin is open in the sight of the world, it is vain to attempt to hide it; all such attempts will but aggravate and increase our shame.

5. A free confession is a condition of a full remission; and when the sin is public, the confession should also be public. If the ministers of England had sinned only in Latin, I would have made shift to admonish them in Latin, or else have said nothing to them. But if they will sin in English, they must hear

of it in English. Unpardoned sin will never let us rest or prosper, though we be at ever so much care and cost to cover it: our sin will surely find us out, though we find not it out. The work of confession is purposely to make known our sin, and freely to take the shame to ourselves; and if 'he that confesseth and forsaketh his sins shall have mercy,' no wonder if 'he that covereth them shall not prosper.' If we be so tender of ourselves, and so loath to confess, God will be the less tender of us, and he will indite our confessions for us. He will either force our consciences to confession, or his judgments shall proclaim our iniquities to the world.

6. Too many who have undertaken the work of the ministry do so obstinately proceed in self-seeking, negligence, pride, and other sins, that it is become our necessary duty to admonish them. If we saw that such would reform without reproof, we would gladly forbear the publishing of their faults. But when reproofs themselves prove so ineffectual, that they are more offended at the reproof than at the sin, and had rather that we should cease reproving than that themselves should cease sinning, I think it is time to sharpen the remedy. For what else should we do? To give up our brethren as incurable were cruelty, as long as there are further means to be used. We must not hate them, but plainly rebuke them, and not suffer sin upon them. To bear with the vices of the ministry is to promote the ruin of the Church; for what speedier way is there for the depraving and undoing of the people, than the depravity of their guides? And how can we more effectually further a reformation, than by endeavouring to reform the leaders of the Church? For my part, I have done as I would be done by; and it is for the safety of the Church, and in tender love to the brethren, whom I venture to reprehend – not to make them contemptible and odious, but to heal the evils that would make them so – that so no enemy may find this matter of reproach among us. But, especially, because our faithful endeavours are of so great necessity to the welfare of the Church, and the saving of men's souls, that it will not consist with a love to either, to be negligent ourselves, or silently to connive at negligence in others. If

thousands of you were in a leaking ship, and those that should pump out the water, and stop the leaks, should be sporting or asleep, or even but favouring themselves in their labours, to the hazarding of you all, would you not awaken them to their work and call on them to labour as for your lives? And if you used some sharpness and importunity with the slothful, would you think that man was in his wits who would take it ill of you, and accuse you of pride, self-conceitedness, or unmannerliness, to presume to talk so saucily to your fellow-workmen, or that should tell you that you wrong them by diminishing their reputation? Would you not say, 'The work must be done, or we are all dead men. Is the ship ready to sink, and do you talk of reputation? or had you rather hazard yourself and us, than hear of your sloth-fulness?' This is our case, brethren. The work of God must needs be done! Souls must not perish, while you mind your worldly business or worldly pleasure, and take your ease, or quarrel with your brethren! Nor must we be silent while men are hastened by you to perdition, and the Church brought into greater danger and confusion, for fear of seeming too uncivil and unmannerly with you, or displeasing your impatient souls! Would you be but as impatient with your sins as with our reproofs, you should hear no more from us, but we should be all agreed! But, neither God nor good men will let you alone in such sins. Yet if you had betaken yourselves to another calling, and would sin to yourselves only, and would perish alone, we should not have so much necessity of molest-ing you, as now we have: but if you will enter into the office of the ministry, which is for the necessary preservation of us all, so that by letting you alone in your sin, we must give up the Church to loss and hazard, blame us not if we talk to you more freely than you would have us to do. If your own body were sick, and you will despise the remedy, or if your own house were on fire, and you will be singing or quarrelling in the streets, I could possibly bear it, and let you alone, (which yet, in charity, I should not easily do,) but, if you will under-take to be the physician of an hospital, or to a whole town that is infected with the plague, or will undertake to quench all the fires that shall be kindled in the town, there is no bearing with your remissness, how much soever it may displease you. Take it how you will, you must be told of it; and if that will not serve, you must be told of it yet more plainly; and, if that will not serve, if you be rejected as well as reprehended, you may thank yourselves. I speak all this to none but the guilty.

And, thus, I have given you those reasons which forced me to publish, in plain English, so much of the sins of the ministry as in the following Treatise I have done. And I suppose the more penitent and humble any are, and the more desirous of the true reformation of the Church, the more easily and fully will they approve such free confessions and reprehensions. But I find it will be impossible to avoid offending those who are at once guilty and impenitent; for there is no way of avoiding this, but by our silence, or their patience: and silent we cannot be, because of God's commands; and patient they will not be, because of their guilt and impenitence. But plain dealers will always be approved in the end; and the time is at hand when you will confess that they were your best friends.

But my principal business is yet behind. I must now take the boldness, brethren, to become your monitor, concerning some of the necessary duties, of which I have spoken in the ensuing discourse. If any of you should charge me with arrogance or immodesty for this attempt, as if hereby I accused you of negligence, or judged myself sufficient to admonish you, I crave your candid interpretation of my boldness, assuring you that I obey not the counsel of my flesh herein, but displease myself as much as some of you; and would rather have the ease and peace of silence, if it would stand with my duty, and the churches' good. But it is the mere necessity of the souls of men, and my desire of their salvation, and of the prosperity of the Church, which forceth me to this arrogance and immodesty, if so it must be called. For who, that hath a tongue, can be silent, when it is for the honour of God, the welfare of his Church, and the everlasting happiness of so many souls?

The *first*, and main point, which I have to propound to you,

is this, Whether it be not the unquestionable duty of the
generality of ministers of these three nations, to set themselves
presently to the work of catechizing, and instructing individually, all that are committed to their care, who will be persuaded to submit thereunto? I need not here stand to prove it,
having sufficiently done this in the following discourse. Can
you think that holy wisdom will gainsay it? Will zeal for
God; will delight in his service, or love to the souls of men,
gainsay it?

1. That people must be taught the principles of religion, and
matters of greatest necessity to salvation, is past doubt
among us.

2. That they must be taught it in the most edifying, ad-
vantageous way, I hope we are agreed.

3. That personal conference, and examination, and instruction, hath many excellent advantages for their good, is no less
beyond dispute.

4. That personal instruction is recommended to us by Scripture, and by the practice of the servants of Christ, and
approved by the godly of all ages, is, so far as I can find,
without contradiction.

5. It is past doubt, that we should perform this great duty to
all the people, or as many as we can; for our love and care of
their souls must extend to all. If there are five hundred or a
thousand ignorant people in your parish or congregation, it is
a poor discharge of your duty, now and then to speak to
some few of them, and to let the rest alone in their ignorance,
if you are able to afford them help.

6. It is no less certain, that so great a work as this is should
take up a considerable part of our time. Lastly, it is equally
certain that all duties should be done in order, as far as may
be, and therefore should have their appointed times. And if we
are agreed to practise, according to these commonly acknowledged truths, we need not differ upon any doubtful circumstances.

I do now, in the behalf of Christ, and for the sake of his
Church, and the immortal souls of men, beseech all the
faithful ministers of Christ, that they will presently and

effectually fall upon this work. Combine for the unanimous performance of it, that it may more easily procure the submission of your people. I must confess, I find, by some experience, that this is the work that, through the grace of God, which worketh by means, must reform indeed; that must expel our common prevailing ignorance; that must bow the stubborn hearts of sinners; that must answer their vain objections, and take off their prejudices; that must reconcile their hearts to faithful ministers, and help on the success of our public preaching; and make true godliness a commoner thing than it has hitherto been. I find that we never took the best course for demolishing the kingdom of darkness, till now. I wonder at myself, how I was so long kept off from so clear and excellent a duty. But the case was with me, as I suppose it is with others. I was long convinced of it, but my apprehensions of the difficulties were too great, and my apprehensions of the duty too small, and so I was long hindered from the performance of it. I imagined the people would scorn it, and none but a few, who had least need, would submit to it, and I thought my strength would never go through with it, having so great burdens on me before; and thus I long delayed it, which I beseech the Lord of mercy to forgive. Whereas, upon trial, I find the difficulties almost nothing (save only through my extraordinary bodily weakness) to that which I imagined; and I find the benefits and comforts of the work to be such, that I would not wish I had forborne it, for all the riches in the world. We spend Monday and Tuesday, from morning almost to night, in the work, taking about fifteen or sixteen families in a week, that we may go through the parish, in which there are upwards of eight hundred families, in a year; and I cannot say yet that one family hath refused to come to me, and but few persons excused themselves, and shifted it off. And I find more outward signs of success with most that do come, than from all my public preaching to them. If you say, It is not so in most places, I answer, I wish that the blame of this may not lie much with ourselves. If, however, some refuse your help, that will not excuse you for not affording it to them that would accept of it. If you ask me what course I take for order and expedition, I may here mention, that, at the delivery of the Catechisms, I take a catalogue of all the persons of understanding in the parish, and the clerk goeth a week before, to every family, to tell them what day to come, and at what hour, (one family at eight o'clock, the next at nine, and the next at ten, &c.) And I am forced by the number to deal with a whole family at once; but ordinarily I admit not any of another family to be present.

Brethren, do I now invite you to this work, without the authority of God, without the consent of all antiquity, without the consent of the Reformed Divines, or without the conviction of your own consciences? See what the Westminster Assembly speak occasionally in the Directory, about the visitation of the sick: 'It is the duty of the minister not only to teach the people committed to his charge in public, but privately, and particularly to admonish, exhort, reprove, and comfort them upon all seasonable occasions, so far as his time, strength, and personal safety will permit. He is to admonish them in time of health to prepare for death. And for that purpose, they are often to confer with their minister about the estate of their souls,' &c. Read this over again, and consider it. Hearken to God, if you would have peace with God. Hearken to conscience, if you would have peace of conscience. I am resolved to deal plainly with you, though I should displease you. It is an unlikely thing that there should be a heart sincerely devoted to God in that man, who, after advertisements and exhortations, will not resolve on so clear and great a duty. I cannot conceive that he who hath one spark of saving grace, and so hath that love to God, and delight to do his will, which is in all the sanctified, could possibly be drawn to oppose or refuse such a work as this; except under the power of such a temptation as Peter was, when he denied Christ, or when he dissuaded him from suffering, and heard a half excommunication, 'Get thee behind me, Satan; thou art an offence unto me: for thou savourest not the things that be of God, but those that be of men.' You have put your hand to the plough; you are doubly devoted to him, as Christians, and as pastors; and dare you, after this, draw back, and refuse his work? You see the work of reformation at a stand; and you are engaged by many obligations to promote it: and dare you now neglect the means by which it must be done? Will you show your faces in a Christian congregation, as ministers of the gospel, and there pray for a reformation, and for the conversion and salvation of your hearers, and for the prosperity of the Church; and when you have done, refuse to use the means by which all this must be effected? I know carnal wit will never want words and show of reason, to gainsay that truth and duty which it abhors. It is easier now to cavil against duty than to perform it: but wait the end, before you pass your final judgment. Can you make yourselves believe that you will have a comfortable review of these neglects, or make a comfortable account of them to God? I dare prognosticate, from the knowledge of the nature of grace, that all the godly ministers in England will make conscience of this duty, and address themselves to it, except those who, by some extraordinary accident, are disabled, or who are under such temptations as aforesaid. I do not hopelessly persuade you to it, but take it for granted that it will be done. And if any lazy, or jealous, or malicious hypocrites, do cavil against it, or hold off, the rest will not do so; but they will take the opportunity, and not resist the warnings of the Lord. And God will uncase the hypocrites ere long, and make them know, to their sorrow, what it was to trifle with him. Woe to them, when they must account for the blood of souls! The reasons which satisfied them here against duty, will not then satisfy them against duty; but will be manifested to have been the effects of their folly, and to have proceeded radically from their corrupted wills, and carnal interest. Nor will their consciences own those reasons at a dying hour, which now they seem to own. Then they shall feel to their sorrow, that there is not that comfort to be had for a departing soul, in the review of such neglected duty, as there is to them that have wholly devoted themselves to the service of the Lord. I AM SURE MY ARGUMENTS FOR THIS DUTY WILL APPEAR STRONGEST AT THE LAST, WHEN THEY SHALL BE VIEWED AT THE HOUR OF DEATH, AT THE DAY OF

JUDGMENT, AND, ESPECIALLY, IN THE LIGHT OF
ETERNITY.

And now, brethren, I earnestly beseech you, in the name of
God, and for the sake of your people's souls, that you will
not slightly slubber over this work, but do it vigorously, and
with all your might; and make it your great and serious
business. Much judgment is required for the managing of it.
Study, therefore, beforehand, how to do it, as you study for
your sermons. I remember how earnest I was with some of the
last parliament, that they would settle catechists in our
assemblies; but truly I am not sorry that it took not effect,
unless for a few of the larger congregations. For I perceive,
that all the life of the work, under God, doth lie in the
prudent effectual management of it, in searching men's
hearts, and setting home the truth to their consciences; and
the ablest minister is weak enough for this, and few of inferior parts would be found competent to it. For I fear nothing
more, than that many ministers, who preach well, will be
found but imperfectly qualified for this work, especially to
manage it with old, ignorant, dead-hearted sinners. And,
indeed, if the ministers be not reverenced by the people, they
will rather slight them, and contest with them, than humbly
learn and submit to them: how much more would they do so
by inferior men? Seeing, then, the work is cast upon us, and
it is we that must do it, or else it must be undone, let us be up
and doing with all our might. When you are speaking to your
people, do it with the greatest prudence and seriousness, and
be as earnest with them as for life or death; and follow it as
closely as you do your public exhortations in the pulpit. I
profess again, it is to me the most comfortable work, except
public preaching, (for there I speak to more, though yet with
less advantage to each individual,) that ever I yet did set my
hand to. And I doubt not but you will find it so too, if you
only perform it faithfully.

My *second* request to the ministers in these kingdoms, is,
that they would at last, without any more delay, unanimously
set themselves to the practice of those parts of Church
discipline which are unquestionably necessary, and part of

their work. It is a sad case, that good men should settle themselves so long in the constant neglect of so great a duty. The common cry is, 'Our people are not ready for it; they will not bear it.' But is not the fact rather, that you will not bear the trouble and hatred which it will occasion? If indeed, you proclaim our churches incapable of the order and government of Christ, what do you but give up the cause to them that withdraw from us, and encourage men to look out for better societies, where that discipline may be had? For though preaching and sacraments may be omitted in some cases, till a fitter season, and accordingly so may discipline; yet it is a hard case to settle in a constant neglect, for so many years together, as we have done, unless there were an absolute impossibility of the work. And if it were so, because of our incapable materials, it would plainly call us to alter our constitution, that the matter may be capable. I have spoken plainly afterwards of this, which I hope you will conscientiously consider of. I now only beseech you, if you would give a comfortable account to the chief Shepherd, and would not be found unfaithful in the house of God, that you do not wilfully or negligently delay it, as if it were a needless thing; nor shrink from it, because of the trouble to the flesh that doth attend it; for as that is a sad sign of hypocrisy, so the costliest duties are usually the most comfortable; and you may be sure that Christ will bear the cost.

My *last* request is, that all the faithful ministers of Christ would, without any more delay, unite and associate for the furtherance of each other in the work of the Lord, and the maintaining of unity and concord in his churches. And that they would not neglect their brotherly meetings to those ends, nor yet spend them unprofitably, but improve them to their edification, and the effectual carrying on the work. Read that excellent letter of Edmund Grindal, Archbishop of Canterbury to Queen Elizabeth, for ministerial meetings and exercises. You will find it in Fuller's History of the Church of England.

Brethren, I crave your pardon for the infirmities of this address; and earnestly longing for the success of your labours,

I shall daily beg of God, that he would persuade you to those duties which I have here recommended to you, and would preserve and prosper you therein, against all the serpentine subtlety and rage that are now engaged to oppose and hinder you.

Your unworthy fellow-servant

15 *April* 1656   RICHARD BAXTER

INTRODUCTORY NOTE

Introductory note

Take heed therefore unto yourselves, and to all the flock, over the which the Holy Ghost hath made you overseers, to feed the church of God, which he hath purchased with his own blood. Acts 20.28

Though some think that Paul's exhortation to these elders doth prove him their ruler, we who are this day to speak to you from the Lord, hope that we may freely do the like, without any jealousies of such a conclusion. Though we teach our people, as officers set over them in the Lord, yet may we teach one another, as brethren in office, as well as in faith. If the people of our charge must 'teach and admonish and exhort each other daily,' no doubt teachers may do it to one another, without any super-eminency of power or degree. We have the same sins to mortify, and the same graces to be quickened and strengthened, as our people have: we have greater works to do than they have, and greater difficulties to overcome, and therefore we have need to be warned and awakened, if not to be instructed, as well as they. So that I confess I think such meetings together should be more frequent, if we had nothing else to do but this. And we should deal as plainly and closely with one another, as the most serious among us do with our flocks, lest if they only have sharp admonitions and reproofs, they only should be sound and lively in the faith. That this was Paul's judgment, I need no other proof, than this rousing, heart-melting exhortation to the Ephesian elders. A short sermon, but not soon learned! Had the bishops and teachers of the Church but thoroughly learned this short exhortation, though to the neglect of many a volume which hath taken up their time, and helped them to greater applause in the world, how happy had it been for the Church, and for themselves!

In further discoursing on this text, I propose to pursue the following method:

First, To consider what it is to take heed to ourselves.

Secondly, To show why we must take heed to ourselves.

Thirdly, To inquire what it is to take heed to all the flock.

Fourthly, To illustrate the manner in which we must take heed to all the flock.

Fifthly, To state some motives why we should take heed to all the flock.

Lastly, To make some application of the whole.

CHAPTER I

The oversight of ourselves

Section 1
The nature of this oversight

Let us consider, What it is to take heed to ourselves.

1. See that the work of saving grace be thoroughly wrought in your own souls. Take heed to yourselves, lest you be void of that saving grace of God which you offer to others, and be strangers to the effectual working of that gospel which you preach; and lest, while you proclaim to the world the necessity of a Saviour, your own hearts should neglect him, and you should miss of an interest in him and his saving benefits. Take heed to yourselves, lest you perish, while you call upon others to take heed of perishing; and lest you famish yourselves while you prepare food for them. Though there is a promise of shining as the stars, to those 'who turn many to righteousness,' that is but on supposition that they are first turned to it themselves. Their own sincerity in the faith is the condition of their glory, simply considered, though their great ministerial labours may be a condition of the promise of their greater glory. Many have warned others that they come not to that place of torment, while yet they hastened to it themselves: many a preacher is now in hell, who hath a hundred times called upon his hearers to use the utmost care and diligence to escape it. Can any reasonable man imagine that God should save men for offering salvation to others, while they refuse it themselves; and for telling others those truths which they

themselves neglect and abuse? Many a tailor goes in rags, that maketh costly clothes for others; and many a cook scarcely licks his fingers, when he hath dressed for others the most costly dishes. Believe it, brethren, God never saved any man for being a preacher, nor because he was an able preacher; but because he was a justified, sanctified man, and consequently faithful in his Master's work. Take heed, therefore, to yourselves first, that you be that which you persuade your hearers to be, and believe that which you persuade them to believe, and heartily entertain that Saviour whom you offer to them. He that bade you love your neighbours as yourselves, did imply that you should love yourselves, and not hate and destroy yourselves and them.

It is a fearful thing to be an unsanctified professor, but much more to be an unsanctified preacher. Doth it not make you tremble when you open the Bible, lest you should there read the sentence of your own condemnation? When you pen your sermons, little do you think that you are drawing up indictments against your own souls! When you are arguing against sin, that you are aggravating your own! When you proclaim to your hearers the unsearchable riches of Christ and his grace, that you are publishing your own iniquity in rejecting them, and your unhappiness in being destitute of them! What can you do in persuading men to Christ, in drawing them from the world, in urging them to a life of faith and holiness, but conscience, if it were awake, would tell you, that you speak all this to your own confusion? If you speak of hell, you speak of your own inheritance: if you describe the joys of heaven, you describe your own misery, seeing you have no right to 'the inheritance of the saints in light.' What can you say, for the most part, but it will be against your own souls? O miserable life! that a man should study and preach against himself, and spend his days in a course of self-condemning! A graceless, inexperienced preacher is one of the most unhappy creatures upon earth: and yet he is ordinarily very insensible of his unhappiness; for he hath so many counters that seem like the gold of saving grace, and so many splendid stones that resemble Christian jewels, that he is seldom troubled with the thoughts of his poverty; but thinks he is 'rich, and increased in goods, and stands in need of nothing, when he is poor, and miserable, and blind, and naked.' He is acquainted with the Holy Scriptures, he is exercised in holy duties, he liveth not in open disgraceful sin, he serveth at God's altar, he reproveth other men's faults, and preacheth up holiness both of heart and life; and how can this man choose but be holy? Oh what aggravated misery is this, to perish in the midst of plenty! – to famish with the bread of life in our hands, while we offer it to others, and urge it on them! That those ordinances of God should be the occasion of our delusion, which are instituted to be the means of our conviction and salvation! and that while we hold the looking-glass of the gospel to others, to show them the face and aspect of their souls, we should either look on the back part of it ourselves, where we can see nothing, or turn it aside, that it may misrepresent us to ourselves! If such a wretched man would take my counsel, he would make a stand, and call his heart and life to an account, and fall a preaching a while to himself, before he preach any more to others. He would consider, whether food in the mouth, that goeth not into the stomach, will nourish; whether he that 'nameth the name of Christ should not depart from iniquity;' whether God will hear his prayers, if 'he regard iniquity in his heart;' whether it will serve the turn at the day of reckoning to say, 'Lord, Lord, we have prophesied in thy name,' when he shall hear these awful words, 'Depart from me, I know you not;' and what comfort it will be to Judas, when he has gone to his own place, to remember that he preached with the other apostles, or that he sat with Christ, and was called by him, 'Friend.' When such thoughts as these have entered into their souls, and kindly worked a while upon their consciences, I would advise them to go to their congregation, and preach over Origen's sermon on Psalm 50.16, 17. 'But unto the wicked God saith, What hast thou to do to declare my statutes, or that thou shouldest take my covenant into thy mouth? seeing thou hatest instruction, and castest my words behind thee.' And when they have read this text, to sit down, and expound and apply it by

their tears; and then to make a full and free confession of their
sin, and lament their case before the whole assembly, and
desire their earnest prayers to God for pardoning and renewing grace; that hereafter they may preach a Saviour whom
they know, and may feel what they speak, and may commend
the riches of the gospel from their own experience.

Alas! it is the common danger and calamity of the Church,
to have unregenerate and inexperienced pastors, and to have
so many men become preachers before they are Christians;
who are sanctified by dedication to the altar as the priests of
God, before they are sanctified by hearty dedication as the
disciples of Christ; and so to worship an unknown God, and
to preach an unknown Christ, to pray through an unknown
Spirit, to recommend a state of holiness and communion with
God, and a glory and a happiness which are all unknown, and
like to be unknown to them for ever. He is like to be but a
heartless preacher, that hath not the Christ and grace that he
preacheth, in his heart. O that all our students in our universities would well consider this! What a poor business is it to
themselves, to spend their time in acquiring some little knowledge of the works of God, and of some of those names which
the divided tongues of the nations have imposed on them, and
not to know God himself, nor exalt him in their hearts, nor
to be acquainted with that one renewing work that should
make them happy! They do but 'walk in a vain show,' and
spend their lives like dreaming men, while they busy their
wits and tongues about abundance of names and notions, and
are strangers to God and the life of saints. If ever God awaken
them by his saving grace, they will have cogitations and
employments so much more serious than their unsanctified
studies and disputations, that they will confess they did but
dream before. A world of business they make themselves
about nothing, while they are wilful strangers to the primitive,
independent, necessary Being, who is all in all. Nothing can
be rightly known, if God be not known; nor is any study well
managed, nor to any great purpose, if God is not studied. We
know little of the creature, till we know it as it stands related
to the Creator: single letters, and syllables uncomposed, are

no better than nonsense. He who overlooketh him who is the 'Alpha and Omega, the beginning and the ending,' and seeth not him in all who is the All of all, doth see nothing at all. All creatures, as such, are broken syllables; they signify nothing as separated from God. Were they separated actually, they would cease to be, and the separation would be an annihilation; and when we separate them in our fancies, we make nothing of them to ourselves. It is one thing to know the creatures as Aristotle, and another thing to know them as a Christian. None but a Christian can read one line of his Physics so as to understand it rightly. It is a high and excellent study, and of greater use than many apprehend; but it is the smallest part of it that Aristotle can teach us.

When man was made perfect, and placed in a perfect world, where all things were in perfect order, the whole creation was then man's book, in which he was to read the nature and will of his great Creator. Every creature had the name of God so legibly engraven on it, that man might run and read it. He could not open his eyes, but he might see some image of God; but no where so fully and lively as in himself. It was, therefore, his work to study the whole volume of nature, but first and most to study himself. And if man had held on in this course, he would have continued and increased in the knowledge of God and himself; but when he would needs know and love the creature and himself in a way of separation from God, he lost the knowledge both of the creature and of the Creator, so far as it could beatify and was worth the name of knowledge; and instead of it, he hath got the unhappy knowledge which he affected, even the empty notions and fantastic knowledge of the creature and himself, as thus separated. And thus, he that lived to the Creator, and upon him, doth now live to and upon the other creatures, and on himself; and thus, 'Every man at his best estate' (the learned as well as the illiterate) 'is altogether vanity. Surely every man walketh in a vain show; surely they are disquieted in vain.' And it must be well observed, that as God laid not aside the relation of a Creator by becoming our Redeemer, nor the right of his propriety and government of us in that relation, but the work of redemption standeth, in some respect, in subordination to that of creation, and the law of the Redeemer to the law of the Creator; so also the duties which we owed to God as Creator have not ceased, but the duties that we owe to the Redeemer, as such, are subordinate thereto. It is the work of Christ to bring us back to God, and to restore us to the perfection of holiness and obedience; and as he is the way to the Father, so faith in him is the way to our former employment and enjoyment of God. I hope you perceive what I aim at in all this, namely, that to see God in his creatures, and to love him, and converse with him, was the employment of man in his upright state; that this is so far from ceasing to be our duty, that it is the work of Christ to bring us, by faith, back to it; and therefore the most holy men are the most excellent students of God's works, and none but the holy can rightly study them or know them. 'His works are great, sought out of all them that have pleasure therein;' but not for themselves, but for him that made them. Your study of physics and other sciences is not worth a rush, if it be not God that you seek after in them. To see and admire, to reverence and adore, to love and delight in God, as exhibited in his works – this is the true and only philosophy; the contrary is mere foolery, and is so called again and again by God himself. This is the sanctification of your studies, when they are devoted to God, and when he is the end, the object, and the life of them all.

And, therefore, I shall presume to tell you, by the way, that it is a grand error, and of dangerous consequence in Christian academies, (pardon the censure from one so unfit to pass it, seeing the necessity of the case commandeth it,) that they study the creature before the Redeemer, and set themselves to physics, and metaphysics, and mathematics, before they set themselves to theology; whereas, no man that hath not the vitals of theology, is capable of going beyond a fool in philosophy. Theology must lay the foundation, and lead the way of all our studies. If God must be searched after, in our search of the creature, (and we must affect no separated knowledge of them) then tutors must read God to their pupils in all;

and divinity must be the beginning, the middle, the end, the life, the all, of their studies. Our physics and metaphysics must be reduced to theology; and nature must be read as one of God's books, which is purposely written for the revelation of himself. The Holy Scripture is the easier book: when you have first learned from it God, and his will, as to the most necessary things, address yourselves to the study of his works, and read every creature as a Christian and a divine. If you see not yourselves, and all things, as living, and moving, and having being in God, you see nothing, whatever you think you see. If you perceive not, in your study of the creatures, that God is all, and in all, and that 'of him, and through him, and to him, are all things,' you may think, perhaps, that you 'know something; but you know nothing as you ought to know.' Think not so basely of your physics, and of the works of God, as that they are only preparatory studies for boys. It is a most high and noble part of holiness, to search after, behold admire, and love the great Creator in all his works. How much have the saints of God been employed in this high and holy exercise! The book of Job, and the Psalms, may show us that our physics are not so little kin to theology as some suppose.

I do, therefore, in zeal for the good of the Church, and their own success in their most necessary labours, propound it for the consideration of all pious tutors, whether they should not as timely, and as diligently, read to their pupils, or cause them to read, the chief parts of practical divinity (and there is no other), as any of the sciences; and whether they should not go together from the very first? It is well that they hear sermons; but that is not enough. If tutors would make it their principal business to acquaint their pupils with the doctrine of salvation, and labour to set it home upon their hearts, that all might be received according to its weight, and read to their hearts as well as to their heads, and so carry on the rest of their instructions, that it may appear they make them but subservient unto this, and that their pupils may feel what they aim at in them all; and so that they would teach all their philosophy *in habitu theologico*, – this might be a happy means to make a happy Church and a happy country. But, when languages and philosophy have almost all their time and diligence, and, instead of reading philosophy like divines, they read divinity like philosophers, as if it were a thing of no more moment than a lesson of music, or arithmetic, and not the doctrine of everlasting life; — this it is that blasteth so many in the bud, and pestereth the Church with unsanctified teachers! Hence it is, that we have so many worldlings to preach of the invisible felicity, and so many carnal men to declare the mysteries of the Spirit; and I would I might not say, so many infidels to preach Christ, or so many atheists to preach the living God: and when they are taught philosophy before or without religion, what wonder if their philosophy be all or most of their religion!

Again, therefore, I address myself to all who have the charge of the education of youth, especially in order to preparation for the ministry. You, that are schoolmasters and tutors, begin and end with the things of God. Speak daily to the hearts of your scholars those things that must be wrought into their hearts, or else they are undone. Let some piercing words fall frequently from your mouths, of God, and the state of their souls, and the life to come. Do not say, they are too young to understand and entertain them. You little know what impressions they may make. Not only the soul of the boy, but many souls may have cause to bless God, for your zeal and diligence, yea, for one such seasonable word. You have a great advantage above others to do them good; you have them before they are grown to maturity, and they will hear you when they will not hear another. If they are destined to the ministry, you are preparing them for the special service of God, and must they not first have the knowledge of him whom they have to serve? Oh think with yourselves, what a sad thing it will be to their own souls, and what a wrong to the Church of God, if they come out from you with common and carnal hearts, to so great and holy and spiritual a work! Of a hundred students in one of our colleges, how many may there be that are serious, experienced, godly young men! If you should send one half of them on a work which they are unfit for, what cruel work will they make in the Church or country! Whereas, if you be the means of their conversion and sanctification, how many souls may bless you, and what greater good can you do the Church? When once their hearts are savingly affected with the doctrine which they study and preach, they will study it more heartily, and preach it more heartily: their own experience will direct them to the fittest subjects, and will furnish them with matter, and quicken them to set it home to the conscience of their hearers. See, therefore, that you make not work for the groans and lamentation of the Church, nor for the great tormentor of the murderers of souls.

2. Content not yourselves with being in a state of grace, but be also careful that your graces are kept in vigorous and lively exercise, and that you preach to yourselves the sermons which you study, before you preach them to others. If you did this for your own sakes, it would not be lost labour; but I am speaking to you upon the public account, that you would do it for the sake of the Church, When your minds are in a holy, heavenly frame, your people are likely to partake of the fruits of it. Your prayers, and praises, and doctrine will be sweet and heavenly to them. They will likely feel when you have been much with God: that which is most on your hearts, is like to be most in their ears. I confess I must speak it by lamentable experience, that I publish to my flock the distempers of my own soul. When I let my heart grow cold, my preaching is cold; and when it is confused, my preaching is confused; and so I can oft observe also in the best of my hearers, that when I have grown cold in preaching, they have grown cold too; and the next prayers which I have heard from them have been too like my preaching. We are the nurses of Christ's little ones. If we forbear taking food ourselves, we shall famish them; it will soon be visible in their leanness, and dull discharge of their several duties. If we let our love decline, we are not like to raise up theirs. If we abate our holy care and fear, it will appear in our preaching: if the matter show it not, the manner will. If we feed on unwholesome food, either errors or fruitless controversies, our hearers are like to

fare the worse for it. Whereas, if we abound in faith, and love, and zeal, how would it overflow to the refreshing of our congregations, and how would it appear in the increase of the same graces in them! O brethren, watch therefore over your own hearts: keep out lusts and passions, and worldly inclinations; keep up the life of faith, and love, and zeal: be much at home, and be much with God. If it be not your daily business to study your own hearts, and to subdue corruption, and to walk with God – if you make not this a work to which you constantly attend, all will go wrong, and you will starve your hearers; or, if you have an affected fervency, you cannot expect a blessing to attend it from on high. Above all, be much in secret prayer and meditation. Thence you must fetch the heavenly fire that must kindle your sacrifices: remember, you cannot decline and neglect your duty, to your own hurt alone; many will be losers by it as well as you. For your people's sakes, therefore, look to your hearts. If a pang of spiritual pride should overtake you, and you should fall into any dangerous error, and vent your own inventions to draw away disciples after you, what a wound may this prove to the Church, of which you have the oversight; and you may become a plague to them instead of a blessing, and they may wish they had never seen your faces. Oh, therefore, take heed to your own judgments and affections. Vanity and error will slyly insinuate, and seldom come without fair pretences: great distempers and apostasies have usually small beginnings. The prince of darkness doth frequently personate an angel of light, to draw the children of light again into darkness. How easily also will distempers creep in upon our affections and our first love, and fear and care abate! Watch, therefore, for the sake of yourselves and others.

But, besides this general course of watchfulness, methinks a minister should take some special pains with his heart, before he is to go to the congregation: if it be then cold, how is he likely to warm the hearts of his hearers? Therefore, go then specially to God for life: read some rousing, awakening book, or meditate on the weight of the subject of which you are to speak, and on the great necessity of your people's

souls, that you may go in the zeal of the Lord into his house.
Maintain, in this manner, the life of grace in yourselves, that
it may appear in all your sermons from the pulpit, – that every
one who comes cold to the assembly, may have some warmth
imparted to him before he depart.

3. Take heed to yourselves, lest your example contradict
your doctrine, and lest you lay such stumbling-blocks before
the blind, as may be the occasion of their ruin; lest you unsay
with your lives, what you say with your tongues; and be the
greatest hinderers of the success of your own labours. It
much hindereth our work, when other men are all the week
long contradicting to poor people in private, that which we
have been speaking to them from the Word of God in public,
because we cannot be at hand to expose their folly; but it will
much more hinder your work, if you contradict yourselves,
and if your actions give your tongue the lie, and if you build
up an hour or two with your mouths, and all the week after
pull down with your hands! This is the way to make men
think that the Word of God is but an idle tale, and to make
preaching seem no better than prating. He that means as he
speaks, will surely do as he speaks. One proud, surly, lordly
word, one needless contention, one covetous action, may cut
the throat of many a sermon, and blast the fruit of all that
you have been doing. Tell me, brethren, in the fear of God,
do you regard the success of your labours, or do you not? Do
you long to see it upon the souls of your hearers? If you do
not, what do you preach for; what do you study for; and what
do you call yourselves the ministers of Christ for? But if you
do, then surely you cannot find in your heart to mar your
work for a thing of nought. What! do you regard the success
of your labours, and yet will not part with a little to the poor,
nor put up with an injury, or a foul word, nor stoop to the
meanest, nor forbear your passionate or lordly carriage, –
no, not for the winning of souls, and attaining the end of all
your labours! You little value success, indeed, that will sell it
at so cheap a rate, or will not do so small a matter to attain it.

It is a palpable error of some ministers, who make such a
disproportion between their preaching and their living; who

study hard to preach exactly, and study little or not at all to live exactly. All the week long is little enough, to study how to speak two hours; and yet one hour seems too much to study how to live all the week. They are loath to misplace a word in their sermons, or to be guilty of any notable infirmity, (and I blame them not, for the matter is holy and weighty,) but they make nothing of misplacing affections, words, and actions, in the course of their lives. Oh how curiously have I heard some men preach; and how carelessly have I seen them live! They have been so accurate as to the preparation of their sermons, that seldom preaching seemed to them a virtue, that their language might be the more polite, and all the rhetorical writers they could meet with were pressed to serve them for the adorning of their style, (and gauds were oft their chiefest ornaments.) They were so nice in hearing others, that no man pleased them that spoke as he thought, or that drowned not affections, or dulled not, or distempered not the heart by the predominant strains of a fantastic wit. And yet, when it came to matter of practice, and they were once out of church, how incurious were the men, and how little did they regard what they said or did, so it were not so palpably gross as to dishonour them! They that preach precisely, would not live precisely! What a difference was there between their pulpit speeches and their familiar discourse? They that were most impatient of barbarisms, solecisms, and paralogisms in a sermon, could easily tolerate them in their life and conversation.

Certainly, brethren, we have very great cause to take heed what we do, as well as what we say: if we will be the servants of Christ indeed, we must not be tongue servants only, but must serve him with our deeds, and be 'doers of the work, that we may be blessed in our deed.' As our people must be 'doers of the word, and not hearers only;' so we must be doers and not speakers only, lest we 'deceive our own selves.' A practical doctrine must be practically preached. We must study as hard how to live well, as how to preach well. We must think and think again, how to compose our lives, as may most tend to men's salvation, as well as our sermons.

When you are studying what to say to your people, if you have any concern for their souls, you will oft be thinking with yourself, 'How shall I get within them? and what shall I say, that is most likely to convince them, and convert them, and promote their salvation?' And should you not as diligently think with yourself, 'How shall I live, and what shall I do, and how shall I dispose of all that I have, as may most tend to the saving of men's souls?' Brethren, if the saving of souls be your end, you will certainly intend it out of the pulpit as well as in it! If it be your end, you will live for it, and contribute all your endeavours to attain it. You will ask concerning the money in your purse, as well as concerning the word of your mouth, 'In what way shall I lay it out for the greatest good, especially to men's souls?' Oh that this were your daily study, how to use your wealth, your friends, and all you have for God, as well as your tongues! Then should we see that fruit of your labours, which is never else like to be seen. If you intend the end of the ministry in the pulpit only, it would seem you take yourselves for ministers no longer than you are there. And, if so, I think you are unworthy to be esteemed ministers at all.

Let me then entreat you, brethren, to do well, as well as say well. Be 'zealous of good works.' Spare not for any cost, if it may promote your Master's work.

(1) Maintain your innocency, and walk without offence. Let your lives condemn sin, and persuade men to duty. Would you have your people more careful of their souls, than you are of yours? If you would have them redeem their time, do not you mis-spend yours. If you would not have them vain in their conference, see that you speak yourselves the things which may edify, and tend to 'minister grace to the hearers.' Order your own families well, if you would have them do so by theirs. Be not proud and lordly, if you would have them to be lowly. There are no virtues wherein your example will do more, at least to abate men's prejudice, than humility and meekness and self-denial. Forgive injuries; and 'be not overcome of evil, but overcome evil with good.' Do as our Lord, 'who, when he was reviled, reviled not again.' If sinners be

stubborn and stout and contemptuous, flesh and blood will
persuade you to take up their weapons, and to master them by
their carnal means: but that is not the way, (further than
necessary self-preservation or public good may require,) but
overcome them with kindness and patience and gentleness.
The former may show that you have more worldly power
than they (wherein yet they are ordinarily too hard for the
faithful); but it is the latter only that will tell them that you
excel them in spiritual excellency. If you believe that Christ
is more worthy of imitation than Caesar or Alexander, and
that it is more glory to be a Christian than to be a conqueror,
yea to be a man than a beast – which often exceed us in
strength – contend with charity, and not with violence; set
meekness and love and patience against force, and not force
against force. Remember, you are obliged to be the servants
of all. 'Condescend to men of low estate.' Be not strange to
the poor of your flock; they are apt to take your strangeness
for contempt. Familiarity, improved to holy ends, may do
abundance of good. Speak not stoutly or disrespectfully to
any one; but be courteous to the meanest, as to your equal in
Christ. A kind and winning carriage is a cheap way of doing
men good.

(2) Let me entreat you to abound in works of charity and
benevolence. Go to the poor, and see what they want, and
show your compassion at once to their soul and body. Buy
them a catechism, and other small books that are likely to do
them good, and make them promise to read them with care
and attention. Stretch your purse to the utmost, and do all the
good you can. Think not of being rich; seek not great things
for yourselves or your posterity. What if you do impoverish
yourselves to do a greater good; will this be loss or gain? If
you believe that God is the safest purse-bearer, and that to
expend in his service is the greatest usury, show them that you
do believe it. I know that flesh and blood will cavil before it
will lose its prey, and will never want somewhat to say
against this duty that is against its interest; but mark what I
say (and the Lord set it home upon your hearts), that man
who hath any thing in the world so dear to him, that he cannot

spare it for Christ, if he call for it, is no true Christian. And because a carnal heart will not believe that Christ calls for it when he cannot spare it, and, therefore, makes that his self-deceiving shift, I say further, that the man who will not be persuaded that duty is duty, because he cannot spare that for Christ which is therein to be expended, is no true Christian; for a false heart corrupteth the understanding, and that again increaseth the delusions of the heart. Do not take it, therefore, as an undoing, to make friends of the mammon of unrighteousness and to lay up treasure in heaven, though you leave yourselves but little on earth. You lose no great advantage for heaven, by becoming poor: 'In pursuing one's way, the lighter one travels the better.'

I know, where the heart is carnal and covetous, words will not wring men's money out of their hands; they can say all this, and more to others; but saying is one thing, and believing is another. But with those that are true believers, methinks such considerations should prevail. O what abundance of good might ministers do, if they would but live in contempt of the world, and the riches and glory thereof, and expend all they have in their Master's service, and pinch their flesh, that they may have wherewith to do good! This would unlock more hearts to the reception of their doctrine, than all their oratory; and, without this, singularity in religion will seem but hypocrisy; and it is likely that it is so. 'He who practises disinterestedness prays to the Lord; he who snatches a man from peril offers a rich sacrifice; these are our sacrifices; these are holy to God. Thus he who is more devout among us is he who is more self-effacing,' saith Minucius Felix.[1] Though we need not do as the papists, who betake themselves to monasteries, and cast away property, yet we must have nothing but what we have for God.

4. Take heed to yourselves, lest you live in those sins which you preach against in others, and lest you be guilty of that which daily you condemn. Will you make it your work to magnify God, and, when you have done, dishonour him as

[1] The author of a work entitled *Octavius*; he lived in the 2nd or 3rd century A.D.

much as others? Will you proclaim Christ's governing power, and yet contemn it, and rebel yourselves? Will you preach his laws, and wilfully break them? If sin be evil, why do you live in it? if it be not, why do you dissuade men from it? If it be dangerous, how dare you venture on it? if it be not, why do you tell men so? If God's threatenings be true, why do you not fear them? if they be false, why do you need-nessly trouble men with them, and put them into such frights without a cause? Do you 'know the judgment of God, that they who commit such things are worthy of death;' and yet will you do them? 'Thou that teachest another, teachest thou not thyself? Thou that sayest a man should not commit adultery,' or be drunk, or covetous, art thou such thyself? 'Thou that makest thy boast of the law, through breaking the law dishonourest thou God?' What! shall the same tongue speak evil that speakest against evil? Shall those lips censure, and slander, and backbite your neighbour, that cry down these and the like things in others? Take heed to yourselves, lest you cry down sin, and yet do not overcome it; lest, while you seek to bring it down in others, you bow to it, and be-come its slaves yourselves: 'For of whom a man is overcome, of the same is he brought into bondage.' 'To whom ye yield yourselves servants to obey, his servants ye are to whom ye obey, whether of sin unto death, or of obedience unto righteousness.' O brethren! it is easier to chide at sin, than to overcome it.

5. Lastly, take heed to yourselves, that you want not the qualifications necessary for your work. He must not be himself a babe in knowledge, that will teach men all those mysterious things which must be known in order to salvation. O what qualifications are necessary for a man who hath such a charge upon him as we have! How many difficulties in divinity to be solved! and these, too, about the fundamental principles of religion! How many obscure texts of Scripture to be expounded! How many duties to be performed, wherein ourselves and others may miscarry, if in the matter, and manner, and end, we be not well informed! How many sins to be avoided, which, without understanding and foresight,

cannot be done! What a number of sly and subtle temptations must we open to our people's eyes, that they may escape them! How many weighty and yet intricate cases of conscience have we almost daily to resolve! And can so much work, and such work as this, be done by raw, unqualified men? O what strong holds have we to batter, and how many of them! What subtle and obstinate resistance must we expect from every heart we deal with! Prejudice hath so blocked up our way, that we can scarcely procure a patient hearing. We cannot make a breach in their groundless hopes and carnal peace, but they have twenty shifts and seeming reasons to make it up again; and twenty enemies, that are seeming friends, are ready to help them. We dispute not with them upon equal terms. We have children to reason with, that cannot understand us. We have distracted men (in spirituals) to argue with, that will bawl us down with raging nonsense. We have wilful, unreasonable people to deal with, who, when they are silenced, are never the more convinced, and who, when they can give you no reason, will give you their resolution; like the man that Salvian[1] had to deal with, who, being resolved to devour a poor man's substance, and being entreated by him to forbear, replied, 'He could not grant his request, for he had made a vow to take it;' so that the preacher, by reason of this most religious evil deed, was fain to depart. We dispute the case against men's wills and passions, as much as against their understandings; and these have neither reason nor ears. Their best arguments are, 'I will not believe you, nor all the preachers in the world, in such things. I will not change my mind, or life; I will not leave my sins; I will never be so precise, come of it what will.' We have not one, but multitudes of raging passions, and contradicting enemies, to dispute against at once, whenever we go about the conversion of a sinner; as if a man were to dispute in a fair or a tumult, or in the midst of a crowd of violent scolds. What equal dealing, and what success, could here be expected? Yet such is our work; and it is a work that must be done.

O brethren! what men should we be in skill, resolution,

[1] A Christian writer living at Marseilles during the 5th century.

and unwearied diligence, who have all this to do? Did Paul cry out, 'Who is sufficient for these things?' And shall we be proud, or careless, or lazy, as if we were sufficient? As Peter saith to every Christian, in consideration of our great approaching change, 'What manner of persons ought we to be in all holy conversation and godliness!' so may I say to every minister, 'Seeing all these things lie upon our hands, what manner of persons ought we to be in all holy endeavours and resolutions for our work!' This is not a burden for the shoulders of a child. What skill doth every part of our work require! – and of how much moment is every part! To preach a sermon, I think, is not the hardest part; and yet what skill is necessary to make the truth plain; to convince the hearers, to let irresistible light in to their consciences, and to keep it there, and drive all home; to screw the truth into their minds, and work Christ into their affections; to meet every objection, and clearly to resolve it; to drive sinners to a stand, and make them see that there is no hope, but that they must unavoidably either be converted or condemned – and to do all this, as regards language and manner, as beseems our work, and yet as is most suitable to the capacities of our hearers. This, and a great deal more that should be done in every sermon, must surely require a great deal of holy skill. So great a God, whose message we deliver, should be honoured by our delivery of it. It is a lamentable case, that in a message from the God of heaven, of everlasting moment to the souls of men, we should behave ourselves so weakly, so unhandsomely, so imprudently, or so slightly, that the whole business should miscarry in our hands, and God should be dishonoured, and his work disgraced, and sinners rather hardened than converted; and all this through our weakness or neglect! How often have carnal hearers gone home jeering at the palpable and dishonourable failings of the preacher! How many sleep under us, because our hearts and tongues are sleepy, and we bring not with us so much skill and zeal as to awake them!

Moreover, what skill is necessary to defend the truth against gainsayers, and to deal with disputing cavillers, according to their several modes and case! And if we fail through weakness, how will they exult over us! Yet that is the smallest matter: but who knows how many weak ones may thereby be perverted, to their own undoing, and to the trouble of the Church? What skill is necessary to deal in private with one poor ignorant soul for his conversion!

O brethren! do you not shrink and tremble under the sense of all this work? Will a common measure of holy skill and ability, of prudence and other qualifications, serve for such a task as this? I know necessity may cause the Church to tolerate the weak; but woe to us, if we tolerate and indulge our own weakness! Do not reason and conscience tell you, that if you dare venture on so high a work as this, you should spare no pains to be qualified for the performance of it? It is not now and then an idle snatch or taste of studies that will serve to make an able and sound divine. I know that laziness hath learned to allege the vanity of all our studies, and how entirely the Spirit must qualify us for, and assist us in our work; as if God commanded us the use of means, and then warranted us to neglect them; as if it were his way to cause us to thrive in a course of idleness, and to bring us to knowledge by dreams when we are asleep, or to take us up into heaven, and show us his counsels, while we think of no such matter, but are idling away our time on earth! O that men should dare, by their laziness, to 'quench the Spirit,' and then pretend the Spirit for the doing of it! 'O outrageous, shameful and unnatural deed!' God hath required us, that we be 'not slothful in business,' but 'fervent in spirit, serving the Lord.' Such we must provoke our hearers to be, and such we must be ourselves. O, therefore, brethren, lose no time! Study, and pray, and confer, and practise; for in these four ways your abilities must be increased. Take heed to yourselves, lest you are weak through your own negligence, and lest you mar the work of God by your weakness.

Section 2
The motives to this oversight

Having showed you what it is to take heed to ourselves, I shall
next lay before you some motives to awaken you to this duty.
1. Take heed to yourselves, for you have a heaven to win or
lose, and souls that must be happy or miserable for ever; and
therefore it concerneth you to begin at home, and to take
heed to yourselves as well as to others. Preaching well may
succeed to the salvation of others, without the holiness of
your own hearts and lives; it is, at least, possible, though less
usual; but it is impossible it should save yourselves. 'Many
will say in that day, Lord, Lord, have we not prophesied in
thy name?' to whom he will answer, 'I never knew you;
depart from me, ye that work iniquity.' O sirs, how many
men have preached Christ, and yet have perished for want of
a saving interest in him! How many, who are now in hell,
have told their people of the torments of hell, and warned
them to escape from it! How many have preached of the
wrath of God against sinners, who are now enduring it!
O what sadder case can there be in the world, than for a
man, who made it his very trade and calling to proclaim
salvation, and to help others to heaven, yet after all to be
himself shut out! Alas! that we should have so many books in
our libraries which tell us the way to heaven; that we should
spend so many years in reading these books, and studying
the doctrine of eternal life, and after all this to miss it! – that
we should study so many sermons of salvation, and yet fall
short of it! – that we should preach so many sermons of
damnation, and yet fall into it? And all because we preached
so many sermons of Christ, while we neglected him; of the
Spirit, while we resisted him; of faith, while we did not
ourselves believe; of repentance and conversion, while we
continued in an impenitent and unconverted state; and of a
heavenly life, while we remained carnal and earthly ourselves.
If we will be divines only in tongue and title, and have not the

Divine image upon our souls, nor give up ourselves to the Divine honour and will, no wonder if we be separated from the Divine presence, and denied the fruition of God for ever. Believe it, sirs, God is no respecter of persons: he saveth not men for their coats or callings; a holy calling will not save an unholy man. If you stand at the door of the kingdom of grace, to light others in, and will not go in yourselves, you shall knock in vain at the gates of glory, that would not enter at the door of grace. You shall then find that your lamps should have had the oil of grace, as well as of ministerial gifts – of holiness, as well as of doctrine – if you would have had a part in the glory which you preached. Do I need to tell you, that preachers of the gospel must be judged by the gospel; and stand at the same bar, and be sentenced on the same terms, and dealt with as severely, as any other men? Can you think to be saved, then, by your clergy; and to come off by a 'He passed for a clergyman,' when there is wanting the 'He believed and lived as a Christian.' Alas, it will not be! You know it will not be. Take heed therefore to yourselves, for your own sakes; seeing you have souls to save or lose, as well as others.

2. Take heed to yourselves, for you have a depraved nature, and sinful inclinations, as well as others. If innocent Adam had need of heed, and lost himself and us for want of it, how much more need have such as we! Sin dwelleth in us, when we have preached ever so much against it; and one degree pre-pareth the heart for another, and one sin inclineth the mind to more. If one thief be in the house, he will let in the rest; because they have the same disposition and design. A spark is the beginning of a flame; and a small disease may cause a greater. A man who knows himself to be purblind, should take heed to his feet. Alas! in our hearts, as well as in our hearers, there is an averseness to God, a strangeness to him, unreasonable and almost unruly passions! In us there are, at the best, the remnants of pride, unbelief, self-seeking, hypocrisy, and all the most hateful, deadly sins. And doth it not then concern us to take heed to ourselves? Is so much of the fire of hell yet unextinguished, that was at first kindled

in us? Are there so many traitors in our very hearts, and is it not necessary for us to take heed? You will scarcely let your little children go themselves while they are weak, without calling upon them to take heed of falling. And, alas! how weak are those of us that seem strongest! How apt to stumble at a very straw! How small a matter will cast us down, by enticing us to folly; or kindling our passions and inordinate desires, by perverting our judgments, weakening our resolutions, cooling our zeal, and abating our diligence! Ministers are not only sons of Adam, but sinners against the grace of Christ, as well as others; and so have increased their radical sin. These treacherous hearts of yours will, one time or other, deceive you, if you take not heed. Those sins that seem now to lie dead will revive: your pride, and worldliness, and many a noisome vice, will spring up, that you thought had been weeded out by the roots. It is most necessary, therefore, that men of so much infirmity should take heed to themselves, and be careful in the oversight of their own souls.

3. Take heed to yourselves, because the tempter will more ply you with his temptations than other men. If you will be the leaders against the prince of darkness, he will spare you no further than God restraineth him. He beareth the greatest malice to those that are engaged to do him the greatest mischief. As he hateth Christ more than any of us, because he is the General of the field, the Captain of our salvation, and doth more than all the world besides against his kingdom; so doth he hate the leaders under him, more than the common soldiers: he knows what a rout he may make among them, if the leaders fall before their eyes. He hath long tried that way of fighting, neither against great nor small comparatively, but of smiting the shepherds, that he may scatter the flock: and so great hath been his success this way, that he will continue to follow it as far as he is able. Take heed, therefore, brethren, for the enemy hath a special eye upon you. You shall have his most subtle insinuations, and incessant solicitations, and violent assaults. As wise and learned as you are, take heed to yourselves, lest he outwit you. The devil is a greater scholar than you, and a nimbler disputant: he can transform himself

into an angel of light to deceive: he will get within you, and trip up your heels before you are aware: he will play the juggler with you undiscerned, and cheat you of your faith or innocency, and you shall not know that you have lost it; nay, he will make you believe it is multiplied or increased, when it is lost. You shall see neither hook nor line, much less the subtle angler himself, while he is offering you his bait. And his bait shall be so fitted to your temper and disposition, that he will be sure to find advantages within you, and make your own principles and inclinations betray you; and whenever he ruineth you, he will make you the instruments of ruin to others. O what a conquest will he think he hath got, if he can make a minister lazy and unfaithful, if he can tempt a minister into covetousness or scandal! He will glory against the Church, and say, 'These are your holy preachers! See what their preciseness is, and whither it brings them.' He will glory against Jesus Christ himself, and say, 'These are thy champions! I can make thy chiefest servants abuse thee; I can make the stewards of thy house unfaithful.' If he did so insult God upon a false surmise, and tell him he could make Job curse him to his face, what will he do if he should prevail against you? And at last he will insult as much over you, that he could draw you to be false to your great trust, and to blemish your holy profession, and to do so much service to him that was your enemy. O, do not so far gratify Satan; do not make him so much sport; suffer him not to use you as the Philistines did Samson, first to deprive you of your strength, and then to put out your eyes, and so to make you the matter of his triumph and derision.

4. Take heed to yourselves, because there are many eyes upon you, and there will be many to observe your falls. You cannot miscarry but the world will ring of it. The eclipses of the sun by day are seldom without witnesses. As you take yourselves for the lights of the churches, you may expect that men's eyes will be upon you. If other men may sin without observation, so cannot you. And you should thankfully consider how great a mercy this is, that you have so many eyes to watch over you, and so many ready to tell you of your

faults; and thus have greater helps than others, at least for restraining you from sin. Though they may do it with a malicious mind, yet you have the advantage of it. God forbid that we should prove so impudent as to do evil in the public view of all, and to sin wilfully while the world is gazing on us! 'They that sleep sleep in the night; and they that be drunken are drunken in the night.' Why, consider that you are ever in the open light: even the light of your own doctrine will expose your evil doings. While you are as lights set upon a hill, think not to lie hid. Take heed therefore to yourselves, and do your work as those that remember that the world looks on them, and that with the quick-sighted eye of malice, ready to make the worst of all, to find the smallest fault where it is, to aggravate it where they find it, to divulge it and to take advantage of it to their own designs, and to make faults where they cannot find them. How cautiously, then, should we walk before so many ill-minded observers!

5. Take heed to yourselves, for your sins have more heinous aggravations than other men's. It was a saying of king Alphonsus, that 'a great man cannot commit a small sin;' much more may we say, that a learned man, or a teacher of others, cannot commit a small sin; or, at least, that the sin is great as committed by him, which is smaller as committed by another.

(1) You are more likely than others to sin against knowledge, because you have more than they; at least, you sin against more light, or means of knowledge. What! do you not know that covetousness and pride are sins? do you not know what it is to be unfaithful to your trust, and, by negligence or self-seeking, to betray men's souls? You know your 'Master's will; and, if you do it not, you shall be beaten with many stripes.' There must needs be the more wilfulness, by how much there is the more knowledge.

(2) Your sins have more hypocrisy in them than other men's, by how much the more you have spoken against them. O what a heinous thing is it in us, to study how to disgrace sin to the utmost, and make it as odious in the eyes of our people as we can, and when we have done, to live in it, and secretly

cherish that which we publicly disgrace! What vile hypocrisy is it, to make it our daily work to cry it down, and yet to keep to it; to call it publicly all naught, and privately to make it our bed-fellow and companion; to bind heavy burdens on others, and not to touch them ourselves with a finger! What can you say to this in judgment? Did you think as ill of sin as you spoke, or did you not? If you did not, why would you dissemblingly speak against it? If you did, why would you keep it and commit it? O bear not that badge of a hypo-critical Pharisee, 'They say, but do not.' Many a minister of the gospel will be confounded, and not be able to look up, by reason of this heavy charge of hypocrisy.

(3) Your sins have more perfidiousness in them than other men's, by how much the more you have engaged yourselves against them. Besides all your common engagements as Christians, you have many more as ministers. How oft have you proclaimed the evil and danger of sin, and called sinners from it? How oft have you denounced against it the terrors of the Lord? All this surely implied that you renounced it yourselves. Every sermon that you preached against it, every exhortation, every confession of it in the congregation, did lay an engagement upon you to forsake it. Every child that you baptized, and every administration of the supper of the Lord, did import your own renouncing of the world and the flesh, and your engagement to Christ. How oft, and how openly, have you borne witness to the odiousness and damnable nature of sin? and yet will you entertain it, notwith-standing all these professions and testimonies of your own? O what treachery is it to make such a stir against it in the pulpit, and, after all, to entertain it in thy heart, and give it the room that is due to God, and even prefer it before the glory of the saints!

6. Take heed to yourselves, because such great works as ours require greater grace than other men's. Weaker gifts and graces may carry a man through in a more even course of life, that is not liable to so great trials. Smaller strength may serve for lighter works and burdens. But if you will venture on the great undertakings of the ministry; if you will lead on

the troops of Christ against Satan and his followers; if you will engage yourselves against principalities and powers, and spiritual wickednesses in high places; if you will undertake to rescue captive sinners out of the devil's paws; do not think that a heedless, careless course will accomplish so great a work as this. You must look to come off with greater shame and deeper wounds of conscience, than if you had lived a common life, if you think to go through such momentous things as these with a careless soul. It is not only the work that calls for heed, but the workman also, that he may be fit for business of such weight. We have seen many men who lived as private Christians, in good reputation for parts and piety, when they took upon them either the magistracy or military employment, where the work was above their gifts, and temptations did overmatch their strength, they proved scandalous disgraced men. And we have seen some private Christians of good esteem, who, having thought too highly of their parts, and thrust themselves into the ministerial office, have proved weak and empty men, and have become greater burdens to the Church than some whom we endeavoured to cast out. They might have done God more service in the higher rank of private men, than they do among the lowest of the ministry. If, then, you will venture into the midst of enemies, and bear the burden and heat of the day, take heed to yourselves.

7. Take heed to yourselves, for the honour of your Lord and Master, and of his holy truth and ways, doth lie more on you than on other men. As you may render him more service, so you may do him more disservice than others. The nearer men stand to God, the greater dishonour hath he by their miscarriages; and the more will they be imputed by foolish men to God himself. The heavy judgments executed on Eli and on his house were because they kicked at his sacrifice and offering: 'Therefore was the sin of the young men very great before the Lord, for men abhorred the offering of the Lord.' It was that great aggravation, of 'causing the enemies of the Lord to blaspheme,' which provoked God to deal more sharply with David, than he would otherwise have done. If you be indeed Christians, the glory of God will be dearer to

you than your lives. Take heed therefore what you do against it, as you would take heed what you do against your lives. Would it not wound you to the heart to hear the name and truth of God reproached for your sakes; to see men point to you, and say, 'There goes a covetous priest, a secret tippler, a scandalous man; these are they that preach for strictness, while they themselves can live as loose as others; they condemn us by their sermons, and condemn themselves by their lives; notwithstanding all their talk, they are as bad as we.' O brethren, could your hearts endure to hear men cast the dung of your iniquities in the face of the holy God, and in the face of the gospel, and of all that desire to fear the Lord? Would it not break your hearts to think that all the godly Christians about you should suffer reproach for your misdoings? Why, if one of you that is a leader of the flock, should be ensnared but once into some scandalous crime, there is scarcely a man or woman that seeketh diligently after their salvation, within the hearing of it, but, besides the grief of their hearts for your sin, are likely to have it cast in their teeth by the ungodly about them, however much they may detest it, and lament it. The ungodly husband will tell his wife, and the ungodly parents will tell their children, and ungodly neighbours and fellow-servants will be telling one another of it, saying, 'These are your godly preachers! See what comes of all your stir. What better are you than others? You are even all alike.' Such words as these must all the godly in the country hear for your sakes. 'It must needs be that offences come; but woe to that man by whom the offence cometh!' O take heed, brethren, of every word you speak, and of every step you tread, for you bear the ark of the Lord, – you are entrusted with his honour! If you that 'know his will, and approve the things that are more excellent, being instructed out of the law, and are confident that ye yourselves are guides of the blind, and lights to them that are in darkness, instructors of the foolish, teachers of babes,' – if you, I say, should live contrary to your doctrine, and 'by breaking the law should dishonour God, the name of God will be blasphemed' among the ignorant and ungodly 'through you.' And you are not unacquainted with that standing decree of heaven, 'Them that honour me I will honour; and they that despise me shall be lightly esteemed.' Never did man dishonour God, but it proved the greatest dishonour to himself. God will find out ways enough to wipe off any stain that is cast upon him; but you will not so easily remove the shame and sorrow from yourselves.

8. Lastly, Take heed to yourselves, for the success of all your labours doth very much depend upon this. God useth to fit men for great works, before he employs them as his instruments in accomplishing them. Now, if the work of the Lord be not soundly done upon your own hearts, how can you expect that he will bless your labours for effecting it in others? He may do it, if he please, but you have much cause to doubt whether he will. I shall here mention some reasons which may satisfy you, that he who would be a means of saving others, must take heed to himself, and that God doth more seldom prosper the labours of unsanctified men.

(1) Can it be expected that God will bless that man's labours, (I mean comparatively, as to other ministers) who worketh not for God, but for himself? Now, this is the case with every unsanctified man. None but converted men do make God their chief end, and do all or any thing heartily for his honour; others make the ministry but a trade to live by. They choose it rather than another calling, because their parents did destine them to it, or because it affordeth them a competent maintenance; because it is a life wherein they have more opportunity to furnish their intellects with all kind of science; or because it is not so toilsome to the body, to those that have a mind to favour their flesh; because it is accompanied with some reverence and respect from men, and because they think it a fine thing to be leaders and teachers, and have others 'receive the law at their mouth.' For such ends as these are they ministers, and for these do they preach; and, were it not for these, or similar objects, they would soon give over. And can it be expected, that God should much bless the labours of such men as these? It is not for him they preach, but themselves, and their own reputation or gain. It is not

him, but themselves, that they seek and serve; and, therefore, no wonder if he leave them to themselves for the success, and if their labours have no greater a blessing than themselves can give, and if the word reach no further than their own strength can make it reach.

(2) Can you think that he is likely to be as successful as others, who dealeth not heartily and faithfully in his work, who believeth not what he saith, and is not truly serious when he seemeth to be most diligent? And can you think that any unsanctified man can be hearty and serious in the ministerial work? A kind of seriousness indeed he may have, such as proceedeth from a common faith or opinion, that the Word is true; or he may be actuated by a natural fervour, or by selfish ends: but the seriousness and fidelity of a sound believer, who ultimately intendeth God's glory, and men's salvation, this he hath not. O sirs, all your preaching and persuading of others, will be but dreaming and vile hypocrisy, till the work be thoroughly done upon your own hearts. How can you set yourselves, day and night, to a work that your carnal hearts are averse to? How can you call, with serious fervour, upon poor sinners to repent and return to God, that never repented or returned yourselves? How can you heartily follow poor sinners, with importunate solicitations to take heed of sin, and to lead a holy life, that never felt yourselves the evil of sin, or the worth of holiness?

These things are never well known till they are felt, nor well felt till they are possessed; and he that feeleth them not himself, is not likely to speak feelingly of them to others, nor to help others to the feeling of them. How can you follow sinners, with compassion in your hearts and tears in your eyes, and beseech them, in the name of the Lord, to stop their course, and return and live, and never had so much compassion on your own soul, as to do this much for yourselves? What! can you love other men better than yourselves? Can you have pity on them, who have no pity upon yourselves? Sirs, do you think they will be heartily diligent to save men from hell, that be not heartily persuaded that there is a hell? Or to bring men to heaven, that do not truly believe that there is a heaven? As Calvin saith on my text; 'For never will the man take diligent care for the salvation of others who neglects his own salvation.' He that hath not so strong a belief of the Word of God, and of the life to come, as will withdraw his own heart from the vanities of this world, and excite him to holy diligence for salvation, cannot be expected to be faithful in seeking the salvation of other men. Surely he that dare damn himself, dare let others alone in the way to damnation; he that, like Judas, will sell his Master for silver, will not stick to make merchandise of the flock; he that will let go his hopes of heaven, rather than leave his worldly and fleshly delights, will hardly leave them for the saving of others. We may naturally conceive, that he will have no pity on others, that is wilfully cruel to himself; that he is not to be trusted with other men's souls, who is unfaithful to his own, and will sell it to the devil for the short pleasures of sin. I CONFESS, THAT MAN SHALL NEVER HAVE MY CONSENT TO HAVE THE CHARGE OF OTHER MEN'S SOULS, AND TO OVERSEE THEM IN ORDER TO THEIR SALVATION, THAT TAKES NOT HEED TO HIMSELF, BUT IS CARELESS OF HIS OWN, except it were in case of absolute necessity, that no better could be had.

(3) Do you think it is a likely thing, that he will fight against Satan with all his might, who is himself a servant to Satan? Will he do any great harm to the kingdom of the devil, who is himself a member and a subject of that kingdom? Will he be true to Christ who is in covenant with his enemy? Now, this is the case of all unsanctified men, of whatsoever rank or profession they be. They are the servants of Satan, and the subjects of his kingdom; it is he that ruleth in their hearts; and are they like to be true to Christ that are ruled by the devil? What prince will choose the friends and servants of his enemy to lead his armies in war against him? This is it that hath made so many preachers of the gospel to be enemies to the work of the gospel which they preach. No wonder if such deride the holy obedience of the faithful; and if while they take on them to preach a holy life, they cast reproaches on them that practise it! O how many such traitors have been

in the Church of Christ in all ages, who have done more against him, under his colours, than they could have done in the open field! They speak well of Christ and of godliness in the general, and yet slyly do what they can to bring them into disgrace, and make men believe that those who set themselves to seek God with all their hearts are a company of enthusiasts or hypocrites. And when they cannot for shame speak that way in the pulpit, they will do it in private among their acquaintance. Alas! how many such wolves have been set over the sheep! If there was a traitor among the twelve in Christ's family, no wonder if there be many now. It cannot be expected that a slave of Satan, 'whose god is his belly, and who mindeth earthly things,' should be any better than 'an enemy to the cross of Christ.' What though he live civilly, and preach plausibly, and maintain outwardly a profession of religion? He may be as fast in the devil's snares, by worldliness, pride, a secret distaste of diligent godliness, or by an unsound heart that is not rooted in the faith, nor unreservedly devoted to Christ, as others are by drunkenness, uncleanness, and similar disgraceful sins. Publicans and harlots do sooner enter heaven than Pharisees, because they are sooner convinced of their sin and misery.

And, though many of these men may seem excellent preachers, and may cry down sin as loudly as others, yet it is all but an affected fervency, and too commonly but a mere useless bawling; for he who cherisheth sin in his own heart doth never fall upon it in good earnest in others. I know, indeed, that a wicked man may be more willing of the reformation of others than of his own, and hence may show a kind of earnestness in dissuading them from their evil ways; because he can preach against sin at an easier rate than he can forsake it, and another man's reformation may consist with his own enjoyment of his lusts. And, therefore, many a wicked minister or parent may be earnest with their people or children to amend, because they lose not their own sinful profits or pleasures by another's reformation, nor doth it call them to that self-denial which their own doth. But yet for all this, there is none of that zeal, resolution, and diligence, which are found in all that are true to Christ. They set not against sin as the enemy of Christ, and as that which endangereth their people's souls. A traitorous commander, that shooteth nothing against the enemy but powder, may cause his guns to make as great a sound or report as those that are loaded with bullets; but he doth no hurt to the enemy. So one of these men may speak as loudly, and mouth it with an affected fervency, but he seldom doth any great execution against sin and Satan. No man can fight well, but where he hateth, or is very angry; much less against them whom he loveth, and loveth above all. Every unrenewed man is so far from hating sin to purpose, that it is his dearest treasure. Hence you may see, that an unsanctified man, who loveth the enemy, is very unfit to be a leader in Christ's army; and to draw others to renounce the world and the flesh, seeing he cleaveth to them himself as his chief good.

(4) It is not likely that the people will much regard the doctrine of such men, when they see that they do not live as they preach. They will think that he doth not mean as he speaks, if he do not live as he speaks. They will hardly believe a man that seemeth not to believe himself. If one bid you run for your lives, because a bear, or an enemy is at your backs, and yet do not mend his own pace, you will be tempted to think that he is but in jest, and that there is really no such danger as he alleges. When preachers tell people of the necessity of holiness, and that without it no man shall see the Lord, and yet remain unholy themselves, the people will think that they do but talk to pass away the hour, and because they must say somewhat for their money, and that all these are but words of course. Long enough may you lift up your voice against sin, before men will believe that there is any such evil or danger in it as you talk of, while they see the same man that reproacheth it, cherishing it in his bosom, and making it his delight. You rather tempt them to think that there is some special good in it, and that you dispraise it as gluttons do a dish which they love, that they may have it all to themselves. As long as men have eyes as well as ears, they will think they *see* your meaning as well as *hear* it; and

they are apter to believe their sight than their hearing, as being the more perfect sense of the two. All that a minister doth, is a kind of preaching; and if you live a covetous or a careless life, you preach these sins to your people by your practice. If you drink, or game, or trifle away your time in vain discourse, they take it as if you said to them, 'Neighbours, this is the life you should all live; on this course you may venture without any danger.' If you are ungodly, and teach not your families the fear of God, nor contradict the sins of the company you are in, nor turn the stream of their vain talking, nor deal with them plainly about their salvation, they will take it as if you preached to them that such things are needless, and that they may boldly do so as well as you. Nay, you do worse than all this, for you teach them to think evil of others that are better than yourselves.

How many a faithful minister, and private Christian, is hated and reproached for the sake of such as you! What say the people to them? 'You are so precise, and tell us so much of sin, and duty, and make such a stir about these matters, while such or such a minister, that is as great a scholar as you, and as good a preacher, will be merry and jest with us, and let us alone, and never trouble himself or us with such discourse. You can never be quiet, but make more ado than needs; and love to frighten men with talk of damnation, when sober, learned, peaceable divines are quiet, and live with us like other men.' Such are the thoughts and talk of people, which your negligence doth occasion. They will give you leave to preach against their sins, and to talk as much as you will for godliness in the pulpit, if you will but let them alone afterwards, and be friendly and merry with them when you have done, and talk as they do, and live as they, and be indifferent with them in your conversation. For they take the pulpit to be but a stage; a place where preachers must show themselves, and play their parts; where you have liberty for an hour to say what you list; and what you say they regard not, if you show them not, by saying it personally to their faces, that you were in good earnest, and did indeed mean them. Is that man then likely to do much good, or fit to be a minister of Christ, that will speak for him an hour on the sabbath, and, by his life, will preach against him all the week besides, yea, and give his public words the lie?

And if any of the people be wiser than to follow the examples of such men, yet the loathsomeness of their lives will make their doctrine the less effectual. Though you know the meat to be good and wholesome, yet it may make a weak stomach rise against it, if the cook or the servant that carrieth it have leprous or even dirty hands. Take heed therefore to yourselves, if ever you mean to do good to others.

Lastly, Consider whether the success of your labours depends not on the assistance and blessing of the Lord. And where hath he made any promise of his assistance and blessing to ungodly men? If he do promise his Church a blessing even by such, yet doth he not promise *them* any blessing. To his faithful servants he hath promised that he will be with them, that he will put his Spirit upon them, and his word into their mouths, and that Satan shall fall before them as lightning from heaven. But where is there any such promise to ungodly ministers? Nay, do you not, by your hypocrisy and your abuse of God, provoke him to forsake you, and to blast all your endeavours, at least as to yourselves, though he may bless them to his chosen? For I do not deny but that God may do good to his Church by wicked men; yet doth he it not so ordinarily, nor so eminently, as by his own servants.

And what I have said of the wicked themselves, doth hold in part of the godly, while they are scandalous and backsliding, in proportion to the measure of their sin.

CHAPTER II

The oversight of the flock

Section 1
The nature of this oversight

Having showed you, What it is to take heed to ourselves, I am to show you, next, What it is to take heed to all the flock.

It was first necessary to take into consideration, what we must be, and what we must do for our own souls, before we come to that which must be done for others: 'He cannot succeed in healing the wounds of others who is himself unhealed by reason of neglecting himself. He neither benefits his neighbours nor himself. He does not raise up others, but himself falls.'[1] Yea, lest all his labours come to naught, because his heart and life are naught that doth perform them. 'For some persons there are who, though expert in spiritual ministry, go about it in a headstrong manner, and while acting intelligently, tread underfoot any good they do. They teach too hurriedly what can only be rendered holy by meditation; and what they proclaim in public they impugn by their conduct. Whence it is that as pastors they walk in paths too rugged for the flock to follow.'[1] When we have led them to the living waters, if we muddy it by our filthy lives, we may lose our labour, and they be never the better.

Before we speak of the work itself, we shall notice somewhat that is pre-supposed in the words before us.

[1] Gregory, *Pastoral Care*, Book IV.

1. It is here implied, that every flock should have its own
pastor, and every pastor his own flock. As every troop or
company in a regiment of soldiers must have its own captain
and other officers, and every soldier knows his own commander and colours; so it is the will of God, that every
church should have its own pastor, and that all Christ's
disciples 'should know their teachers that are over them in the
Lord.' Though a minister is an officer in the Church universal, yet is he in a special manner the overseer of that particular church which is committed to his charge. When we
are ordained ministers without a special charge, we are licensed
and commanded to do our best for all, as we shall have
opportunity for the exercise of our gifts: but when we have
undertaken a particular charge, we have restrained the exercise
of our gifts so specially to that congregation, that we must
allow others no more than it can spare of our time and help,
except where the public good requireth it, which must, no
doubt, be first regarded. From this relation of pastor and
flock, arise all the duties which they mutually owe to each
other.

2. When we are commanded to take heed to all the flock, it is
plainly implied, that flocks must ordinarily be no greater
than we are capable of overseeing, or 'taking heed to.' God
will not lay upon us natural impossibilities: he will not bind
men to leap up to the moon, to touch the stars, or to number
the sands of the sea. If the pastoral office consists in overseeing
all the flock, then surely the number of souls under the care
of each pastor must not be greater than he is able to take such
heed to as is here required. Will God require one bishop to
take the charge of a whole county, or of so many parishes or
thousands of souls, as he is not able to know or to oversee?
Yea, and to take the sole government of them, while the
particular teachers of them are free from that undertaking?
Will God require the blood of so many parishes at one man's
hands, if he do not that which ten, or twenty, or a hundred,
or three hundred men can no more do, than I can move a
mountain? Then woe to poor prelates! Is it not, then, a most
doleful case, that learned, sober men should plead for this

as a desirable privilege; that they should wilfully draw on themselves such a burden; and that they do not rather tremble at the thoughts of so great an undertaking? O, happy had it been for the Church, and happy for the bishops themselves, if this measure, that is intimated by the apostle here, had still been observed: that the diocese had been no greater than the elders or bishops could oversee and rule, so that they might have taken heed to all the flock: or that pastors had been multiplied as churches increased, and the number of overseers been proportioned to the number of souls, that they might not have let the work be undone, while they assumed the empty titles, and undertook impossibilities! And that they had rather prayed the Lord of the harvest to send forth more labourers, even so many as were proportioned to the work, and not to have undertaken all themselves. I should scarcely commend the prudence or humility of that labourer, let his parts be ever so great, that would not only undertake to gather in all the harvest in this county himself, and that upon pain of death, yea, of damnation, but would also earnestly contend for this prerogative.

But it may be said, there are others to teach, though one only have the rule.

To this I answer: Blessed be God it is so; and no thanks to some of them. But is not government of great concernment to the good of souls, as well as preaching? If it be not, then what use is there for church governors? If it be, then they that nullify it by undertaking impossibilities, do go about to ruin the churches and themselves. If only preaching be necessary, let us have none but mere preachers: what needs there then such a stir about government? But if discipline, in its place, be necessary too, what is it but enmity to men's salvation to exlcude it? and it is unavoidably excluded, when it is made to be his work that is naturally incapable of performing it. The general that will command an army alone, may as well say, Let it be destroyed for want of command: and the schoolmaster that will oversee or govern all the schools in the county alone, may as well say, Let them all be ungoverned: and the physician that will undertake the care of all the sick people in a whole nation, or county, when he is not able to visit the hundredth man of them, may as well say, Let them perish.

Yet still it must be acknowledged, that in case of necessity, where there are not more to be had, one man may undertake the charge of more souls than he is well able to oversee particularly. But then he must undertake only to do what he can for them, and not to do all that a pastor ordinarily ought to do. This is the case of some of us, who have greater parishes than we are able to take that special heed to which their state requireth. I profess for my own part, I am so far from their boldness that dare venture on the sole government of a county, that I would not, for all England, have undertaken to be one of the two that should do all the pastoral work that God requireth, in the parish where I live, had I not this to satisfy my conscience, that, through the Church's necessities, more cannot be had; and therefore, I must rather do what I can, than leave all undone because I cannot do all. But cases of unavoidable necessity are not to be the ordinary condition of the Church; or at least, it is not desirable that it should so be. O happy Church of Christ, were the labourers but able and faithful, and proportioned in number to the number of souls; so that the pastors were so many, or the particular churches so small, that we might be able to 'take heed to all the flock.'

Having noticed these things, which are presupposed, we shall now proceed to consider the duty which is recommended in the text, *Take heed to all the flock*.

It is, you see, *all* the flock, or every individual member of our charge. To this end it is necessary, that we should know every person that belongeth to our charge; for how can we take heed to them, if we do not know them? We must labour to be acquainted, not only with the persons, but with the state of all our people, with their inclinations and conversations; what are the sins of which they are most in danger, and what duties they are most apt to neglect, and what temptations they are most liable to; for if we know not their temperament or disease, we are not likely to prove successful physicians.

Being thus acquainted with all the flock, we must afterward take heed to them. One would imagine that every reasonable man would be satisfied of this, and that it would need no further proof. Doth not a careful shepherd look after every individual sheep? and a good schoolmaster after every individual scholar? and a good physician after every particular patient? and a good commander after every individual soldier? Why then should not the shepherds, the teachers, the physicians, the guides of the churches of Christ, take heed to every individual member of their charge? Christ himself, the great and good Shepherd, that hath the whole to look after, doth yet take care of every individual; like him whom he describes in the parable, who left 'the ninety and nine sheep in the wilderness, to seek after one that was lost.' The prophets were often sent to single men. Ezekiel was made a watchman over individuals, and was commanded to say to the wicked, 'Thou shalt surely die.' Paul taught his hearers not only 'publicly but from house to house:' and in another place he tells us, that he 'warned every man, and taught every man, in all wisdom, that he might present every man perfect in Christ Jesus.' Many other passages of Scripture make it evident that it is our duty to take heed to every individual of our flock; and many passages in the ancient Councils do plainly show that this was the practice of the primitive times. But I shall quote only one from Ignatius: 'Let assemblies,' says he, 'be often gathered; inquire after all by name: despise not servant-men or maids.' You see it was then considered as a duty to look after every member of the flock by name, not excepting the meanest servant-man or maid.

But, some one may object, 'The congregation that I am set over is so great that it is impossible for me to know them all, much more to take heed to all individually.'

To this I answer, Is it necessity or is it not, that hath cast you upon such a charge? If it be not, you excuse one sin by another. How durst you undertake that which you knew yourself unable to perform, when you were not forced to it? It would seem you had some other ends in undertaking it, and never intended to be faithful to your trust. But if you think that you were necessitated to undertake it, I would ask you, might you not have procured assistance for so great a charge? Have you done all that you could with your friends and neighbours, to get maintenance for another to help you? Have you not as much maintenance yourself, as might serve yourself and another? What though it will not serve to maintain you in fulness? Is it not more reasonable that you should pinch your flesh and family, then undertake a work that you cannot perform, and neglect the souls of so many of your flock? I know, that what I say will seem hard to some; but to me it is an unquestionable thing, that, if you have but a hundred pounds a year, it is your duty to live upon part of it, and allow the rest to a competent assistant, rather than that the flock which you are over should be neglected. If you say, that is a hard measure, and that your wife and children cannot so live, I answer, Do not many families in your parish live on less? Have not many able ministers in the prelates' days been glad of less, with liberty to preach the gospel? There are some yet living, as I have heard, who have offered the bishops to enter into bond to preach for nothing, if they might but have liberty to preach the gospel. If you shall still say, that you cannot live so meanly as poor people do, I further ask, Can your parishioners better endure damnation, than you can endure want and poverty? What! do you call yourselves ministers of the gospel, and yet are the souls of men so base in your eyes, that you had rather they should eternally perish, than that you and your family should live in a low and poor condition? Nay, should you not rather beg your bread, than put so great a matter as men's salvation upon a hazard, or disadvantage? Yea, as hazard the damnation of but one soul? O sirs, it is a miserable thing when men study and talk of heaven and hell, and the fewness of the saved, and the difficulty of salvation, and be not all the while in good earnest. If you were, you could never surely stick at such matters as these, and let your people go down to hell, that you might live in higher style in this world. Remember this, the next time you are preaching to them, that they cannot be saved without knowledge; and hearken whether conscience does not tell you, 'It is likely they might be brought to knowledge, if they had but diligent instruction and exhortation privately, man by man; and if there were another minister to assist me, this might be done: and if I would live sparingly and deny my flesh, I might have an assistant. Dare I, then, let my people live in that ignorance which I myself have told them is damning, rather than put myself and family to a little want?'

Must I turn to my Bible to show a preacher where it is written, that a man's soul is worth more than a world, much more therefore than a hundred pounds a year, much more are many souls more worth? Or that both we and all that we have are God's, and should be employed to the utmost for his service? Or that it is inhuman cruelty to let souls go to hell, for fear my wife and children should fare somewhat the harder, or live at lower rates; when, according to God's ordinary way of working by means, I might do much to prevent their misery, if I would but a little displease my flesh, which all, who are Christ's, have crucified with its lusts? Every man must render to God the things that are God's, and that, let it be remembered, is all he is and all he possesses. How are all things sanctified to us, but in the separation and dedication of them to God? Are they not all his talents, and must be employed in his service? Must not every Christian first ask, In what way may I most honour God with my substance? Do we not preach these things to our people? Are they true as to them, and not as to us? Yea more, is not the church-maintenance devoted, in a special manner, to the service of God for the church? And should we not then use it for the utmost furtherance of that end? If any minister who hath two hundred pounds a year can prove that a hundred pounds of it may do God more service, if it be laid out on himself, or wife and children, than if it maintain one or two suitable assistants to help forward the salvation of the flock, I shall not presume to reprove his expenses; but where this cannot be proved, let not the practice be justified.

And I must further say, that this poverty is not so intolerable and dangerous a thing as it is pretended to be. If you have but food and raiment, must you not therewith be content? and what would you have more than that which may fit you for the work of God? It is not 'being clothed in purple and fine linen, and faring sumptuously every day,' that is necessary for this end. 'A man's life consisteth not in the abundance of the things that he possesseth.' If your clothing be warm, and your food be wholesome, you may be as well supported by it to do God service as if you had the fullest satisfaction to your flesh. A patched coat may be warm, and bread and water are wholesome food. He that wanteth not these, hath but a poor excuse to make for hazarding men's souls, that he may live on dainties.

But, while it is our duty to take heed to all the flock, we must pay special attention to some classes in particular. By many, this is very imperfectly understood, and therefore I shall dwell a little upon it.

1. We must labour, in a special manner, for the conversion of the unconverted.

The work of conversion is the first and great thing we must drive at; after this we must labour with all our might. Alas! the misery of the unconverted is so great, that it calleth loudest to us for compassion. If a truly converted sinner do fall, it will be but into sin which will be pardoned, and he is not in that hazard of damnation by it as others are. Not but that God hateth their sins as well as others', or that he will bring them to heaven, let them live ever so wickedly; but the spirit that is within them will not suffer them to live wickedly, nor to sin as the ungodly do. But with the unconverted it is far otherwise. They 'are in the gall of bitterness, and in the bond of iniquity,' and have yet no part nor fellowship in the pardon of their sins, or the hope of glory. We have, therefore, a work of greater necessity to do for them, even 'to open their eyes, and to turn them from darkness to light, and from the power of Satan unto God; that they may receive forgiveness of sins, and an inheritance among them that are sanctified.' He that seeth one man sick of a mortal disease, and another only pained with the toothache, will be moved more

to compassionate the former, than the latter; and will surely
make more haste to help him, though he were a stranger, and
the other a brother or a son. It is so sad a case to see men in a
state of damnation, wherein, if they should die, they are lost
for ever, that methinks we should not be able to let them
alone, either in public or private, whatever other work we
may have to do. I confess, I am frequently forced to neglect
that which should tend to the further increase of knowledge
in the godly, because of the lamentable necessity of the
unconverted. Who is able to talk of controversies, or of nice
unnecessary points, or even of truths of a lower degree of
necessity, how excellent soever, while he seeth a company of
ignorant, carnal, miserable sinners before his eyes, who must
be changed or damned? Methinks I even see them entering
upon their final woe! Methinks I hear them crying out for
help, for speediest help! Their misery speaks the louder,
because they have not hearts to ask for themselves. Many a
time have I known, that I had some hearers of higher fancies,
that looked for rarities, and were addicted to despise the
ministry, if I told them not somewhat more than ordinary;
and yet I could not find in my heart to turn from the necessities of the impenitent, for the humouring of them; nor even
to leave speaking to miserable sinners for their salvation, in
order to speak to such novelists; no, nor so much as should
otherwise be done, to weak saints for their confirmation and
increase in grace. Methinks, as Paul's 'spirit was stirred
within him, when he saw the Athenians wholly given to
idolatry,' so it should cast us into one of his paroxysms, to
see so many men in the utmost danger of being everlastingly
undone. Methinks, if by faith we did indeed look upon them
as within a step of hell, it would more effectually untie our
tongues, than Croesus' danger, as they tell us, did his son's.[1]
He that will let a sinner go down to hell for want of speaking
to him, doth set less by souls than did the Redeemer of

---

[1] Croesus, King of Lydia (6th century B.C.) was about to be killed by a Persian
soldier, when the horror of the sight loosened the tongue of Croesus' dumb
son, and he cried out, 'Fellow, slay not Croesus'. The power of speech there-
after remained with the youth.

souls; and less by his neighbour, than common charity will allow him to do by his greatest enemy. O, therefore, brethren, whomsoever you neglect, neglect not the most miserable! Whatever you pass over, forget not poor souls that are under the condemnation and curse of the law, and who may look every hour for the infernal execution, if a speedy change do not prevent it. O call after the impenitent, and ply this great work of converting souls, whatever else you leave undone.

2. We must be ready to give advice to inquirers, who come to us with cases of conscience; especially the great case which the Jews put to Peter, and the gaoler to Paul and Silas, 'What must we do to be saved?' A minister is not to be merely a public preacher, but to be known as a counsellor for their souls, as the physician is for their bodies, and the lawyer for their estates: so that each man who is in doubts and straits, may bring his case to him for resolution; as Nicodemus came to Christ, and as it was usual with the people of old to go to the priest, 'whose lips must keep knowledge, and at whose mouth they must ask the law, because he is the messenger of the Lord of hosts.' But as the people have become unacquainted with this office of the ministry, and with their own duty and necessity in this respect, it belongeth to us to acquaint them with it, and publicly to press them to come to us for advice about the great concerns of their souls. We must not only be willing to take the trouble, but should draw it upon ourselves, by inviting them to come. What abundance of good might we do, could we but bring them to this! And, doubtless, much might be done in it, if we did our duty. How few have I ever heard of, who have heartily pressed their people to their duty in this way! Oh! it is a sad case that men's souls should be so injured and hazarded by the total neglect of so great a duty, and that ministers should scarcely ever tell them of it, and awaken them to it. Were your hearers but duly sensible of the need and importance of this, you would have them more frequently knocking at your doors, and making known to you their sad complaints, and begging your advice. I beseech you, then, press them more

to this duty for the future; and see that you perform it carefully when they do seek your help. To this end it is very necessary that you be well acquainted with practical cases, and especially that you be acquainted with the nature of saving grace, and able to assist them in trying their state, and in resolving the main question that concerns their everlasting life or death. One word of seasonable, prudent advice, given by a minister to persons in necessity, may be of more use than many sermons. 'A word fitly spoken,' says Solomon, 'how good is it!'

3. We must study to build up those who are already truly converted. In this respect our work is various, according to the various states of Christians.

(1) There are many of our flock that are young and weak, who, though they are of long standing, are yet of small proficiency or strength. This, indeed, is the most common condition of the godly. Most of them content themselves with low degrees of grace, and it is no easy matter to get them higher. To bring them to higher and stricter opinions is easy, that is, to bring them from the truth into error, on the right hand as well as on the left; but to increase their knowledge and gifts is not easy, and to increase their graces is the hardest of all. It is a very sad thing for Christians to be weak: it exposeth us to dangers; it abateth our consolations and delight in God, and taketh off the sweetness of wisdom's ways; it maketh us less serviceable to God and man, to bring less honour to our Master, and to do less good to all about us. We get small benefit in the use of the means of grace. We too easily play with the serpent's baits, and are ensnared by his wiles. A seducer will easily shake us, and evil may be made to appear to us as good, truth as falsehood, sin as duty; and so on the contrary. We are less able to resist and stand in an encounter; we sooner fall; we hardlier rise; and are apter to prove a scandal and reproach to our profession. We less know ourselves, and are more apt to be mistaken as to our own estate, not observing corruptions when they have got advantage of us. We are dishonourable to the gospel by our very weakness, and little useful to any about us. In a word,

though we live to less profit to ourselves or others, yet are we unwilling and too unready to die.

Now, seeing the case of weakness in the converted is so sad, how diligent should we be to cherish and increase their grace! The strength of Christians is the honour of the Church. When they are inflamed with the love of God, and live by a lively working faith, and set light by the profits and honours of the world, and love one another with a pure heart fervently, and can bear and heartily forgive a wrong, and suffer joyfully for the cause of Christ, and study to do good, and walk inoffensively and harmlessly in the world, are ready to be servants to all men for their good, becoming all things to all men in order to win them to Christ, and yet abstaining from the appearance of evil, and seasoning all their actions with a sweet mixture of prudence, humility, zeal, and heavenly mindedness – oh, what an honour are such to their profession! What an ornament to the Church; and how serviceable to God and man! Men would sooner believe that the gospel is from heaven, if they saw more such effects of it upon the hearts and lives of those who profess it. The world is better able to read the nature of religion in a man's life than in the Bible. 'They that obey not the word, may be won by the conversation' of such as are thus eminent for godliness. It is, therefore, a most important part of our work, to labour more in the polishing and perfecting of the saints, that they may be strong in the Lord, and fitted for their Master's service.

(2) Another class of converts that need our special help, are those who labour under some particular corruption, which keeps under their graces, and makes them a trouble to others, and a burden to themselves. Alas! there are too many such persons. Some are specially addicted to pride, and others to worldly-mindedness; some to sensual desires, and others to frowardness or other evil passions. Now it is our duty to give assistance to all these; and partly by dissuasions, and clear discoveries of the odiousness of the sin, and partly by suitable directions about the remedy, to help them to a more complete conquest of their corruptions. We are leaders of Christ's army against the powers of hell, and must resist all the works

of darkness wherever we find them, even though it should be in the children of light. We must be no more tender of the sins of the godly, than of the ungodly, nor any more befriend them or favour them. By how much more we love their persons, by so much the more must we manifest it, by making opposition to their sins. And yet we must look to meet with some tender persons here, especially when iniquity hath got any head, and made a party, and many have fallen in love with it; they will be as pettish and as impatient of reproof as some worse men, and perhaps will interest even piety itself in their faults. But the ministers of Christ must do their duty, notwithstanding their peevishness; and must not so far hate their brother, as to forbear rebuking him, or suffer sin to lie upon his soul. It must, no doubt, be done with much prudence, yet done it must be.

(3) Another class who demand special help are declining Christians, that are either fallen into some scandalous sin, or else abate their zeal and diligence, and show that they have lost their former love. As the case of backsliders is very sad, so our diligence must be very great for their recovery. It is sad to them to lose so much of their life, and peace, and serviceableness to God; and to become so serviceable to Satan and his cause. It is sad to us to see that all our labour is come to this; and that, when we have taken so much pains with them, and have had so much hopes of them, all should be so far frustrated. It is saddest of all, to think that God should be so dishonoured by those whom he hath so loved, and for whom he hath done so much; and that Christ should be so wounded in the house of his friends. Besides, partial backsliding hath a natural tendency to total apostasy, and would effect it, if special grace did not prevent it.

Now, the more sad the case of such Christians is, the more must we exert ourselves for their recovery. We must 'restore those that are overtaken in a fault, in the spirit of meekness,' and yet see that the sore be thoroughly searched and healed, and the joint be well set again, what pain soever it may cost. We must look especially to the honour of the gospel, and see that they give such evidence of true repentance, and make such free and full confession of their sin, that some reparation be thereby made to the Church and their holy profession, for the wound they have given to religion. Much skill is required for restoring such a soul.

(4) The last class whom I shall here notice, as requiring our attention, are the strong; for they, also, have need of our assistance: partly to preserve the grace they have; partly to help them in making further progress; and partly to direct them in improving their strength for the service of Christ, and the assistance of their brethren; and, also, to encourage them to persevere, that they may receive the crown.

All these are the objects of the ministerial work, and in respect to each of them, we must 'take heed to all the flock.'

4. We must have a special eye upon families, to see that they are well ordered, and the duties of each relation performed. The life of religion, and the welfare and glory of both the Church and the State, depend much on family government and duty. If we suffer the neglect of this, we shall undo all. What are we like to do ourselves to the reforming of a congregation, if all the work be cast on us alone; and masters of families neglect that necessary duty of their own, by which they are bound to help us? If any good be begun by the ministry in any soul, a careless, prayerless, worldly family is like to stifle it, or very much hinder it; whereas, if you could but get the rulers of families to do their duty, to take up the work where you left it, and help it on, what abundance of good might be done! I beseech you, therefore, if you desire the reformation and welfare of your people, do all you can to promote family religion. To this end, let me entreat you to attend to the following things:

(1) Get information how each family is ordered, that you may know how to proceed in your endeavours for their further good.

(2) Go occasionally among them, when they are likely to be most at leisure, and ask the master of the family whether he prays with them, and reads the Scripture, or what he doth? Labour to convince such as neglect this, of their sin; and if

you have opportunity, pray with them before you go, and give them an example of what you would have them do. Perhaps, too, it might be well to get a promise from them, that they will make more conscience of their duty for the future.

(3) If you find any, through ignorance and want of practice, unable to pray, persuade them to study their own wants, and to get their hearts affected with them, and, in the meanwhile, advise them to use a form of prayer, rather than not pray at all. Tell them, however, that it is their sin and shame that they have lived so negligently, as to be so unacquainted with their own necessities as not to know how to speak to God in prayer, when every beggar can find words to ask an alms; and, therefore, that a form of prayer is but for necessity, as a crutch to a cripple, while they cannot do well without it; but that they must resolve not to be content with it, but to learn to do better as speedily as possible, seeing that prayer should come from the feelings of the heart, and be varied according to our necessities and circumstances.

(4) See that in every family there are some useful moving books, beside the Bible. If they have none, persuade them to buy some: if they be not able to buy them, give them some if you can. If you are not able yourself, get some gentlemen, or other rich persons, that are ready to good works, to do it. And engage them to read them at night, when they have leisure, and especially on the Lord's day.

(5) Direct them how to spend the Lord's day; how to despatch their worldly business, so as to prevent encumbrances and distractions; and when they have been at church, how to spend the time in their families. The life of religion dependeth much on this, because poor people have no other free considerable time; and, therefore, if they lose this, they lose all, and will remain ignorant and brutish. Persuade the master of every family to cause his children and servants to repeat the Catechism to him, every Sabbath evening, and to give him some account of what they have heard at church during the day.

Neglect not, I beseech you, this important part of your

work. Get masters of families to do their duty, and they will not only spare you a great deal of labour, but will much further the success of your labours. If a captain can get the officers under him to do their duty, he may rule the soldiers with much less trouble, than if all lay upon his own shoulders. You are not like to see any general reformation, till you procure family reformation. Some little religion there may be, here and there; but while it is confined to single persons, and is not promoted in families, it will not prosper, nor promise much future increase.

5. We must be diligent in visiting the sick, and helping them to prepare either for a fruitful life, or a happy death. Though this should be the business of all our life and theirs, yet doth it, at such a season, require extraordinary care both of them and us. When time is almost gone, and they must now or never be reconciled to God, oh, how doth it concern them to redeem those hours, and to lay hold on eternal life! And when we see that we are like to have but a few days or hours more to speak to them, in order to their everlasting welfare, who, that is not a block or an infidel, would not be much with them, and do all he can for their salvation in that short space?

Will it not awaken us to compassion, to look on a languishing man, and to think that within a few days his soul will be in heaven or in hell? Surely it will try the faith and seriousness of ministers, to be much about dying men! They will thus have opportunity to discern whether they themselves are in good earnest about the matters of the life to come. So great is the change that is made by death, that it should awaken us to the greatest sensibility to see a man so near it, and should excite in us the deepest pangs of compassion, to do the office of inferior angels for the soul, before it departs from the body, that it may be ready for the convoy of superior angels to the 'inheritance of the saints in light.' When a man is almost at his journey's end, and the next step brings him to heaven or hell, it is time for us, while there is hope, to help him if we can.

And as their present necessity should move us to embrace that opportunity for their good, so should the advantage that sickness and the prospect of death affordeth. Even the stoutest sinners will hear us on their death-bed, though they scorned us before. They will then let fall their fury, and be as gentle as lambs, who were before as untractable as lions. I find not one in ten, of the most obstinate scornful wretches in my parish, but when they come to die, will humble themselves, confess their faults, and seem penitent, and promise, if they should recover, to reform their lives. Cyprian saith to those in health, 'He who everyday reminds himself that he is dying, despises the present and hastens to things to come. Much more he who feels himself to be in the very act of dying.' O how resolvedly will the worst of sinners seem to cast away their sins and promise reformation, and cry out of their folly, and of the vanity of this world, when they see that death is in good earnest with them, and away they must without delay! Perhaps you will say, that these forced changes are not cordial, and that, therefore, we have no great hope of doing them any saving good. I confess it is very common for sinners to be frightened into ineffectual purposes, but not so common to be at such a season converted to the Saviour. It is a remark of Augustine, 'He cannot die badly who lives well; and scarcely shall he die well who lives badly.' Yet 'scarcely' and 'never' are not all one. It should make both them and us the more diligent in the time of health, because it is 'scarcely'; but yet we should bestir us at the last, in the use of the best remedies, because it is not 'never'.

But as I do not intend to furnish a directory for the whole ministerial work, I will not stop to tell you particularly what must be done for men in their last extremity; but shall notice only three or four things, as specially worthy of your attention.

(1) Stay not till their strength and understanding are gone, and the time so short that you scarcely know what to do; but go to them as soon as you hear they are sick, whether they send for you or not.

(2) When the time is so short, that there is no opportunity to instruct them in the principles of religion in order, be sure to ply the main points, and to dwell on those truths which

are most calculated to promote their conversion, showing them the glory of the life to come, and the way by which it was purchased for us, and the great sin and folly of their having neglected it in time of health; but yet the possibility that remaineth of their still obtaining it, if they will believe in Christ, the only Saviour, and repent of their sins.

(3) If they recover, be sure to remind them of their promises and resolutions in time of sickness. Go to them purposely to set these home to their consciences; and whenever, afterwards, you see them remiss, go to them, and put them in mind of what they said when they were stretched on a sick-bed. And because it is of such use to them who recover, and hath been the means of the conversion of many a soul, it is very necessary that you go to them whose sickness is not mortal, as well as to those who are dying, that so you may have some advantage to move them to repentance, and may afterward have this to plead against their sins; as a bishop of Cologne is said to have answered the Emperor Sigismund, when he asked him what was the way to be saved, 'He must be what he purposed, or promised to be, when he was last troubled with the stone and the gout.'

6. We must reprove and admonish those who live offensively or impenitently. Before we bring such matters before the church, or its rulers, it is ordinarily most fit for the minister to try himself what he can do in private to bow the sinner to repentance, especially if it be not a public crime. Here there is required much skill, and a difference must be made, according to the various tempers of the offenders; but with the most it will be necessary to speak with the greatest plainness and power, to shake their careless hearts, and make them see what it is to dally with sin; to let them know the evil of it, and its sad effects as regards both God and themselves.

7. The last part of our oversight, which I shall notice, consisteth in the exercise of Church discipline. This consisteth, after the aforesaid private reproofs, in more public reproof, combined with exhortation to repentance, in prayer for the offender, in restoring the penitent, and in excluding and avoiding the impenitent.

(1) In the case of public offences, and even of those of a more private nature, when the offender remains impenitent, he must be reproved before all, and again invited to repentance. This is not the less our duty, because we have made so little conscience of the practice of it. It is not only Christ's command to tell the church, but Paul's to 'rebuke before all;' and the Church did constantly practise it, till selfishness and formality caused them to be remiss in this and other duties. There is no room to doubt whether this be our duty, and as little is there any ground to doubt whether we have been unfaithful as to the performance of it. Many of us, who would be ashamed to omit preaching or praying half so much, have little considered what we are doing, while living in the wilful neglect of this duty, and other parts of discipline, so long as we have done. We little think how we have drawn the guilt of swearing, and drunkenness, and fornication, and other crimes upon our own heads, by neglecting to use the means which God has appointed for the cure of them.

If any shall say, There is little likelihood that public reproof will do them good, that they will rather be enraged by the shame of it; I answer –

[a] It ill becomes a creature to implead the ordinances of God as useless, or to reproach God's service instead of doing it, and to set his wits in opposition to his Maker. God can render useful his own ordinances, or else he would never have appointed them.

[b] The usefulness of discipline is apparent, in the shaming of sin and humbling the sinner, and in manifesting the holiness of Christ, and of his doctrine and Church, before all the world.

[c] What will you do with such sinners? Will you give them up as hopeless? That would be more cruel than administering reproof to them. Will you use other means? Why, it is supposed that all other means have been used without success; for this is the last remedy.

[d] The principal use of this public discipline is not for the offender himself, but for the Church. It tendeth exceedingly to deter others from the like crimes, and so to keep the congregation and their worship pure. Seneca could say, 'He

who excuses present evils transmits them to posterity.' And elsewhere, 'He who spares the guilty harms the good.'

(2) With reproof we must join exhortation of the offender to repentance, and to the public profession of it for the satisfaction of the church. As the church is bound to avoid communion with impenitent scandalous sinners, so, when they have had evidence of their sin, they must also have some evidence of their repentance; for we cannot know them to be penitent without evidence; and what evidence can the church have but their profession of repentance, and afterwards their actual reformation?

Much prudence, I confess, is to be exercised in such proceedings, lest we do more hurt than good; but it must be such Christian prudence as ordereth duties, and suiteth them to their ends, not such carnal prudence as shall enervate or exclude them. In performing this duty, we should deal humbly, even when we deal most sharply, and make it appear that it is not from any ill will, nor any lordly disposition, nor from revenge for any injury, but a necessary duty which we cannot conscientiously neglect; and, therefore, it may be meet to show the people the commands of God obliging us to do what we do, in some such words as the following:

'Brethren, sin is so hateful an evil in the eyes of the most holy God, how light soever impenitent sinners make of it, that he hath provided the everlasting torments of hell for the punishment of it; and no lesser means can prevent that punishment than the sacrifice of the Son of God, applied to those who truly repent of and forsake it; and therefore God, who calleth all men to repentance, hath commanded us to "exhort one another daily, while it is called To-day, lest any be hardened through the deceitfulness of sin," (Hebrews 3.13) and that we do not hate our brother in our heart, but in any wise rebuke our neighbour, and not suffer sin upon him, (Leviticus 19.17) and that if our brother offend us, we should tell him his fault between him and us; and if he hear us not, we should take two or three more with us; and if he hear not them, we should tell the church; and if he hear not the church, he must be to us as a heathen man and a publican;

(Matthew 18.15–17) and those that sin, we must rebuke before all, that others may fear, (1 Timothy 5.20) and rebuke with all authority: (Titus 2.15) yea, were it an apostle of Christ that should sin openly, he must be reproved openly, as Paul did Peter; (Galatians 2.11, 14) and if they repent not, we must avoid them, and with such not so much as eat, (2 Thessalonians 3.6, 11, 12, 14; 1 Corinthians 5.11–13.)

'Having heard of the scandalous conduct of A.B. of this church, or parish, and having received sufficient proof that he hath committed the odious sin of ——, we have seriously dealt with him to bring him to repentance; but, to the grief of our hearts, we perceive no satisfactory result of our endeavours; but he seemeth still to remain impenitent (or he still liveth in the same sin, though he verbally professes repentance). We therefore judge it our duty to proceed to the use of that further remedy which Christ hath commanded us to try; and hence we beseech him, in the name of the Lord, without further delay, to lay to heart the greatness of his sin, the wrong he hath done to Christ and to himself, and the scandal and grief that he hath caused to others. And I do earnestly beseech him, for the sake of his own soul, that he will consider, what it is that he can gain by his sin and impenitency, and whether it will pay for the loss of everlasting life; and how he thinks to stand before God in judgment, or to appear before the Lord Jesus, when death shall snatch his soul from his body, if he be found in this impenitent state. And I do beseech him, for the sake of his own soul, and, as a messenger of Jesus Christ, require him, as he will answer the contrary at the bar of God, that he lay aside the stoutness and impenitency of his heart, and unfeignedly confess and lament his sin before God and this congregation. And this desire I here publish, not out of any ill will to his person, as the Lord knoweth, but in love to his soul, and in obedience to Christ, who hath made it my duty; desiring that, if it be possible, he may be saved from his sin, and from the power of Satan, and from the everlasting wrath of God, and may be reconciled to God and to his church; and, therefore, that he may be humbled by true contrition, before he be humbled by remediless condemnation.'

To this purpose I conceive our public admonitions should proceed; and, in some cases, where the sinner considereth his sin to be small, it may be necessary to point out the aggravations of it, particularly by citing some passages of Scripture which speak of its evil and its danger.

(3) With these reproofs and exhortations, we must join the prayers of the congregation in behalf of the offender. This should be done in every case of discipline, but particularly if the offender will not be present to receive admonition, or gives no evidence of repentance, and shows no desire for the prayers of the congregation. In such cases, especially, it will be meet that we beg the prayers of the congregation for him ourselves, entreating them to consider what a fearful condition the impenitent are in, and to have pity on a poor soul that is so blinded and hardened by sin and Satan, that he cannot pity himself; and to think what it is for a man to appear before the living God in such a case, and, therefore, that they would join in earnest prayer to God, that he would open his eyes, and soften, and humble his stubborn heart, before he be in hell beyond remedy. And, accordingly, let us be very earnest in prayer for him, that the congregation may be excited affectionately to join with us; and who knows but God may hear our prayers, and the sinner's heart may relent under them, more than under all our exhortations?

It is, in my judgment, a very laudable course of some churches, that use, for the next three days together, to desire the congregation to join in earnest prayer to God for the opening of the sinner's eyes, and the softening of his heart, and the saving of him from impenitency and eternal death.

If ministers would be conscientious in performing this duty entirely and self-denyingly, they might make something of it, and expect a blessing upon it; but when we shrink from all that is dangerous or ungrateful in our work, and shift off all that is costly or troublesome, we cannot expect that any great good should be effected by such a carnal, partial use of means; and though some may here and there be wrought upon, yet we cannot look that the gospel should run and be glorified when we do our duty so lamely and so defectively.

(4) We must restore the penitent to the fellowship of the church. As we must not teach an offender to make light of discipline by too much facility, so neither must we discourage him by too much severity. If he appear to be truly sensible of the sinfulness of his conduct, and penitent on account of it, we must see that he confess his guilt, and that he promise to fly from such sins for the time to come, to watch more narrowly and to walk more warily, to avoid temptation, to distrust his own strength, and to rely on the grace which is in Christ Jesus.

We must assure him of the riches of God's love, and the sufficiency of Christ's blood to pardon his sins, if he believe and repent.

We must see that he begs to be restored to the communion of the church, and desires their prayers to God for his pardon and salvation.

We must charge the church that they imitate Christ, in forgiving and in retaining the penitent person; or, if he were cast out, in restoring him to their communion; and that they must never reproach him with his sins, nor cast them in his teeth, but forgive them, even as Christ doth.

Finally, we must give God thanks for his recovery, and pray for his confirmation and future preservation.

(5) The last part of discipline is the excluding from the communion of the church those who, after sufficient trial, remain impenitent.

Exclusion from church communion, commonly called ex-communication, is of divers sorts or degrees, which are not to be confounded; but that which is most commonly to be practised amongst us, is, only to remove an impenitent sinner from our communion, till it shall please the Lord to give him repentance.

In this exclusion or removal, the minister or governors of the church are authoritatively to charge the people, in the name of the Lord, to have no communion with him, and to pronounce him one whose communion the church is bound to avoid; and it is the people's duty carefully to avoid him, provided the pastor's charge contradict not the Word of God.

Nevertheless, we must pray for the repentance and restoration even of the excommunicated; and if God shall give them repentance, we must gladly receive them again into the communion of the church.

Would we were but so far faithful in the practice of this discipline, as we are satisfied both of the matter and manner of it; and did not dispraise and reproach it by our negligence, while we write and plead for it with the highest commendations! It is worthy of our consideration, who is like to have the heavier charge about this matter at the bar of God – whether those who have reproached and hindered discipline by their tongues, because they knew not its nature and necessity; or we who have so vilified it by our constant omission, while with our tongues we have magnified it? If hypocrisy be no sin, or if the knowledge of our Master's will by no aggravation of disobedience, then we may be in a better case than they; but if these be great evils, we must be much worse than the very persons whom we so loudly condemn. I will not advise the zealous maintainers, and obstinate neglecters of discipline, to unsay all that they have said, till they are ready to do as they say; nor to recant their defences of discipline, till they mean to practise it; nor to burn all the books which they have written for it, and all the records of their cost and hazards for it, lest they rise up in judgment against them, to their confusion. But I would persuade them, without any more delay, to conform their practice to these testimonies which they have given, lest the more they are proved to have commended discipline, the more they are proved to have condemned themselves for neglecting it.

It hath somewhat amazed me to hear some, that I took for reverend, godly divines, reproach, as a sect, the Sacramentarians and Disciplinarians. And, when I desired to know whom they meant, they told me they meant them that will not give the sacrament to all the parish, and them that will make distinctions by their discipline. I had thought the tempter had obtained a great victory, if he had got but one godly pastor of a church to neglect discipline, as well as if he had got him to neglect preaching; much more if he had got him to approve of that neglect: but it seems that he hath got some to scorn at the performers of the duty which they neglect. Sure I am, if it were well understood how much of the pastoral authority and work consisteth in church guidance, it would be also discerned, that to be against discipline, is near to being against the ministry; and to be against the ministry is near to being absolutely against the church; and to be against the church, is near to being absolutely against Christ. Blame not the harshness of the inference, till you can avoid it, and free yourselves from the charge of it before the Lord.

Section 2
The manner of this oversight

Having thus considered the nature of this oversight, we shall next speak of the manner; not of each part distinctly, lest we be tedious, but of the whole in general.

1. The ministerial work must be carried on purely for God and the salvation of souls, not for any private ends of our own. A wrong end makes all the work bad as from us, how good soever it may be in its own nature. It is not serving God, but ourselves, if we do it not for God, but for ourselves. They who engage in this as a common work, to make a trade of it for their worldly livelihood, will find that they have chosen a bad trade, though a good employment. Self-denial is of absolute necessity in every Christian, but it is doubly necessary in a minister, as without it he cannot do God an hour's faithful service. Hard studies, much knowledge, and excellent preaching, if the ends be not right, is but more glorious hypocritical sinning. The saying of Bernard is commonly known: 'Some desire to know merely for the sake

of knowing, and that is shameful curiosity. Some desire to know that they may sell their knowledge, and that too is shameful. Some desire to know for reputation's sake, and that is shameful vanity. But there are some who desire to know that they may edify others, and that is praiseworthy; and there are some who desire to know that they themselves may be edified, and that is wise.'

2. The ministerial work must be carried on diligently and laboriously, as being of such unspeakable consequence to ourselves and others. We are seeking to uphold the world, to save it from the curse of God, to perfect the creation, to attain the ends of Christ's death, to save ourselves and others from damnation, to overcome the devil, and demolish his kingdom, to set up the kingdom of Christ, and to attain and help others to the kingdom of glory. And are these works to be done with a careless mind, or a lazy hand? O see, then, that this work be done with all your might! Study hard, for the well is deep, and our brains are shallow; and, as Cassiodorus[1] says: 'Here the common level of knowledge is not to be the limit; here a true ambition is demonstrated; the more a deep knowledge is sought after, the greater the honour in attaining it.' But especially be laborious in the practice and exercise of your knowledge. Let Paul's words ring continually in your ears, 'Necessity is laid upon me; yea, woe is unto me, if I preach not the gospel!' Ever think with yourselves what lieth upon your hands: 'If I do not bestir myself, Satan may prevail, and the people everlastingly perish, and their blood be required at my hand. By avoiding labour and suffering, I shall draw on myself a thousand times more than I avoid; whereas, by present diligence, I shall prepare for future blessedness.' No man was ever a loser by God.

3. The ministerial work must be carried on prudently and orderly. Milk must go before strong meat; the foundation must be laid before we attempt to raise the superstructure. Children must not be dealt with as men of full stature. Men must be brought into a state of grace, before we can expect from them the works of grace. The work of conversion, and

[1] Italian statesman and historian of the 6th century.

repentance from dead works, and faith in Christ, must be first and frequently and thoroughly taught. We must not ordinarily go beyond the capacities of our people, nor teach them the perfection, that have not learned the first principles of religion: for, as Gregory of Nyssa[1] saith: 'We teach not infants the deep precepts of science, but first letters, and then syllables, &c. So the guides of the Church do first propound to their hearers certain documents, which are as the elements; and so by degrees do open to them the more perfect and mysterious matters.' Therefore did the Church take so much pains with their catechumens, before they baptized them, and would not lay unpolished stones into the building.

4. Throughout the whole course of our ministry, we must insist chiefly upon the greatest, most certain, and most necessary truths, and be more seldom and sparing upon the rest. If we can but teach Christ to our people, we shall teach them all. Get them well to heaven, and they will have knowledge enough. The great and commonly acknowledged truths of religion are those that men must live upon, and which are the great instruments of destroying men's sins, and raising the heart to God. We must, therefore, ever have our people's necessities before our eyes. To remember the 'one thing needful' will take us off gauds and needless ornaments, and unprofitable controversies. Many other things are desirable to be known; but this must be known, or else our people are undone for ever. I confess I think NECESSITY should be the great disposer of a minister's course of study and labour. If we were sufficient for everything, we might attempt everything, and take in order the whole Encyclopaedia: but life is short, and we are dull, and eternal things are necessary, and the souls that depend on our teaching are precious. I confess, necessity hath been the conductor of my studies and life. It chooseth what book I shall read, and tells me when, and how long. It chooseth my text, and makes my sermon, both for matter and manner, so far as I can keep out my own corruption. Though I know the constant expectation of death hath been a great cause of this, yet I know no reason why the

[1] A Cappadocian Father (4th century).

most healthy man should not make sure of the most necessary things first, considering the uncertainty and shortness of all men's lives. Xenophon thought, 'there was no better teacher than necessity, which teacheth all things most diligently.' Who can, in studying, preaching, or labouring, be doing other matters, if he do but know that this MUST be done? Who can trifle or delay, that feeleth the urgent spurs of necessity? As the soldier saith, 'No lengthy discussing, but speedy and strong contending is needed where necessity urges on', so much more must we, as our business is more important. Doubtless this is the best way to redeem time, to see that we lose not an hour, when we spend it only on necessary things. This is the way to be most profitable to others, though not always to be most pleasing and applauded; because, through men's frailty, it is true what Seneca says, that 'We are attracted to novelties rather than to great things.'

Hence it is, that a preacher must be oft upon the same things, because the matters of necessity are few. We must not either feign necessaries, or fall much upon unnecessaries, to satisfy them that look for novelties, though we must clothe the same truths with a grateful variety in the manner of our delivery. The great volumes and tedious controversies that so much trouble us and waste our time, are usually made up more of opinions than of necessary verities; for, as Ficinus[1] saith, 'Necessity is shut up within narrow limits; not so with opinion': and, as Gregory Nazianzen[2] and Seneca often say, 'Necessaries are common and obvious; it is superfluities that we waste our time for, and labour for, and complain that we attain them not.' Ministers, therefore, must be observant of the case of their flocks, that they may know what is most necessary for them, both for matter and for manner; and usually the matter is to be first regarded, as being of more importance than the manner. If you are to choose what authors to read yourselves, will you not rather take those that tell you what you know not, and that speak the most necessary truths in the clearest manner, though it be in barbarous or

[1] Italian philosopher (15th century).
[2] A Cappadocian Father (4th century).

unhandsome language, than those that will most learnedly
and elegantly tell you that which is false or vain, and 'by a
great effort say nothing.' I purpose to follow Augustine's
counsel: 'Give first place to the meaning of the Word, so that
the soul is given preference over the body; from which it
follows that we seek the more true as much as the more dis-
cerning discourses to be met with, just as we seek the more
sensible, as much as the more handsome, to be our friends.'
And surely, as I do in my studies for my own edification, I
should do in my teaching for other men's. It is commonly
empty, ignorant men who want the matter and substance of
true learning, that are over curious and solicitous about
words and ornaments, when the old, experienced, and most
learned men, abound in substantial verities delivered usually
in the plainest dress. As Aristotle makes it the reason why
women are more addicted to pride in apparel than men, that,
being conscious of little inward worth, they seek to make it
up with outward borrowed ornaments; so is it with empty,
worthless preachers, who affect to be esteemed that which they
are not, and have no other way to procure that esteem.

5. All our teaching must be as plain and simple as possible.
This doth best suit a teacher's ends. He that would be understood must speak to the capacity of his hearers. Truth loves
the light, and is most beautiful when most naked. It is the
sign of an envious enemy to hide the truth; and it is the work
of a hypocrite to do this under pretence of revealing it; and
therefore painted obscure sermons (like painted glass in
windows which keeps out the light) are too oft the marks of
painted hypocrites. If you would not teach men, what do you
in the pulpit? If you would, why do you not speak so as to
be understood? I know the height of the matter may make a
man not understood, when he hath studied to make it as
plain as he can; but that a man should purposely cloud the
matter in strange words, and hide his mind from the people,
whom he pretendeth to instruct, is the way to make fools
admire his profound learning, and wise men his folly, pride,
and hypocrisy. Some men conceal their sentiments, under the
pretence of necessity, because of men's prejudices, and the

unpreparedness of common understandings to receive the truth. But truth overcomes prejudice by the mere light of evidence, and there is no better way to make a good cause prevail, than to make it as plain, and as generally and thoroughly known as we can; it is this light that will dispose an unprepared mind. It is, at best, a sign that a man hath not well digested the matter himself, if he is not able to deliver it plainly to others. I mean as plainly as the nature of the matter will bear, in regard of capacities prepared for it by pre-requisite truths; for I know that some men cannot at present understand some truths, if you speak them as plainly as words can express them; as the easiest rules in grammar, most plainly taught, will not be understood by a child that is but learning his alphabet.

6. Our work must be carried on with great humility. We must carry ourselves meekly and condescendingly to all; and so teach others, as to be as ready to learn of any that can teach us, and so both teach and learn at once; not proudly venting our own conceits, and disdaining all that any way contradict them, as if we had attained to the height of knowledge, and were destined for the chair, and other men to sit at our feet. Pride is a vice that ill beseems them that must lead men in such an humble way to heaven: let us, therefore, take heed, lest, when we have brought others thither, the gate should prove too strait for ourselves. For, as Grotius saith, 'Pride is born in heaven, but as if unmindful that the way from that place is closed, it is impossible for it to return afterwards!' God, that thrust out a proud angel, will not entertain there a proud preacher. Methinks we should remember, at least the title of a *Minister*, which, though the popish priests disdain, yet so do not we. It is this pride at the root that feedeth all the rest of our sins. Hence the envy, the contention, and un-peaceableness of ministers; hence the stops to all reformation; all would lead, and few will follow or concur. Hence, also, is the non-proficiency of too many ministers, because they are too proud to learn. Humility would teach them another lesson. I may say of ministers as Augustine to Jerome, even of the aged among them, 'Although it is more fitting for the

aged to teach than to learn, much more is it fitting to learn than to be ignorant.'

7. There must be a prudent mixture of severity and mildness both in our preaching and discipline; each must be predominant, according to the quality or character of the person, or matter, that we have in hand. If there be *no* severity, our reproofs will be despised. If *all* severity, we shall be taken as usurpers of dominion, rather than persuaders of the minds of men to the truth.

8. We must be serious, earnest, and zealous in every part of our work. Our work requireth greater skill, and especially greater life and zeal than any of us bring to it. It is no small matter to stand up in the face of a congregation, and to deliver a message of salvation or damnation, as from the living God, in the name of the Redeemer. It is no easy matter to speak so plainly, that the most ignorant may understand us; and so seriously that the deadest hearts may feel us; and so convincingly, that the contradicting cavillers may be silenced. The weight of our matter condemneth coldness and sleepy dulness. We should see that we be well awakened ourselves, and our spirits in such a plight as may make us fit to awaken others. If our words be not sharpened, and pierce not as nails, they will hardly be felt by stony hearts. To speak slightly and coldly of heavenly things is nearly as bad as to say nothing of them at all.

9. The whole of our ministry must be carried on in tender love to our people. We must let them see that nothing pleaseth us but what profiteth them; and that what doeth them good doth us good; and that nothing troubleth us more than their hurt. We must feel toward our people, as a father toward his children: yea, the tenderest love of a mother must not surpass ours. We must even travail in birth, till Christ be formed in them. They should see that we care for no outward thing, neither wealth, nor liberty, nor honour, nor life, in comparison of their salvation; but could even be content, with Moses, to have our names blotted out of the book of life, i.e. to be removed from the number of the living: rather than they should not be found in the Lamb's book of life. Thus should

we, as John saith, be ready to 'lay down our lives for the
brethren,' and, with Paul, not count our lives dear to us, so
we may but 'finish our course with joy, and the ministry
which we have received of the Lord Jesus.' When the people
see that you unfeignedly love them, they will hear any thing
and bear any thing from you; as Augustine saith, 'Love God,
and do what you please.' We ourselves will take all things
well from one that we know doth entirely love us. We will
put up with a blow that is given us in love, sooner than with a
foul word that is spoken to us in malice or in anger. Most
men judge of the counsel, as they judge of the affection of
him that gives it: at least, so far as to give it a fair hearing. Oh,
therefore, see that you feel a tender love to your people in
your breasts, and let them perceive it in your speeches, and
see it in your conduct. Let them see that you spend, and are
spent, for their sakes; and that all you do is for them, and not
for any private ends of your own. To this end the works of
charity are necessary, as far as your estate will reach; for bare
words will hardly convince men that you have any great
love to them. But, if you are not able to give, show that you
are willing to give if you had it, and do that sort of good you
can. But see that your love be not carnal, flowing from pride,
as one that is a suitor for himself rather than for Christ, and,
therefore, doth love because he is loved, or that he may be
loved. Take heed, therefore, that you do not connive at the
sins of your people, under pretence of love, for that were to
cross the nature and end of love. Friendship must be cemented
by piety. A wicked man cannot be a true friend; and, if you
befriend their wickedness, you show that you are wicked
yourselves. Pretend not to love them, if you favour their sins,
and seek not their salvation. By favouring their sins, you will
show your enmity to God; and then how can you love your
brother? If you be their best friends, help them against their
worst enemies. And think not all sharpness inconsistent with
love: parents correct their children, and God himself 'chastens
every son whom he receiveth.' Augustine saith, 'Better it is to
love even with the accompaniment of severity, than to mislead
by (excess of) lenity.'

10. We must carry on our work with patience. We must bear with many abuses and injuries from those to whom we seek to do good. When we have studied for them, and prayed for them, and exhorted them, and beseeched them with all earnestness and condescension, and given them what we are able, and tended them as if they had been our children, we must look that many of them will requite us with scorn and hatred and contempt, and account us their enemies, because we 'tell them the truth.' Now, we must endure all this patiently, and we must unweariedly hold on in doing good, 'in meekness instructing those that oppose themselves, if God, peradventure, will give them repentance to the acknowledging of the truth.' We have to deal with distracted men who will fly in the face of their physician, but we must not, therefore, neglect their cure. He is unworthy to be a physician, who will be driven away from a phrenetic patient by foul words. Yet, alas, when sinners reproach and slander us for our love, and are more ready to spit in our faces, than to thank us for our advice, what heart-risings will there be, and how will the remnants of old Adam (pride and passion) struggle against the meekness and patience of the new man! And how sadly do many ministers come off under such trials!

11. All our work must be managed reverently, as beseemeth them that believe the presence of God, and use not holy things as if they were common. Reverence is that affection of the soul which proceedeth from deep apprehensions of God and indicateth a mind that is much conversant with him. To manifest irreverence in the things of God is to manifest hypocrisy, and that the heart agreeth not with the tongue. I know not how it is with others, but the most reverent preacher, that speaks as if he saw the face of God, doth more affect my heart, though with common words, than an irreverent man with the most exquisite preparations. Yea, though he bawl it out with never so much seeming earnestness, if reverence be not answerable to fervency, it worketh but little. Of all preaching in the world, (that speaks not stark lies) I hate that preaching which tends to make the hearers laugh, or to move their minds with tickling levity,

and affect them as stage-plays used to do, instead of affecting them with a holy reverence of the name of God. Jerome says, 'Teach in thy church, not to get the applause of the people, but to set in motion the groan; the tears of the hearers are thy praises.' The more of God appeareth in our duties, the more authority will they have with men. We should, as it were, suppose we saw the throne of God, and the millions of glorious angels attending him, that we may be awed with his majesty when we draw near him in holy things, lest we profane them and take his name in vain.

12. All our work must be done spiritually, as by men possessed of the Holy Ghost. There is in some men's preaching a spiritual strain, which spiritual hearers can discern and relish; whereas, in other men's, this sacred tincture is so wanting, that, even when they speak of spiritual things, the manner is such as if they were common matters. Our evidence and illustrations of divine truth must also be spiritual, being drawn from the Holy Scriptures, rather than from the writings of men. The wisdom of the world must not be magnified against the wisdom of God; philosophy must be taught to stoop and serve, while faith doth bear the chief sway. Great scholars in Aristotle's school must take heed of glorying too much in their master, and despising those that are below them, lest they themselves prove lower in the school of Christ, and 'least in the kingdom of God,' while they would be great in the eyes of men. As wise a man as any of them would glory in nothing but the cross of Christ, and determined to know nothing but him crucified. They that are so confident that Aristotle is in hell, should not too much take him for their guide in the way to heaven. It is an excellent memorandum that Gregory hath left: 'God in the first place gathers together the unlearned; afterwards the wise ones. And not of orators does he make fishermen, but of fishermen he produces orators.' The most learned men should think of this.

Let all writers have their due esteem, but compare none of them with the Word of God. We will not refuse their service, but we must abhor them as rivals or competitors. It is the sign of a distempered heart that loseth the relish of Scripture excellency. For there is in a spiritual heart a co-naturality to the Word of God, because this is the seed which did regenerate him. The Word is that seal which made all the holy impressions that are in the hearts of true believers, and stamped the image of God upon them; and, therefore, they must needs be like that Word and highly esteem it as long as they live.

13. If you would prosper in your work, be sure to keep up earnest desires and expectations of success. If your hearts be not set on the end of your labours, and you long not to see the conversion and edification of your hearers, and do not study and preach in hope, you are not likely to see much success. As it is a sign of a false, self-seeking heart, that can be content to be still doing, and yet see no fruit of his labour; so I have observed that God seldom blesseth any man's work so much as his, whose heart is set upon the success of it. Let it be the property of a Judas to have more regard to the bag than to his work, and not to care much for what they pretend to care; and to think, if they have their salaries, and the love and commendations of their people, they have enough to satisfy them: but, let all who preach for Christ and men's salvation, be unsatisfied till they have the thing they preach for. He never had the right ends of a preacher, who is indifferent whether he obtain them, and is not grieved when he misseth them, and rejoiced when he can see the desired issue. When a man doth only study what to say, and how, with commendation, to spend the hour, and looks no more after it, unless it be to know what people think of his abilities, and thus holds on from year to year, I must needs think that this man doth preach for himself, and not for Christ, even when he preacheth Christ, how excellently soever he may seem to do it. No wise or charitable physician is content to be always giving physic, and to see no amendment among his patients, but to have them all die upon his hands: nor will any wise and honest schoolmaster be content to be still teaching, though his scholars profit not by his instructions; but both of them would rather be weary of the employment.

I know that a faithful minister may have comfort when he

wants success; and 'though Israel be not gathered, our reward is with the Lord;' and our acceptance is not according to the fruit, but according to our labour: but then, he that longeth not for the success of his labours can have none of this comfort, because he was not a faithful labourer. What I say is only for them that are set upon the end, and grieved if they miss it. Nor is this the full comfort that we must desire, but only such a part as may quiet us, though we miss the rest. What if God will accept a physician, though the patient die? He must, notwithstanding that, work in compassion, and long for a better issue, and be sorry if he miss it. For it is not merely our own reward that we labour for, but other men's salvation. I confess, for my part, I marvel at some ancient reverend men, that have lived twenty, thirty, or forty years with an unprofitable people, among whom they have scarcely been able to discern any fruits of their labours, how they can, with so much patience, continue among them. Were it my case, though I durst not leave the vineyard, nor quit my calling, yet I should suspect that it was God's will I should go somewhere else, and another come in my place that might be fitter for them; and I should not be easily satisfied to spend my days in such a manner.

14. Our whole work must be carried on under a deep sense of our own insufficiency, and of our entire dependence on Christ. We must go for light, and life, and strength to him who sends us on the work. And when we feel our own faith weak, and our hearts dull, and unsuitable to so great a work as we have to do, we must have recourse to him, and say, 'Lord, wilt thou send me with such an unbelieving heart to persuade others to believe? Must I daily plead with sinners about everlasting life and everlasting death, and have no more belief or feeling of these weighty things myself? O, send me not naked and unprovided to the work; but, as thou commandest me to do it, furnish me with a spirit suitable thereto.' Prayer must carry on our work as well as preaching: he preacheth not heartily to his people, that prayeth not earnestly for them. If we prevail not with God to give them faith and repentance, we shall never prevail with them to believe and

repent. When our own hearts are so far out of order, and
theirs so far out of order, if we prevail not with God to mend
and help them, we are like to make but unsuccessful work.

15. Having given you these concomitants of our ministerial
work, as singly to be performed by every minister, let me
conclude with one other, that is necessary to us as we are
fellow-labourers in the same work; and that is this, we must be
very studious of union and communion among ourselves, and
of the unity and peace of the churches that we oversee. We
must be sensible how needful this is to the prosperity of the
whole, the strengthening of our common cause, the good
of the particular members of our flock, and the further en-
largement of the kingdom of Christ. And, therefore, ministers
must smart when the Church is wounded, and be so far from
being the leaders in divisions, that they should take it as a
principal part of their work to prevent and heal them. Day
and night should they bend their studies to find out means to
close such breaches. They must not only hearken to motions
for unity, but propound them and prosecute them; not only
entertain an offered peace, but even follow it when it flieth
from them. They must, therefore, keep close to the ancient
simplicity of the Christian faith, and the foundation and
centre of catholic unity. They must abhor the arrogancy of
them that frame new engines to rack and tear the Church of
Christ under pretence of obviating errors and maintaining the
truth. The Scripture sufficiency must be maintained, and
nothing beyond it imposed on others; and if papists ,or others,
call to us for the standard and rule of our religion, it is the
Bible that we must show them, rather than any confessions of
churches, or writings of men. We must learn to distinguish
between certainties and uncertainties, necessaries and unnecessaries, catholic verities and private opinions; and to lay
the stress of the Church's peace upon the former, not upon the
latter. We must avoid the common confusion of speaking of
those who make no difference between verbal and real errors,
and hate that 'madness formerly among theologians,' who tear
their brethren as heretics, before they understand them. And
we must learn to see the true state of controversies, and

reduce them to the very point where the difference lieth, and not make them seem greater than they are. Instead of quarrelling with our brethren, we must combine against the common adversaries; and all ministers must associate and hold communion, and correspondence, and constant meetings to these ends; and smaller differences of judgment are not to interrupt them. They must do as much of the work of God, in unity and concord, as they can, which is the use of synods; not to rule over one another, and make laws, but to avoid misunderstandings, and consult for mutual edification, and maintain love and communion, and go on unanimously in the work that God hath already commanded us. Had the ministers of the gospel been men of peace, and of catholic, rather than factious spirits, the Church of Christ had not been in the case it now is. The nations of Lutherans and Calvinists abroad, and the differing parties here at home, would not have been plotting the subversion of one another, nor remain at that distance, and in that uncharitable bitterness, nor strengthen the common enemy, and hinder the building and prosperity of the Church as they have done.

Section 3
Motives to the oversight of the flock

Having considered the manner in which we are to take heed to the flock, I shall now proceed to lay before you some motives to this oversight; and here I shall confine myself to those contained in my text.

1. The first consideration which the text suggesteth to us, is drawn from our relation to the flock: We are *overseers* of it. (1) The nature of our office requireth us to 'take heed to the flock.' What else are we overseers for? ' "Bishop" is a title which intimates more of labour than of honour,' says Poly-

dore Virgil.[1] To be a bishop, or pastor, is not to be set up as an idol for the people to bow to, or as idle 'slow bellies,' to live to our fleshly delight and ease; but it is to be the guide of sinners to heaven. It is a sad case that men should be of a calling of which they know not the nature, and undertake they know not what. Do these men consider what they have undertaken, that live in ease and pleasure, and have time to take their superfluous recreations and to spend an hour and more at once, in loitering, or in vain discourse, when so much work doth lie upon their hands? Brethren, do you consider what you have taken upon you? Why, you have undertaken the conduct, under Christ, of a band of his soldiers 'against principalities and powers, and spiritual wickedness in high places.' You must lead them on to the sharpest conflicts; you must acquaint them with the enemies' stratagems and assaults; you must watch yourselves, and keep them watching. If you miscarry, they and you may perish. You have a subtle enemy, and therefore you must be wise. You have a vigilant enemy, and therefore you must be vigilant. You have a malicious and violent and unwearied enemy, and therefore you must be resolute, courageous and indefatigable. You are in a crowd of enemies, encompassed by them on every side, and if you heed one and not all, you will quickly fall. And oh, what a world of work have you to do! Had you but one ignorant old man or woman to teach, what a hard task would it be, even though they should be willing to learn! But if they be as unwilling as they are ignorant, how much more difficult will it prove! But to have such a multitude of ignorant persons, as most of us have, what work will it find us! What a pitiful life is it, to have to reason with men that have almost lost the use of reason, and to argue with them that neither understand themselves nor you! O brethren, what a world of wickedness have we to contend against in one soul; and what a number of these worlds! And when you think you have done something, you leave the seed among the fowls of the air; wicked men are at their elbows to rise up and contradict all you have said. You

---

[1] An Italian-English ecclesiastic and historian (16th century).

speak but once to a sinner, for ten or twenty times that the emissaries of Satan speak to them.

Moreover, how easily do the business and cares of the world choke the seed which you have sown. And if the truth had no enemy but what is in themselves, how easily will a frozen carnal heart extinguish those sparks which you have been long in kindling! yea, for want of fuel, and further help, they will go out of themselves. And when you think your work doth happily succeed, and have seen men confessing their sins, and promising reformation, and living as new creatures and zealous converts, alas! they may, after all this, prove unsound and false at the heart, and such as were but superficially changed and took up new opinions and new company, without a new heart. O how many, after some considerable change, are deceived by the profits and honours of the world, and are again entangled by their former lusts! How many do but change a disgraceful way of flesh-pleasing, for a way that is less dishonourable, and maketh not so great a noise in their consciences! How many grow proud before they acquire a thorough knowledge of religion; and, confident in the strength of their unfurnished intellects, greedily snatch at every error that is presented to them under the name of truth; and, like chickens that straggle from the hen, are carried away by that infernal kite, while they proudly despise the guidance and advice of those that Christ hath set over them for their safety! O brethren, what a field of work is there before us! Not a person that you see but may find you work. In the saints themselves, how soon do the Christian graces languish if you neglect them; and how easily are they drawn into sinful ways, to the dishonour of the gospel, and to their own loss and sorrow! If this be the work of a minister, you may see what a life he hath to lead. Let us, then, be up and doing, with all our might; difficulties must quicken, not discourage us in so necessary a work. If we cannot do all, let us do what we can; for, if we neglect it, woe to us, and to the souls committed to our care! Should we pass over all these other duties, and, by a plausible sermon only, think to prove ourselves faithful ministers, and to put off God and man with such a shell and vizor, our reward will prove as superficial as our work.

(2) Consider that it is by your own voluntary undertaking and engagement that all this work is laid upon you. No man forced you to be overseers of the Church. And doth not common honesty bind you to be true to your trust?

(3) Consider that you have the honour to encourage you to the labour. And a great honour it is to be the ambassadors of God, and the instruments of men's conversion, to 'save their souls from death, and to cover a multitude of sins.' The honour, indeed, is but the attendant of the work. To do, therefore, as the prelates of the Church in all ages have done, to strive for precedency, and fill the world with contentions about the dignity and superiority of their seats, doth show that we much forget the nature of that office which we have undertaken. I seldom see ministers strive so furiously, who shall go first to a poor man's cottage to teach him and his family the way to heaven; or who shall first endeavour the conversion of a sinner, or first become the servant of all. Strange, that notwithstanding all the plain expressions of Christ, men will not understand the nature of their office! If they did, would they strive who would be the pastor of a whole county and more, when there are so many thousand poor sinners in it that cry for help, and they are neither able nor willing to engage for their relief? Nay, when they can patiently live in the house with profane persons, and not follow them seriously and incessantly for their conversion? And that they would have the name and honour of the work of a county, who are unable to do all the work of a parish, when the honour is but the appendage of the work? Is it names and honour, or the work and end, that they desire? Oh! if they would faithfully, humbly, and self-denyingly lay out themselves for Christ and his Church, and never think of titles and reputation, they should then have honour whether they would or not; but by gaping after it, they lose it: for, this is the case of virtue's shadow, 'What follows I fly; what flies, the same I follow.'

(4) Consider that you have many other excellent privileges of the ministerial office to encourage you to the work. If

therefore you will not do the work, you have nothing to do with the privileges. It is something that you are maintained by other men's labours. This is for your work, that you may not be taken off from it, but, as Paul requireth, may 'give yourselves wholly to these things,' and not be forced to neglect men's souls, whilst you are providing for your own bodies. Either do the work, then, or take not the maintenance.

But you have far greater privileges than this. Is it nothing to be brought up to learning, when others are brought up to the cart and plough? and to be furnished with so much delightful knowledge, when the world lieth in ignorance? Is it nothing to converse with learned men, and to talk of high and glorious things, when others must converse with almost none but the most vulgar and illiterate? But especially, what an excellent privilege is it, to live in studying and preaching Christ! to be continually searching into his mysteries, or feeding on them! to be daily employed in the consideration of the blessed nature, works, and ways of God! Others are glad of the leisure of the Lord's day, and now and then of an hour besides, when they can lay hold upon it. But we may keep a continual Sabbath. We may do almost nothing else, but study and talk of God and glory, and engage in acts of prayer and praise, and drink in his sacred, saving truths. Our employment is all high and spiritual. Whether we be alone, or in company, our business is for another world. O that our hearts were but more tuned to this work! What a blessed, joyful life should we then live! How sweet would our study be to us! How pleasant the pulpit! And what delight would our conference about spiritual and eternal things afford us! To live among such excellent helps as our libraries afford, to have so many silent wise companions whenever we please – all these, and many other similar privileges of the ministry, bespeak our unwearied diligence in the work.

(5) By your work you are related to Christ, as well as to the flock. You are the stewards of his mysteries, and rulers of his household; and he that entrusted you, will maintain you in his work. But then, 'it is required of a steward that a man be found faithful.' Be true to him, and never doubt but he will

be true to you. Do you feed his flock, and he will sooner feed you as he did Elijah, than leave you to want. If you be in prison, he will open the doors; but then you must relieve imprisoned souls. He will give you 'a tongue and wisdom that no enemy shall be able to resist;' but then you must use it faithfully for him. If you will put forth your hand to relieve the distressed, he will wither the hand that is stretched out against you. The ministers of England, I am sure, may know this by large experience. Many a time hath God rescued them from the jaws of the devourer. Oh, the admirable preservations and deliverances that they have had from cruel Papists, from tyrannical persecutors, and from misguided, passionate men! Consider, brethren, why it is that God hath done all this. Is it for your persons, or for his Church? What are you to him more than other men, but for his work and people's sakes? Are you angels? Is your flesh formed of better clay than your neighbours? Are you not of the same generation of sinners, that need his grace as much as they? Up then, and work as the redeemed of the Lord, as those that are purposely rescued from ruin for his service. If you believe that God hath rescued you for himself, live to him, as being unreservedly his who hath delivered you.

2. The second motive in the text is drawn from the efficient cause of this relation. It is the Holy Ghost that hath made us overseers of his Church, and, therefore, it behoveth us to take heed to it. The Holy Ghost makes men bishops or overseers of the Church in three several respects: By qualifying them for the office; by directing the ordainers to discern their qualifications, and know the fittest men; and by directing them, the people and themselves, for the affixing them to a particular charge. All these things were then done in an extraordinary way, by inspiration, or at least very often. The same are done now by the ordinary way of the Spirit's assistance. But it is the same Spirit still; and men are made overseers of the Church (when they are rightly called) by the Holy Ghost, now as well as then. It is a strange conceit, therefore, of the Papists, that ordination by the hands of man is of more absolute necessity in the ministerial office, than the

calling of the Holy Ghost. God hath determined in his Word, that there shall be such an office, and what the work and power of that office shall be, and what sort of men, as to their qualifications, shall receive it. None of these can be undone by man, or made unnecessary. God also giveth men the qualifications which he requireth; so that, all that the Church hath to do, whether pastors or people, ordainers or electors, is but to discern and determine which are the men that God hath thus qualified, and to accept of them that are so provided, and, upon consent, to install them solemnly in this office.

What an obligation, then, is laid upon us, by our call to the work! If our commission be sent from heaven, it is not to be disobeyed. When the apostles were called by Christ from their secular employments, they immediately left friends, and house, and trade, and all, and followed him. When Paul was called by the voice of Christ, he 'was not disobedient to the heavenly vision.' Though our call is not so immediate or extraordinary, yet it is from the same Spirit. It is no safe course to imitate Jonah, in turning our back upon the commands of God. If we neglect our work, he hath a spur to quicken us; if we run away from it, he hath messengers enough to overtake us, and bring us back, and make us do it; and it is better to do it at first than at last.

3. The third motive in the text is drawn from the dignity of the object which is committed to our charge. It is the *Church of* G O D which we must oversee – that Church for which the world is chiefly upheld, which is sanctified by the Holy Ghost, which is the mystical body of Christ, that Church with which angels are present, and on which they attend as ministering spirits, whose little ones have their angels beholding the face of God in heaven. Oh what a charge is it that we have undertaken! And shall we be unfaithful to it? Have we the stewardship of God's own family, and shall we neglect it? Have we the conduct of those saints that shall live for ever with God in glory, and shall we neglect them? God forbid! I beseech you, brethren, let this thought awaken the negligent. You that draw back from painful, displeasing, suffering duties, and put off men's souls with ineffectual formalities, do you

think this is honourable treatment of Christ's spouse? Are the souls of men thought meet by God to see his face, and live for ever in heaven, and are they not worthy of your utmost cost and labour on earth? Do you think so basely of the Church of God, as if it deserved not the best of your care and help? Were you the keepers of sheep or swine, you would scarcely let them go, and say, They are not worth the looking after; especially if they were your own. And dare you say so of the souls of men, of the Church of God? Christ walketh among them: remember his presence, and see that you are diligent in your work. They are 'a chosen generation, a royal priesthood, a holy nation, a peculiar people, to show forth the praises of him that hath called them.' And yet will you neglect them? What a high honour is it to be but one of them, yea, but a door-keeper in the house of God! But to be the priest of these priests, and the ruler of these kings – this is such an honour as multiplieth your obligations to diligence and fidelity in so noble an employment.

4. The last motive that is mentioned in my text, is drawn from the price that was paid for the Church which we oversee: 'Which God,' says the apostle, 'hath purchased with his own blood.' Oh what an argument is this to quicken the negligent, and to condemn those who will not be quickened to their duty by it! 'Oh,' saith one of the ancient doctors, 'if Christ had but committed to my keeping one spoonful of his blood in a fragile glass, how curiously would I preserve it, and how tender would I be of that glass! If then he have committed to me the purchase of his blood, should I not as carefully look to my charge?' What! sirs, shall we despise the blood of Christ? Shall we think it was shed for them who are not worthy of our utmost care? You may see here, it is not a little fault that negligent pastors are guilty of. As much as in them lieth, the blood of Christ would be shed in vain. They would lose him those souls which he hath so dearly purchased.

Oh, then, let us hear these arguments of Christ, whenever we feel ourselves grow dull and careless: 'Did I die for these souls, and wilt not thou look after them? Were they worth my blood, and are they not worth thy labour? Did I come down from heaven to earth, "to seek and to save that which was lost;" and wilt thou not go to the next door, or street, or village, to seek them? How small is thy condescension and labour compared to mine! I debased myself to this, but it is thy honour to be so employed. Have I done and suffered so much for their salvation, and was I willing to make thee a fellow-worker with me, and wilt thou refuse to do that little which lieth upon thy hands?' Every time we look upon our congregations, let us believingly remember that they are the purchase of Christ's blood, and therefore should be regarded by us with the deepest interest and the most tender affection. Oh, think what a confusion it will be to a negligent minister, at the last day, to have this blood of the Son of God pleaded against him; and for Christ to say, 'It was the purchase of my blood of which thou didst make so light, and dost thou think to be saved by it thyself?' O brethren, seeing Christ will bring his blood to plead with us, let it plead us to our duty, lest it plead us to damnation.

I have now done with the motives which I find in the text itself. There are many more that might be gathered from the rest of this exhortation of the apostle, but we must not stay to take in all. If the Lord set home but these few upon our hearts, I doubt not we shall see reason to mend our pace; and the change will be such on our hearts and in our ministry, that ourselves and our congregations will have cause to bless God for it. I know myself to be unworthy to be your monitor; but a monitor you must have; and it is better for us to hear of our sin and duty from anybody than from nobody. Receive the admonition, and you will see no cause in the monitor's unworthiness to repent of it. But if you reject it, the unworthiest messenger may bear that witness against you another day which will then confound you.

CHAPTER III

Application

Section 1
The use of humiliation

Reverend and dear brethren, our business here this day is to humble our souls before the Lord for our past negligence, and to implore God's assistance in our work for the time to come. Indeed, we can scarcely expect the latter without the former. If God will help us in our future duty, he will first humble us for our past sin. He that hath not so much sense of his faults as unfeignedly to lament them, will hardly have so much more as to move him to reform them. The sorrow of repentance may exist without a change of heart and life; because a passion may be more easily wrought, than a true conversion. But the change cannot take place without some good measure of the sorrow. Indeed, we may here justly begin our confessions; it is too common with us to expect that from our people, which we do little or nothing in ourselves. What pains do we take to humble them, while we ourselves are unhumbled! How hard do we expostulate with them to wring out of them a few penitential tears, (and all too little) while yet our own eyes are dry! Alas! how we set them an example of hard-heartedness, while we are endeavouring by our words to melt and mollify them! Oh, if we did but study half as much to affect and amend our own hearts, as we do those of our hearers, it would not be with many of us as it is! It is a great deal too little that we do for their humiliation;

but I fear it is much less that some of us do for our own. Too many do somewhat for other men's souls, while they seem to forget that they have souls of their own to regard. They so carry the matter, as if their part of the work lay in calling for repentance, and the hearers' in repenting; theirs in bespeaking tears and sorrow, and other men's in weeping and sorrowing; theirs in crying down sin, and the people's in forsaking it; theirs in preaching duty, and the hearers' in practising it.

But we find that the guides of the Church in Scripture did confess their own sins, as well as the sins of the people. Ezra confessed the sins of the priests, as well as of the people, weeping and casting himself down before the house of God. Daniel confessed his own sin, as well as the people's. I think, if we consider well the duties already stated, and how imperfectly we have performed them, we need not demur upon the question, whether we have cause of humiliation? I must needs say, though I condemn myself in saying it, that he who readeth but this one exhortation of Paul to the elders of the church at Ephesus, and compareth his life with it, must be stupid and hard-hearted, if he do not melt under a sense of his neglects, and be not laid in the dust before God and forced to bewail his great omissions, and to fly for refuge to the blood of Christ, and to his pardoning grace. I am confident, brethren, that none of you do in judgment approve of the libertine doctrine, that crieth down the necessity of confession, contrition, and humiliation, yea, and in order to the pardon of sin! Is it not a pity, then, that our hearts are not as orthodox as our heads? But I see we have but half learned our lesson, when we know it, and can say it. When the understanding hath learned it, there is more ado to teach our wills and affections, our eyes, our tongues, and hands. It is a sad thing that so many of us preach our hearers asleep; but it is sadder still, if we have studied and preached ourselves asleep, and have talked so long against hardness of heart, till our own has grown hardened under the noise of our own reproofs.

And that you may see that it is not a causeless sorrow that God requireth of us, I shall call to your remembrance our manifold sins, and set them in order before you, that we may deal plainly and faithfully in a free confession of them, and that God who is 'faithful and just may forgive them, and cleanse us from all iniquity.' In this I suppose I have your hearty consent, and that you will be so far from being offended with me, though I should disgrace your persons, and others in this office, that you will readily subscribe the charge, and be humble self-accusers; and so far am I from justifying myself by the accusation of others, that I do unfeignedly put my name with the first in the bill of indictment. For how can a wretched sinner, one chargeable with so many and so great transgressions, presume to justify himself before God? Or how can he plead guiltless, whose conscience hath so much to say against him? If I cast shame upon the ministry, it is not on the office, but on our persons, by opening that sin which is our shame. The glory of our high employment doth not communicate any glory to our sin; for 'sin is a reproach to any people.' And be they pastors or people, it is only they that 'confess and forsake their sins that shall have mercy,' while 'he that hardeneth his heart shall fall into mischief.'

The great sins that we are guilty of, I shall not undertake to enumerate; and therefore my passing over any particular one, is not to be taken as a denial or justification of it. But I shall consider it as my duty, to instance some few which cry loud for humiliation and speedy reformation.

Only I must needs first premise this profession, that, notwithstanding all the faults which are now amongst us, I do not believe that ever England had so able and faithful a ministry since it was a nation, as it hath at this day; and I fear that few nations on earth, if any, have the like. Sure I am, the change is so great within these twelve years, that it is one of the greatest joys that ever I had in the world to behold it. Oh, how many congregations are now plainly and frequently taught, that lived then in great obscurity! How many able, faithful men are there now in a county, in comparison of what were then! How graciously hath God prospered the studies of many young men, who were little children in the beginning of the late troubles, so that now they cloud the

most of their seniors! How many miles would I have gone
twenty years ago, and less, to have heard one of those ancient
reverend divines, whose congregations are now grown thin,
and their parts esteemed mean, by reason of the notable
improvement of their juniors! And in particular, how merci-
fully hath the Lord dealt with this poor county of Worcester,
in raising up so many who do credit to the sacred office, and
self-denyingly and freely, zealously and unweariedly, lay out
themselves for the good of souls! I bless the Lord that hath
placed me in such a neighbourhood, where I may have the
brotherly fellowship of so many able, faithful, humble,
unanimous, and peaceable men. Oh that the Lord would long
continue this admirable mercy to this unworthy county! And
I hope I shall rejoice in God while I have a being, for the
common change in other parts, that I have lived to see: that
so many hundred faithful men are so hard at work for the
saving of souls, although with the muttering and gnashing of
teeth of the enemy; and that more are springing up apace. I
know there are some men, whose parts I reverence, who
being, in point of government, of another mind from them,
will be offended at my very mention of this happy alteration:
but I must profess, if I were absolutely prelatical, if I knew my
heart, I could not choose for all that but rejoice. What! not
rejoice at the prosperity of the Church, because the men do
differ in one opinion about its order? Should I shut my eyes
against the mercies of the Lord? The souls of men are not so
contemptible to me, that I should envy them the bread of life,
because it is broken to them by a hand that had not the
prelatical approbation. O that every congregation were thus
supplied! But every thing cannot be done at once. They had
a long time to settle a corrupted ministry; and when the
ignorant and scandalous are cast out, we cannot create abilities
in others for the supply; we must stay the time of their
preparation and growth; and then, if England drive not away
the gospel by their abuse, even by their wilful unreformed-
ness, and hatred of the light, they are like to be the happiest
nation under heaven. For, as for all the sects and heresies
that are creeping in and daily troubling us, I doubt not but the

gospel, managed by an able self-denying ministry, will effectually disperse and shame them all.

But you may say, this is not confessing sin, but applauding those whose sins you pretend to confess. To this I answer, it is the due acknowledgment of God's kindness, and thanksgiving for his admirable mercies, that I may not seem unthankful in confession, much less to cloud or vilify God's graces, while I open the frailties that in many do accompany them; for many things are sadly out of order in the best, as will appear from the following particulars.

1. One of our most heinous and palpable sins is PRIDE. This is a sin that hath too much interest in the best of us, but which is more hateful and inexcusable in us than in other men. Yet is it so prevalent in some of us, that it inditeth our discourses, it chooseth our company, it formeth our countenances, it putteth the accent and emphasis upon our words. It fills some men's minds with aspiring desires, and designs: it possesseth them with envious and bitter thoughts against those who stand in their light, or who by any means eclipse their glory, or hinder the progress of their reputation. Oh what a constant companion, what a tyrannical commander, what a sly and subtle insinuating enemy, is this sin of pride! It goes with men to the draper, the mercer, the tailor: it chooseth them their cloth, their trimming, and their fashion. Fewer ministers would ruffle it out in the fashion in hair and habit, if it were not for the command of this tyrannous vice. And I would that this were all, or the worst. But, alas! how frequently doth it go with us to our study, and there sit with us and do our work! How oft doth it choose our subject, and, more frequently still, our words and ornaments! God commandeth us to be as plain as we can, that we may inform the ignorant; and as convincing and serious as we are able, that we may melt and change their hardened hearts. But pride stands by and contradicteth all, and produceth its toys and trifles. It polluteth rather than polisheth; and, under pretence of laudable ornaments, dishonoureth our sermons with childish gauds: as if a prince were to be decked in the habit of a stage-player, or a painted fool. It persuadeth us to paint the window,

that it may dim the light: and to speak to our people that which they cannot understand; to let them know that we are able to speak unprofitably. If we have a plain and cutting passage, it taketh off the edge, and dulls the life of our preaching, under pretence of filing off the roughness, unevenness, and superfluity. When God chargeth us to deal with men as for their lives, and to beseech them with all the earnestness that we are able, this cursed sin controlleth all, and condemneth the most holy commands of God, and saith to us, 'What! will you make people think you are mad? will you make them say you rage or rave? Cannot you speak soberly and moderately?' And thus doth pride make many a man's sermons; and what pride makes, the devil makes; and what sermons the devil will make and to what end, we may easily conjecture. Though the matter be of God, yet if the dress, and manner, and end be from Satan, we have no great reason to expect success.

And when pride hath made the sermon, it goes with us into the pulpit, it formeth our tone, it animateth us in the delivery, it takes us off from that which may be displeasing, how necessary soever, and setteth us in pursuit of vain applause. In short, the sum of all is this, it maketh men, both in studying and preaching, to seek themselves, and deny God, when they should seek God's glory, and deny themselves. When they should inquire, What shall I say, and how shall I say it, to please God best, and do most good? it makes them ask, What shall I say, and how shall I deliver it, to be thought a learned able preacher, and to be applauded by all that hear me? When the sermon is done, pride goeth home with them, and maketh them more eager to know whether they were applauded, than whether they did prevail for the saving of souls. Were it not for shame, they could find in their hearts to ask people how they liked them, and to draw out their commendations. If they perceive that they are highly thought of, they rejoice, as having attained their end; but if they see that they are considered but weak or common men, they are displeased, as having missed the prize they had in view.

But even this is not all, nor the worst, if worse may be.

Oh, that ever it should be said of godly ministers, that they are so set upon popular air, and on sitting highest in men's estimation, that they envy the talents and names of their brethren who are preferred before them, as if all were taken from their praise that is given to another; and as if God had given them his gifts, to be the mere ornaments and trappings of their persons, that they may walk as men of reputation in the world, and as if all his gifts to others were to be trodden down and vilified, if they seem to stand in the way of their honour! What? a saint, a preacher of Christ, and yet envy that which hath the image of Christ, and malign his gifts for which he should have the glory, and all because they seem to hinder our glory? Is not every true Christian a member of the body of Christ, and, therefore, partaketh of the blessings of the whole, and of each particular member thereof? and doth not every man owe thanks to God for his brethren's gifts, not only as having himself a part in them, as the foot hath the benefit of the guidance of the eye; but also because his own ends may be attained by his brethren's gifts, as well as by his own? For if the glory of God, and the Church's felicity, be not his end, he is not a Christian. Will any workman malign another, because he helpeth him to do his master's work? Yet, alas! how common is this heinous crime among the ministers of Christ! They can secretly blot the reputation of those that stand in the way of their own; and what they cannot for shame do in plain and open terms, lest they be proved liars and slanderers, they will do in generals, and by malicious intimations, raising suspicions where they cannot fasten accusations. And some go so far, that they are unwilling that any one who is abler than themselves should come into their pulpits, lest they should be more applauded than themselves. A fearful thing it is, that any man, who hath the least of the fear of God, should so envy God's gifts, and had rather than his carnal hearers should remain unconverted, and the drowsy unawakened, than that it should be done by another who may be preferred before him. Yea, so far doth this cursed vice prevail, that in great congregations, which have need of the help of many preachers, we can scarcely, in many places, get two of equality to live together in love and quietness, and unanimously to carry on the work of God. But unless one of them be quite below the other in parts, and content to be so esteemed, or unless he be a curate to the other, and ruled by him, they are contending for precedency, and envying each other's interest, and walking with strangeness and jealousy towards one another, to the shame of their profession, and the great wrong of their people. I am ashamed to think of it, that when I have been labouring to convince persons of public interest and capacity, of the great necessity of more ministers than one in large congregations, they tell me, they will never agree together. I hope the objection is unfounded as to the most; but it is a sad case that it should be true of any. Nay, some men are so far gone in pride, that when they might have an equal assistant to further the work of God, they had rather take all the burden upon themselves, though more than they can bear, than that any one should share with them in the honour, or that their interest in the esteem of the people should be diminished.

Hence also it is that men do so magnify their own opinions, and are as censorious of any that differ from them in lesser things, as if it were all one to differ from them and from God. They expect that all should conform to their judgment, as if they were the rulers of the Church's faith; and while we cry down papal infallibility, too many of us would be popes ourselves, and have all stand to our determination, as if we were infallible. It is true, we have more modesty than expressly to say so; we pretend that it is only the evidence of truth, that appeareth in our reasons, that we expect men should yield to, and our zeal is for the truth and not for ourselves: but as that must needs be taken for truth which is ours, so our reasons must needs be taken for valid; and if they be but freely examined, and be found fallacious, as we are exceedingly backward to see it ourselves, because they are ours, so we are angry that it should be disclosed to others. We so espouse the cause of our errors, as if all that were spoken against them were spoken against our persons, and we were

heinously injured to have our arguments thoroughly con-
futed, by which we injured the truth and the souls of men. The
matter is come to this pass, through our pride, that if an error
or fallacious argument do fall under the patronage of a
reverend name, (which is nothing rare,) we must either allow
it the victory, and give away the truth, or else become injurious to that name that doth patronize it; for though you
meddle not with their persons, yet do they put themselves
under all the strokes which you give their arguments; and feel
them as sensibly as if you had spoken of themselves, because
they think it will follow in the eyes of others, that weak
arguing is a sign of a weak man. If, therefore, you consider
it your duty to shame their errors and false reasonings, by dis-
covering their nakedness, they take it as if you shamed their
persons; and so their names must be a garrison or fortress
to their mistakes, and their reverence must defend all their
sayings from attack.

So high indeed are our spirits, that when it becomes the
duty of any one to reprove or contradict us, we are commonly impatient both of the matter and the manner. We love
the man who will say as we say, and be of our opinion, and
promote our reputation, though, in other respects, he be less
worthy of our esteem. But he is ungrateful to us who contradicteth us and differeth from us, and dealeth plainly with
us as to our miscarriages and telleth us of our faults. Especially in the management of our public arguings, where the eye
of the world is upon us, we can scarcely endure any contradiction or plain dealing. I know that railing language is to be
abhorred, and that we should be as tender of each other's
reputation, as our fidelity to the truth will permit. But our
pride makes too many of us think all men contemn us, that
do not admire us, yea, and admire all we say, and submit
their judgments to our most palpable mistakes. We are so
tender, that a man can scarcely touch us but we are hurt;
and so high-minded, that a man who is not versed in compli-
menting, and skilled in flattery above the vulgar rate, can
scarcely tell how to handle us so observantly, and fit our

expectations at every turn, without there being some word, or some neglect, which our high spirits will fasten on, and take as injurious to our honour.

I confess I have often wondered that this most heinous sin should be made so light of, and thought so consistent with a holy frame of heart and life, when far less sins are, by ourselves, proclaimed to be so damnable in our people. And I have wondered more, to see the difference between godly preachers and ungodly sinners, in this respect. When we speak to drunkards, worldlings, or ignorant unconverted persons, we disgrace them to the utmost, and lay it on as plainly as we can speak, and tell them of their sin, and shame, and misery; and we expect that they should not only bear all patiently, but take all thankfully. And most that I deal with do take it patiently; and many gross sinners will commend the closest preachers most, and will say that they care not for hearing a man that will not tell them plainly of their sins. But if we speak to godly ministers against their errors or their sins, if we do not honour them and reverence them, and speak as smoothly as we are able to speak, yea, if we mix not commendations with our reproofs, and if the applause be not predominant, so as to drown all the force of the reproof or confutation, they take it as almost an insufferable injury.

Brethren, I know this is a sad confession, but that all this should exist among us, should be more grievous to us than to be told of it. Could the evil be hid, I should not have disclosed it, at least so openly in the view of all. But, alas! it is long ago open to the eyes of the world. We have dishonoured ourselves by idolizing our honour; we print our shame, and preach our shame, thus proclaiming it to the whole world. Some will think that I speak overcharitably when I call such persons godly men, in whom so great a sin doth so much prevail. I know, indeed, that where it is predominant, not hated, and bewailed, and mortified in the main, there can be no true godliness; and I beseech every man to exercise a strict jealousy and search of his own heart. But if all be graceless that are guilty of any, or of most of the fore-mentioned discoveries of pride, the Lord be merciful to the ministers of this land, and give us quickly another spirit; for grace is then a rarer thing than most of us have supposed it to be.

Yet I must needs say, that I do not mean to involve all the ministers of Christ in this charge. To the praise of Divine grace be it spoken, we have some among us, who are eminent for humility and meekness, and who, in these respects, are exemplary to their flocks and to their brethren. It is their glory, and shall be their glory; and maketh them truly honourable and lovely in the eyes of God and of all good men, and even in the eyes of the ungodly themselves. O that the rest of us were but such! But, alas! this is not the case with all of us.

O that the Lord would lay us at his feet, in the tears of unfeigned sorrow for this sin! Brethren, may I expostulate this case a little with my own heart and yours, that we may see the evil of our sin, and be reformed! Is not pride the sin of devils – the first-born of hell? Is it not that wherein Satan's image doth much consist? and is it to be tolerated in men who are so engaged against him and his kingdom as we are? The very design of the gospel is to abase us; and the work of grace is begun and carried on in humiliation. Humility is not a mere ornament of a Christian, but an essential part of the new creature. It is a contradiction in terms, to be a Christian, and not humble. All who will be Christians must be Christ's disciples, and 'come to him to learn;' and the lesson which he teacheth them is, to 'be meek and lowly.' Oh, how many precepts and admirable examples hath our Lord and Master given us to this end! Can we behold him washing and wiping his servants' feet, and yet be proud and lordly still? Shall he converse with the meanest of the people, and shall we avoid them as below our notice, and think none but persons of wealth and honour fit for our society? How many of us are oftener found in the houses of gentlemen than in the cottages of the poor, who most need our help? There are many of us who would think it below us, to be daily with the most needy and beggarly people, instructing them in the way of life and salvation; as if we had taken charge of the souls of the rich only! Alas! what is it that we have to be proud of? Is it of our body? Why, is it not made of the like materials as the brutes; and must it not shortly be as loathsome and abominable as a carcase? Is it of our graces? Why, the more we are proud of them, the less we have to be proud of. When so much of the nature of grace consists in humility, it is a great absurdity to be proud of it. Is it of our knowledge and learning? Why, if we have any knowledge at all, we must needs know how much reason we have to be humble; and if we know more than others, we must know more reason than others to be humble. How little is it that the most learned know, in comparison of that of which they are ignorant! To know that things are past your reach, and to know how ignorant you are, one would think should be no great cause of pride. However, do not the devils know more than you? And will you be proud of that in which the devils excel you? Our very business is to teach the great lesson of humility to our people; and how unfit, then, is it that we should be proud ourselves? We must study humility, and preach humility; and must we not possess and practise humility? A proud preacher of humility is at least a self-condemning man.

What a sad case is it, that so vile a sin is not more easily discerned by us, but many who are most proud, can blame it in others, and yet take no notice of it in themselves! The world takes notice of some among us, that they have aspiring minds, and seek for the highest room, and must be the rulers, and bear the sway wherever they come, or else there is no living or acting with them. In any consultations, they come not to search after truth, but to dictate to others, who, perhaps, are fit to teach them. In a word, they have such arrogant domineering spirits, that the world rings of it, and yet they will not see it in themselves!

Brethren, I desire to deal closely with my own heart and yours. I beseech you consider whether it will save us to speak well of the grace of humility while we possess it not, or to speak against the sin of pride while we indulge in it? Have not many of us cause to inquire diligently, whether sincerity will consist with such a measure of pride as we feel? When we are telling the drunkard that he cannot be saved unless he become temperate, and the fornicator that he cannot be saved unless he become chaste, have we not as great reason, if we are proud, to say to ourselves, that we cannot be saved unless we become humble? Pride, in fact, is a greater sin than drunkenness or whoredom; and humility is as necessary as sobriety and chastity. Truly, brethren, a man may as certainly, and more slyly, make haste to hell, in the way of earnest preaching of the gospel, and seeming zeal for a holy life, as in a way of drunkenness and filthiness. For what is holiness, but a devotedness to God and a living to him? and what is a damnable state, but a devotedness to carnal self and a living to ourselves? And doth any one live more to himself, or less to God, than the proud man? And may not pride make a preacher study for himself and pray and preach, and live to himself, even when he seemeth to surpass others in the work? It is not the work without the right principle and end that will prove us upright. The work may be God's, and yet we may do it, not for God, but for ourselves. I confess I feel such continual danger on this point, that if I do not watch, lest I should study for myself, and preach for myself, and write for myself, rather than for Christ, I should soon miscarry; and after all, I justify not myself, when I must condemn the sin.

Consider, I beseech you, brethren, what baits there are in the work of the ministry, to entice a man to selfishness, even in the highest works of piety. The fame of a godly man is as great a snare as the fame of a learned man. But woe to him that takes up the fame of godliness instead of godliness! 'Verily I say unto you, they have their reward.' When the times were all for learning and empty formalities, the temptation of the proud did lie that way. But now, when, through the unspeakable mercy of God, the most lively practical preaching is in credit, and godliness itself is in credit, the temptation of the proud is to pretend to be zealous preachers and godly men. Oh, what a fine thing is it to have the people crowding to hear us, and affected with what we say, and yielding up to us their judgments and affections! What a taking thing is it to be cried up as the ablest and godliest man in the country, to be famed through the land for the highest spiritual excellencies! Alas! brethren, a little grace combined with such inducements, will serve to make you join yourselves with the forwardest, in promoting the cause of Christ in the world. Nay, pride may do it without special grace.

Oh, therefore, be jealous of yourselves; and, amidst all your studies, be sure to study humility. 'He that exalteth himself shall be humbled, and he that humbleth himself shall be exalted.' I commonly observe that almost all men, whether good or bad, do loathe the proud, and love the humble. So far indeed doth pride contradict itself, that, conscious of its own deformity, it often borrows the homely dress of humility. We have the more cause to be jealous of it, because it is a sin most deeply rooted in our nature, and as hardly as any extirpated from the soul.

2. We do not so seriously, unreservedly, and laboriously lay out ourselves in the work of the Lord as beseemeth men of our profession and engagements. I bless the Lord that there are so many who do this work with all their might. But, alas! how imperfectly and how negligently do the most, even of those that we take for godly ministers, go through their work! How few of us do so behave ourselves in our office, as men that are wholly devoted thereto, and who have consecrated all they have to the same end! And because you shall see my grounds for this confession, I shall mention some instances of our sinful negligence.

(1) If we were duly devoted to our work, we should not be so negligent in our studies. Few men are at the pains that are necessary for the right informing of their understanding, and fitting them for their further work. Some men have no delight in their studies, but take only now and then an hour, as an unwelcome task which they are forced to undergo, and are glad when they are from under the yoke. Will neither the natural desire of knowledge, nor the spiritual desire of knowing God and things Divine, nor the consciousness of our great ignorance and weakness, nor the sense of the weight of our ministerial work – will none of all these things keep us closer to our studies, and make us more painful in seeking after truth? O what abundance of things are there that a minister

should understand! and what a great defect is it to be ignorant of them! and how much shall we miss such knowledge in our work! Many ministers study only to compose their sermons, and very little more, when there are so many books to be read, and so many matters that we should not be unacquainted with. Nay, in the study of our sermons we are too negligent, gathering only a few naked truths, and not considering of the most forcible expressions by which we may set them home to men's consciences and hearts. We must study how to convince and get within men, and how to bring each truth to the quick, and not leave all this to our extemporary promptitude, unless in cases of necessity. Certainly, brethren, experience will teach you that men are not made learned or wise without hard study and unwearied labour and experience.

(2) If we were heartily devoted to our work, it would be done more vigorously, and more seriously, than it is by the most of us. How few ministers do preach with all their might, or speak about everlasting joys and everlasting torments in such a manner as may make men believe that they are in good earnest! It would make a man's heart ache, to see a company of dead, drowsy sinners sitting under a minister, and not hear a word that is likely to quicken or awaken them. Alas! we speak so drowsily and so softly, that sleepy sinners cannot hear. The blow falls so light that hard-hearted sinners cannot feel. The most of ministers will not so much as exert their voice, and stir up themselves to an earnest utterance. But if they do speak loud and earnestly, how few do answer it with weight and earnestness of matter! And yet without this, the voice doth little good; the people will esteem it but mere bawling, when the matter doth not correspond. It would grieve one to the heart to hear what excellent doctrine some ministers have in hand, while yet they let it die in their hands for want of close and lively application; what fit matter they have for convincing sinners, and how little they make of it; what good they might do if they would set it home, and yet they cannot or will not do it.

O sirs, how plainly, how closely, how earnestly, should we deliver a message of such moment as ours, when the everlast-

ing life or everlasting death of our fellow-men is involved in
it! Methinks we are in nothing so wanting as in this seriousness; yet is there nothing more unsuitable to such a business,
than to be slight and dull. What! speak coldly for God, and for
men's salvation? Can we believe that our people must be
converted or condemned, and yet speak in a drowsy tone?
In the name of God, brethren, labour to awaken your own
hearts, before you go to the pulpit, that you may be fit to
awaken the hearts of sinners. Remember they must be awakened or damned, and that a sleepy preacher will hardly
awaken drowsy sinners. Though you give the holy things of
God the highest praises in words, yet, if you do it coldly, you
will seem by your manner to unsay what you said in the
matter. It is a kind of contempt of great things, especially
of so great things, to speak of them without much affection
and fervency. The manner, as well as the words, must set
them forth. If we are commanded, 'Whatsoever thy hand
findeth to do, do it with all thy might,' then certainly such
a work as preaching for men's salvation should be done with
all our might. But, alas, how few in number are such men! It
is only here and there, even among good ministers, that we
find one who has an earnest, persuasive, powerful way of
speaking, that the people can feel him preach when they hear
him.

Though I move you not to a constant loudness in your
delivery (for that will make your fervency contemptible), yet
see that you have a constant seriousness; and when the matter
requireth it (as it should do, in the application at least), then
lift up your voice, and spare not your spirits. Speak to your
people as to men that must be awakened, either here or in
hell. Look around upon them with the eye of faith, and with
compassion, and think in what a state of joy or torment they
must all be for ever; and then, methinks, it will make you
earnest, and melt your heart to a sense of their condition. Oh,
speak not one cold or careless word about so great a business
as heaven or hell. Whatever you do, let the people see that
you are in good earnest. Truly, brethren, they are great works
which have to be done, and you must not think that trifling

will despatch them. You cannot break men's hearts by jesting with them, or telling them a smooth tale, or pronouncing a gaudy oration. Men will not cast away their dearest pleasures at the drowsy request of one that seemeth not to mean as he speaks, or to care much whether his request be granted or not. If you say that the work is God's, and he may do it by the weakest means, I answer, It is true, he may do so; but yet his ordinary way is to work by means, and to make not only the matter that is preached, but also the manner of preaching instrumental to the work.

With the most of our hearers, the very pronunciation and tone of speech is a great point. The best matter will scarcely move them, if it be not movingly delivered. See, especially, that there be no affectation, but that you speak as familiarly to them as you would do, if you were talking to any of them personally. The want of a familiar tone and expression is a great fault in most of our deliveries, and that which we should be very careful to amend. When a man hath a reading or de- claiming tone, like a school-boy saying his lesson, or repeating an oration, few are moved with any thing that he says. Let us, therefore, rouse up ourselves to the work of the Lord, and speak to our people as for their lives, and save them as by violence, 'pulling them out of the fire.' Satan will not be charmed out of his possession: we must lay siege to the souls of sinners, which are his garrison, and find out where his chief strength lieth, and lay the battery of God's ordnance against it, and ply it close, till a breach is made; and then suffer them not by their shifts to repair it again. As we have reason- able creatures to deal with, and as they abuse their reason against the truth, we must see that our sermons be all convinc- ing, and that we make the light of Scripture and Reason shine so bright in the faces of the ungodly, that it may even force them to see, unless they wilfully shut their eyes. A sermon full of mere words, how neatly soever it be composed, while it wants the light of evidence, and the life of zeal, is but an image or a well-dressed carcase.

In preaching, there is a communion of souls, and a com- munication of somewhat from ours to theirs. As we and they have understandings and wills and affections, so must the bent of our endeavours be to communicate the fullest light of evidence from our understandings to theirs, and to warm their hearts, by kindling in them holy affections as by a communication from our own. The great things which we have to commend to our hearers have reason enough on their side, and lie plain before them in the Word of God. We should, therefore, be furnished with all kind of evidence, so that we may come as with a torrent upon their understandings, and with our reasonings and expostulations to pour shame upon all their vain objections, and bear down all before us, that they may be forced to yield to the power of truth.

(3) If we are heartily devoted to the work of God, why do we not compassionate the poor unprovided congregations around us, and take care to help them to find able ministers; and, in the mean time, go out now and then to their assistance, when the business of our particular charge will give us any leave? A sermon in the more ignorant places, purposely for the work of conversion, delivered by the most lively, powerful preachers, might be a great help where constant means are wanting.

3. Another sad discovery that we have not so devoted ourselves and all we have to the service of God as we ought, is our prevailing regard to our worldly interests in opposition to the interest and work of Christ. This I shall manifest in three instances:

(1) The temporizing of ministers. I would not have any to be contentious with those that govern them, nor to be disobedient to any of their lawful commands. But it is not the least reproach of ministers, that the most of them, for worldly advantage, do always suit themselves to the party which is most likely to promote their ends. If they look for secular advantages, they suit themselves to the secular power; if for popular applause, they suit themselves to the Church party that is most in credit. This, alas! is an epidemical malady. In Constantine's days how prevalent were the Orthodox! In Constantius' days they almost all turned Arians, so that there were very few bishops that did not apostatize or betray the

truth, even of the very men that had been in the Council of Nicaea. Indeed when not only Liberius,[1] but great Ossius[2] himself fell, who had been the president in so many orthodox councils, what better could be expected of weaker men? Were it not for secular advantage, how should it come to pass that ministers, in all countries of the world, are either all, or almost all, of that religion that is most in credit, and most consistent with their worldly interests? Among the Greeks, they are all of the Greek profession: among the Papists, they are almost all Papists: in Norway, Sweden, and Denmark, they are almost all Lutherans: and so in other countries. It is strange that they should be all in the right in one country, and all in the wrong in another, if carnal advantages did not sway much with men, when they engage in the search of truth. The variety of intellect, and numberless other circumstances, would unavoidably occasion a great variety of opinions on various points. But let the prince, and the stream of men in power, go one way, and you shall have the generality of ministers agree with them to a hair, and that without any extraordinary search. How generally did the common sort of ministers change their religion with the prince, at several times, in this land! Not all, indeed, as our Martyrology can witness, but yet the most. And the same tractable distemper doth still follow us; so that it occasioneth our enemies to say, that reputation and preferment are our religion and our reward. (2) We too much mind worldly things, and shrink from duties that will injure or hinder our temporal interests. How common is it for ministers to drown themselves in worldly business! Too many are such as the sectaries would have us to be, who tell us that we should go to the plough and labour for our living, and preach without so much study. This is a lesson which is easily learned. Men show no anxiety to cast off care, that their own souls and the Church may have all their care.

And especially, how commonly are those duties neglected, that are likely, if performed, to diminish our estates! Are there

[1] Bishop of Rome from 352 to 366.
[2] Bishop of Cordova (d. 357).

not many, for example, that dare not, that will not, set up the
exercise of discipline in their churches, because it may hinder
the people from paying them their dues? They will not offend
sinners with discipline, lest they offend them in their estates.
I find money is too strong an argument for some men to
answer, that yet can proclaim 'the love of it to be the root of
all evil,' and can make long orations of the danger of covetousness. I will at present say no more to them but this: If it was
so deadly a sin in Simon Magus to offer to buy the gift of
God with money, what is it to sell his gift, his cause, and the
souls of men for money? And what reason have we to fear,
lest our money perish with us!

(3) Our barrenness in works of charity, and in improving all
we have for our Master's service. If worldly interest did not
much prevail against the interest of Christ and the Church,
surely most ministers would be more fruitful in good works,
and would more lay out what they have for his glory.
Experience hath fully proved that works of charity do most
powerfully remove prejudice, and open the heart to words of
piety. If men see that you are addicted to do good, they will
the more easily believe that you are good, and that it is good
which you persuade them to. When they see that you love
them, and seek their good, they will the more easily trust you.
And when they see that you seek not the things of the world,
they will the less suspect your intentions, and the more easily
be drawn by you to seek that which you seek. Oh, how much
good might ministers do, if they did set themselves wholly
to do good, and would dedicate all their faculties and substance to that end! Say not that it is a small matter to do good
to men's bodies, and that this will but win them to us, and not
to God; for it is prejudice that is a great hindrance of men's
conversion, and this will help to remove it. We might do
men more good, if they were but willing to learn of us; and
this will make them willing, and then our further diligence
may profit them. I beseech you, brethren, do not think that
it is ordinary charity that is expected from you, any more than
ordinary piety. You must, in proportion to your talents, go
much beyond others. It is not enough to give a little to a poor

man: others do that as well as you. But what singular thing
do you do with your estates for your Master's service? I
know you cannot give away that which you have not; but
methinks all that you have should be devoted to God. I know
the great objection is, 'We have a wife and children to provide
for: a little will not serve them at present, and we are not
bound to leave them beggars.' To this I answer:

[*a*] There are few texts of Scripture more abused than that
of the apostle, 'He that provideth not for his own, and specially for those of his own house, hath denied the faith, and is
worse than an infidel.' This is made a pretence for gathering
up portions, and providing a full estate for posterity, when the
apostle speaketh only against them that did cast their poor
kindred and family on the Church, to be maintained out of the
common stock, when they were able to do it themselves;
as if one that hath a widow in his house that is his mother or
daughter, and would have her to be kept by the parish, when
he hath enough himself. The following words show that it is
present provision, and not future portions, that the apostle
speaketh of, when he bids 'them that have widows relieve
them, and let not the church be charged, that it may relieve them
that are widows indeed.'

[*b*] You may so educate your children as other persons do,
that they may be able to gain their own livelihood by some
honest trade or employment, without other great provisions.
I know that your charity and care must begin at home, but
it must not end there. You are bound to do the best you can to
educate your children, so as they may be capable of being
most serviceable to God, but not to leave them rich, nor to
forbear other necessary works of charity, merely to make
a larger provision for them. There must be some proportion
between the provision we make for our families, and for the
Church of Christ. A truly charitable self-denying heart, that
hath devoted itself, and all that it hath, to God, would be the
best judge of the due proportions, and would see which way
of expense is likely to do God the greatest service, and that
way it would take.

[*c*] I confess I would not have men lie too long under tempta-

tions to incontinency, lest they wound themselves and their profession by their falls. But yet methinks it is hard that men can do no more to mortify the concupiscence of the flesh, that they may live in a single condition, and have none of those temptations from wife and children, to hinder them from furthering their ministerial ends by charitable works. If he that marrieth not doth better than he that doth marry, surely ministers should labour to do that which is best. And if he that can 'receive this saying,' must receive it, we should endeavour after it. This is one of the highest points of the Romish policy, which alleges that it is the duty of bishops, priests, and other religious orders, not to marry, by which means they have no posterity to drain the church's revenues, nor to take up their care; but they make the public cause to be their interest, and they lay out themselves for it while they live, and leave all they have to it when they die. It is a pity that for a better cause we can no more imitate them in self-denial, where it might be done.

[d] But they that must marry, should take such as can maintain themselves and their children, or maintain them at the rate which their temporal means will afford, and devote as much of the church's means to the church's service as they can.

I would put no man upon extremes. But in this case, flesh and blood doth even make good men so partial, that they take their duties, and duties of very great worth and weight, to be extremes. If worldly vanities did not blind us, we might see when a public, or other greater good, did call us to deny ourselves and our families. Why should we not live more nearly and poorer in the world, rather than leave those works undone, which may be of greater use than our plentiful provision? But we consult in points of duty with flesh and blood; and what counsel it will give us, we may easily know. It will tell us we must have a competency; and many pious men's competency is but little below the rich man's rates in the parable (Luke 16.19). If they be not clothed in the best, and 'fare sumptuously every day,' they have not a competency. A man that preacheth an immortal crown, should not seek much after transitory vanity. And he that preacheth the contempt of riches should himself contemn them and show it by his life. And he that preacheth self-denial and mortification should practise these virtues in the eyes of them to whom he preacheth, if he would have his doctrine believed. All Christians are sanctified; and, therefore, themselves, and all that they have, are consecrated 'to the Master's use.' But ministers are doubly sanctified: they are devoted to God, both as Christians and as ministers; and, therefore, they are doubly obligated to honour him with all they have.

Oh, brethren, what abundance of good works are before us, and to how few of them do we put our hands! I know the world expecteth more from us than we have; but if we cannot answer the expectations of the unreasonable, let us do what we can to answer the expectations of God, and of conscience, and of all just men. 'This is the will of God, that with well doing we should put to silence the ignorance of foolish men.'

Those ministers especially, that have larger incomes, must be larger in doing good. I will give but one instance at this time. There are some ministers who have a hundred and fifty, two hundred, or three hundred pounds a-year of salary, and have so large parishes, that they are not able to do a quarter of the ministerial work, nor once in a year to deal personally with half their people for their instruction, and yet they will content themselves with public preaching, as if that were all that was necessary, and leave almost all the rest undone, to the everlasting danger or damnation of multitudes, rather than maintain one or two diligent men to assist them. Or if they have an assistant, it is but some young man who is but poorly qualified for the work, and not one that will faithfully and diligently watch over the flock, and afford them that personal instruction which is so necessary. If this be not serving ourselves of God, and selling men's souls for our fuller maintenance in the world, what is? Methinks such men should fear, lest, while they are accounted excellent preachers and godly ministers by men, they should be accounted cruel soul-murderers by Christ; and lest the cries of those souls which they have betrayed to damnation, should ring in their ears for ever and ever. Will preaching a good sermon serve the turn, while you never look more after them, but deny them that closer help that is necessary, and alienate that maintenance to your own flesh, which should provide relief for so many souls? How can you open your mouths against oppressors, when you yourselves are so great oppressors, not only of men's bodies, but of their souls? How can you preach against unmercifulness, while you are so unmerciful? And how can you talk against unfaithful ministers, while you are so unfaithful yourselves? The sin is not small because it is unobserved, and is not odious in the eyes of men, or because the charity which you withhold is such as the people blame you not for withholding. Satan himself, their greatest enemy, hath their consent all along in the work of their perdition. It is no extenuation, therefore, of your sin, that you have their consent: for that you may sooner have for their everlasting hurt, than for their everlasting good.

And now, sirs, I beseech you to take what has been said into consideration; and see whether this be not the great and lamentable sin of the ministers of the gospel, that they be not fully devoted to God, and give not up themselves, and all that they have, to the carrying on of the blessed work which they have undertaken; and whether flesh-pleasing, and self-seeking, and an interest distinct from that of Christ, do not make us neglect much of our duty, and serve God in the cheapest and most applauded part of his work, and withdraw from that which would subject us to cost and sufferings? And whether this do not show, that too many of us are earthly that seem to be heavenly, and mind the things below, while they preach the things above, and idolize the world while they call men to contemn it? And as Salvian saith, 'No one neglects salvation more than he who prefers something above God': Despisers of God will prove despisers of their own salvation.

4. We are sadly guilty of undervaluing the unity and peace of the whole Church. Though I scarcely meet with any one who will not speak for unity and peace, or, at least, that will expressly speak against it, yet is it not common to meet with

those who are studious to promote it; but too commonly do we find men averse to it, and jealous of it, if not themselves the instruments of division. The Papists have so long abused the name of the catholic Church, that, in opposition to them, many either put it out of their creeds, or only retain the name while they understand not, or consider not the nature of the thing; or think it is enough to believe that there is such a body, though they behave not themselves as members of it. If the Papists will idolize the Church, shall we therefore deny it, disregard it, or divide it? It is a great and a common sin throughout the Christian world, to take up religion in a way of faction; and instead of a love and tender care of the universal Church, to confine that love and respect to a party. Not but that we must prefer, in our estimation and communion, the purer parts before the impure, and refuse to participate with any in their sins; yet the most infirm and diseased part should be compassionated and assisted to the utmost of our power; and communion must be held as far as is lawful, and nowhere avoided, but upon the urgency of necessity; as we must love those of our neighbourhood that have the plague or leprosy, and afford them all the relief we can, and acknowledge all our just relations to them, and communicate to them, though we may not have local communion with them; and in other diseases which are not so infectious, we may be the more with them for their help, by how much the more they need it.

Of the multitude that say they are of the catholic Church, it is rare to meet with men of a catholic spirit. Men have not a universal consideration of, and respect to, the whole Church, but look upon their own party as if it were the whole. If there be some called Lutherans, some Calvinists, some subordinate divisions among these, and so of other parties among us, most of them will pray hard for the prosperity of their party, and rejoice and give thanks when it goes well with them; but if any other party suffer, they little regard it, as if it were no loss at all to the Church. If it be the smallest parcel that possesseth not many nations, no, nor cities on earth, they are ready to carry it, as if they were the whole Church, and as if it went well with the Church when it goes well with them. We cry down the Pope as Antichrist, for including the Church in the Romish pale, and no doubt but it is abominable schism: but, alas! how many do imitate them too far, while they reprove them! And as the Papists foist the word *Roman* into their creed, and turn the catholic Church into the Roman Catholic church, as if there were no other catholics, and the Church were of no larger extent, so is it with many others as to their several parties. Some will have it to be the Lutheran catholic church, and some the Reformed catholic church; some the Anabaptist catholic church, and so of some others. And if they differ not among themselves, they are little troubled at differing from others, though it be from almost all the Christian world. The peace of their party they take for the peace of the Church. No wonder, therefore, if they carry it no further.

How rare is it to meet with a man that smarteth or bleedeth with the Church's wounds, or sensibly taketh them to heart as his own, or that ever had solicitous thoughts of a cure! No; but almost every party thinks that the happiness of the rest consisteth in turning to them; and because they be not of their mind, they cry, Down with them! and are glad to hear of their fall, as thinking that is the way to the Church's rising, that is, their own. How few are there who understand the true state of controversies between the several parties; or that ever well discerned how many of them are but verbal, and how many are real! And if those that understand it do, in order to right information and accommodation, disclose it to others, it is taken as an extenuation of their error, and as a carnal compliance with them in their sin. Few men grow zealous for peace till they grow old, or have much experience of men's spirits and principles, and see better the true state of the Church, and the several differences, than they did before. And then they begin to write their *Irenicons*, and many such are extant at this day. As a young man in the heat of his lust and passion was judged to be no fit auditor of moral philosophy, so we find that those same young men who may be zealous for peace and unity, when they are grown more experienced, are zealous for their factions against these in their youthful heat. And therefore, such peace-makers as these before-mentioned do seldom do much greater good than to quiet their own consciences in the discharge of so great a duty, and to moderate some few, and save them from further guilt, and to leave behind them, when they are dead, a witness against a wilful, self-conceited, unpeaceable world.

Nay, commonly it bringeth a man under suspicion either of favouring some heresy or abating his zeal, if he do but attempt a pacificatory work. As if there were no zeal necessary for the great fundamental verities of the Church's unity and peace, but only for parties, and some particular truths.

And a great advantage the devil hath got this way, by employing his own agents, the unhappy Socinians, in writing so many treatises for catholic and arch-catholic unity and peace, which they did for their own ends; by which means the enemy of peace hath brought it to pass, that whoever maketh motion for peace, is presently under suspicion of being one that hath need of it for an indulgence to his own errors. A fearful case, that heresy should be credited, as if none were such friends to unity and peace as they; and that so great and necessary a duty, upon which the Church's welfare doth so depend, should be brought into such suspicion or disgrace.

Brethren, I speak not all this without apparent reason. We have as sad divisions among us in England, considering the piety of the persons, and the smallness of the matter of our discord, as most nations under heaven have known. The most that keeps us at odds is but the right form and order of Church government. Is the distance so great, that Presbyterian, Episcopalian, and Independent might not be well agreed? Were they but heartily willing and forward for peace, they might. I know they might. I have spoken with some moderate men of all the parties, and I perceive, by their concessions, it were an easy work. Were men's hearts but sensible of the Church's case, and unfeignedly touched with love to one another, and did they but heartily set themselves to seek it, the settling of a safe and happy peace were an easy work. If we could not in every point agree, we might easily narrow our differences, and hold communion upon our agreement in the main; determining on the safest way for managing our few and small disagreements, without the danger or trouble of the Church. But is this much done? It is not done. To the shame of all our faces be it spoken, it is not done. Let each party flatter themselves now as they please, it will be recorded to the shame of the ministry of England while the gospel shall abide in the world.

And oh what heinous aggravations do accompany this sin! Never men, since the apostles' days, I think, did make greater profession of godliness. The most of them are bound by solemn oaths and covenants, for unity and reformation: they all confess the worth of peace, and most of them will preach for it, and talk for it, while yet they sit still and neglect it, as if it were not worth the looking after. They will read and preach on those texts that command us to 'follow peace with all men,' and 'as much as in us lieth, to live peaceably with them:' and yet they are so far from following it, and doing all they possibly can for it, that many snarl at it, and malign and censure any that endeavour to promote it; as if all zeal for peace did proceed from an abatement of our zeal for holiness; and as if holiness and peace were so fallen out, that there were no reconciling them: when yet it has been found, by long experience, that concord is a sure friend to piety, and piety always moves to concord; while, on the other hand, errors and heresies are bred by discord, as discord is bred and fed by them. We have seen, to our sorrow, that where the servants of God should have lived together as one – of one heart, and one soul, and one lip – and should have promoted each other's faith and holiness, and admonished and assisted each other against sin, and rejoiced together in the hope of future glory, we have, on the contrary, lived in mutual jealousies, and drowned holy love in bitter contentions, and studied to disgrace and undermine one another, and to increase our own parties by right or wrong. We, that were wont to glory of our love to the brethren as a mark of our sincerity in the faith, have now turned it into the love of a party only; and those that are against that party have more of our spleen and envy

and malice, than our love. I know this is not so with all, nor prevalently with any true believer; but yet it is so common, that it may cause us to question the sincerity of many that are thought by themselves and others to be most sincere.

And it is not ourselves only that are scorched in this flame, but we have drawn our people into it, and cherished them in it, so that most of the godly in the nation are fallen into parties, and have turned much of their ancient piety into vain opinions and disputes and envyings and animosities. Yea, whereas it was wont to be made the certain mark of a graceless wretch to deride the godly, how few are there now that stick at secretly deriding and slandering those that are not of their opinions! A pious Prelatical man can reverently scorn and slander a Presbyterian; and a Presbyterian an Independent; and an Independent both. And, what is the worst of all, the common ignorant people take notice of all this, and do not only deride us, but are hardened by us against religion; and when we go about to persuade them to be religious, they see so many parties, that they know not which to join; and think that it is as good to be of none at all, as of any, since they are uncertain which is the right; and thus thousands are grown into a contempt of all religion, by our divisions; and many poor carnal wretches begin to think themselves in the better case of the two, because they hold to their old formalities, when we hold to nothing.

I know that some of these men are learned and reverend, and intend not such mischievous ends as these. The hardening of men in ignorance is not their design. But this is the thing effected. To intend well in doing ill is no rarity. Who can, in reverence to any man on earth, sit still and hold his tongue, while he seeth people thus run to their own destruction, and the souls of men undone by the contentions of divines for their several parties and interests? The Lord that knows my heart, knows, (if I know it myself,) that as I am not of any one of these parties, so I speak not a word of this in a factious partiality for one party, or against another, as such, much less in spleen against any person; but if I durst in conscience, I would have silenced all this, for fear of giving them offence whom I must honour. But what am I but a servant of Christ? and what is my life worth, but to do him service? and whose favour can recompense me for the ruin of the Church? and who can be silent while souls are undone? Not I, for my part, while God is my Master, and his word my rule; his work my business; and the success of it, for the saving of souls, my end. Who can be reconciled to that which so lamentably crosseth his Master's interest, and his main end in life? Nor yet would I have spoken any of this, had it been only in respect to my own charge, where, I bless God, the sore is but small, in comparison of what it is in many other places. But the knowledge of some neighbouring congregations, and of others more remote, hath drawn out these observations from me.

We may talk of peace, indeed, as long as we live, but we shall never obtain it but by returning to the apostolical simplicity. The Papists' faith is too big for all men to agree upon, or even all their own, if they enforced it not with arguments drawn from the fire, the halter, and the strappado. And many Anti-papists do too much imitate them in the tedious length of their subscribed confessions, and the novelty of their impositions, when they go furthest from them in the quality of the things imposed. When we once return to the ancient simplicity of faith, then, and not till then, shall we return to the ancient love and peace. I would therefore recommend to all my brethren, as the most necessary thing to the Church's peace, that they unite in necessary truths, and bear with one another in things that may be borne with; and do not make a larger creed, and more necessaries, than God hath done. To this end, let me entreat you to attend to the following things:

(1) Lay not too great a stress upon controverted opinions, which have godly men, and, especially, whole churches, on both sides.

(2) Lay not too great a stress on those controversies that are ultimately resolvable into philosophical uncertainties, as are some unprofitable controversies about freewill, the manner of the Spirit's operations and the Divine decrees.

(3) Lay not too great a stress on those controversies that are

merely verbal, and which if they were anatomized, would appear to be no more. Of this sort are far more (I speak it confidently upon certain knowledge) that make a great noise in the world, and tear the Church, than almost any of the eager contenders that ever I spoke with do seem to discern, or are like to believe.

(4) Lay not too much stress on any point of faith which was disowned by or unknown to the whole Church of Christ, in any age, since the Scriptures were delivered to us.

(5) Much less should you lay great stress on those of which any of the more pure or judicious ages were wholly ignorant.

(6) And least of all should you lay much stress on any point which no one age since the apostles did ever receive, but all commonly held the contrary.

I know it is said that a man may subscribe the Scripture, and the ancient creeds, and yet maintain Socinianism, or other heresies. To which I answer, So he may another test which your own brains shall contrive: and while you make a snare to catch heretics, instead of a test for the Church's communion, you will miss your end; and the heretic, by the slipperiness of his conscience, will break through, and the tender Christian may possibly be ensnared. And by your new creed the Church is like to have new divisions, if you keep not close to the words of Scripture.

He that shall live to that happy time when God will heal his broken churches, will see all this that I am pleading for reduced to practice, and this moderation takes place of the new-dividing zeal, and the doctrine of the sufficiency of Scripture established; and all men's confessions and comments valued only as subservient helps, and not made the test of Church communion, any further than they are the same with Scripture. Till, however, the healing age come, we cannot expect that healing truths will be entertained, because there are not healing spirits in the leaders of the Church. But when the work is to be done, the workmen will be fitted for it; and blessed will be the agents of so glorious a work.

5. Lastly, We are sadly negligent in performing acknowledged duties, for example, church discipline. If there be any

work of reformation to be set afoot, how many are there that will go no further than they are drawn! It were well if all would do even that much. And when a work is like to prove difficult and costly, how backward are we to it, and how many excuses do we make for the omission of it! What hath been more talked of, and prayed for, and contended about in England, for many years past, than discipline? There are, in fact, but few men who do not seem zealous in disputing for one side or other; some for the Prelatical way, some for the Presbyterian, and some for the Congregational. And yet, when we come to the practice of it, for aught I see, we are quite agreed: most of us are for no way. It hath made me wonder, sometimes, to look on the face of England, and see how few congregations in the land have any considerable execution of discipline, and to think withal what volumes have been written for it; and how almost all the ministry of the nation are engaged for it. How zealously they have contended for it, and made many a just exclamation against the opposers of it, and yet, notwithstanding all this, they will do little or nothing in the exercise of it. I have marvelled what should make them so zealous in siding for that which their practice shows their hearts are against. But I see a disputing zeal is more natural than a holy, obedient, practising zeal.

How many ministers are there in England that know not their own charge, and cannot tell who are the members of it; that never cast out one obstinate sinner, nor brought one to public confession and promise of reformation, nor even admonished one publicly to call him to such repentance! But they think they do their duty, if they give them not the sacrament of the Lord's supper, (when it is perhaps avoided voluntarily by the persons themselves); and in the mean time, we leave them stated members of our churches, (for church membership does not consist merely in partaking of the Lord's supper, else what are children who have been baptized in their infancy?) and grant them all other communion with the Church, and call them not to personal repentance for their sin. Is it not God's ordinance that they should be personally rebuked and admonished, and publicly called to repentance, and be cast out if they remain impenitent? If these be no duties, why have we made such a noise and stir in the world about them? If they be duties, why do we not practise them? Many of them avoid the very hearing of the Word. The ancient discipline of the Church was stricter, when the Sixth General Council at Trull[1] ordained, that 'Whosoever was three days together from church, without urgent necessity, was to be excommunicated.'

Brethren, I desire not to offend any party, but I must needs say that these sins are not to be cloaked over with excuses, extenuations, or denials. We have long cried up discipline, and every party its particular way. Would you have people value your form of government, or would you not? No doubt but you would. Now, if you would have them value it, it must be for some excellency. Show them then that excellency. What is it? Wherein doth it consist? And if you would have them believe you, show it to them, not merely on paper, but in practice; not simply in words, but in deeds. How can the people know the worth of discipline, without the thing? Is it a name and a shadow that you have made all this noise about? How can they think that to be good, which doth no good? Truly, I fear we take not the right way to maintain our cause; that we even betray it, while we are hot disputers for it. Speak truly: is it not these two things that keep up the reputation of the long-contended-for discipline among men; namely, with the godly, the mere reputation of their ministers that stand for it, and with many of the ungodly, the non-execution of it, because they find it to be toothless, and not so troublesome to them as they expected? If once our Government come to be upholden by the votes of those who should be corrected or ejected by it, and the worst men be friends to it because it is a friend to them in their ungodliness, we shall then engage the Lord against it, and he will appear as engaged against us. Set all the execution of discipline together that hath been practised in a whole county, ever since it was so con-

[1] In 692 a Synod was held in the domed room ('trullus') of the Imperial Palace at Constantinople to complete the disciplinary work of the Sixth General Council of 680.

tended for, and I doubt it will not appear so observable as to draw godly people into a liking of it for its effects. How can you wonder, if many that desire deeds and not words, reformation, and not merely the name of reformation, do turn over to the separated congregations, when you show them nothing but the bare name of discipline in yours?

All Christians value God's ordinances, and think them not vain things; and, therefore, are unwilling to live without them. Discipline is not a needless thing to the Church: if you will not make a difference between the precious and the vile, by discipline, people will do it by separation. If you will keep many scores or hundreds in your churches, that are notoriously ignorant, and utterly destitute of religion, and never publicly (nor, perhaps, privately) reprove them, nor call them to repentance, nor cast them out, you need not marvel if some timorous souls should run out of your churches, as from a ruinous edifice, which they fear is ready to fall upon their heads. Consider, I pray you, if you should act in the same manner with them as to the sacrament, as you do as to discipline, and should only show them the bread and wine, and never let them taste of these memorials of their Redeemer's love, could you expect that the name of a sacrament would satisfy them, or that they would like your communion? Why should you then think that they will be satisfied with the empty sound of the word *church-government*?

Besides, consider what a disadvantage you cast upon your cause, in all your disputations with men of different views. If your principles be better than theirs, and their practice be better than yours, the people will suppose that the question is whether the name or the thing, the shadow or the substance, be more desirable, and they will take your way to be a mere delusive formality, because they see you but formal in the use of it, yea, that you use it not at all. In what I now say, I speak not against your form of government, but for it; and tell you, that it is you who are against it that seem so earnest for it, while you more disgrace it for want of exercise, than you credit it by all your arguments. And you will find, before you have done, that the faithful execution of it would be your strongest argument. Till then, the people will understand you, as if you openly proclaimed, We would have no public admonitions, confessions, or excommunications; our way is to do no good, but to set up the naked name of a government.

I desire not to spur on any one to an unseasonable performance of this great duty. But will it never be a fit season? Would you forbear sermons and sacraments so many years on pretence of unseasonableness? Will you have a better season for it when you are dead? How many are dead already, before they ever did anything in this important work, though they were long preparing for it! I know some have more discouragements and hindrances than others; but what discouragements and hindrances can excuse us from such a duty? Besides the reasons which we have already stated, let these few be seriously considered:

(1) How sad a sign do we make it to be in preaching to our people, to live in the wilful and continued omission of any known duty! And shall we do so year after year, nay, all our days? If excuses will take off the danger of this sign, what man will not find them as well as you?

(2) We plainly manifest laziness and sloth, if not unfaithfulness in the work of Christ. I speak from experience. It was laziness that kept me so long from this duty, and pleaded hard against it. It is indeed a troublesome and painful work, and such as calls for some self-denial, because it will bring upon us the displeasure of the wicked. But dare we prefer our carnal ease and quietness, or the love and peace of wicked men, before our service to Christ our Master? Can slothful servants expect a good reward? Remember, brethren, that we of this county have thus promised before God, in the second article of our agreement: 'We agree and resolve, by God's help, that so far as God doth make known our duty to us, we will faithfully endeavour to discharge it, and will not desist through any fears or losses in our estates, or the frowns and displeasure of men, or any the like carnal inducements whatsoever.' I pray you study this promise, and compare your performance with it. And do not think that you were ensnared by thus engaging; for God's law hath laid an

obligation on you to the very same duty, before your engagement did it. Here is nothing but what others are bound to, as well as you.

(3) The neglect of discipline hath a strong tendency to delude immortal souls, by making those think they are Christians that are not, while they are permitted to live with the character of such, and are not separated from the rest by God's ordinance: and it may make the scandalous think their sin a tolerable thing, which is so tolerated by the pastors of the church.

(4) We corrupt Christianity itself in the eyes of the world, and do our part to make them believe that Christ is no more for holiness than Satan, or that the Christian religion exacteth holiness no more than the false religions of the world. For if the holy and unholy are all permitted to be sheep of the same fold, without any means being used to separate them, we defame the Redeemer, as if he were guilty of it, and as if this were the nature of his precepts.

(5) We keep up separation, by permitting the worst to be uncensured in our churches, so that many honest Christians think they are obliged to withdraw from us. I have spoken with some members of the separated churches, who were moderate men, and have argued with them against separation; and they have assured me, that they were of the Presbyterian judgment, or had nothing to say against it, but they joined themselves to other churches from pure necessity, thinking that discipline, being an ordinance of Christ, must be used by all that can, and, therefore, they durst no longer live without it when they might have it; and they could find no Presbyterian churches that executed discipline, as they wrote for it: and they told me, that they separated only *pro tempore*, till the Presbyterians will use discipline, and then they will willingly return to them again. I confess I was sorry that such persons had any such occasion to withdraw from us. It is not keeping offenders from the sacrament that will excuse us from the further exercise of discipline, while they are members of our churches.

(6) We do much to bring the wrath of God upon ourselves

and our congregations, and so to blast the fruit of our labours. If the angel of the church of Thyatira was reproved for suffering seducers in the church, we may be reproved, on the same ground, for suffering open, scandalous, impenitent sinners.

And what are the hindrances that now keep the ministers of England from the execution of that discipline, for which they have so much contended? The great reason, as far as I can learn, is, 'The difficulty of the work, and the trouble or suffering that we are like to incur by it. We cannot publicly reprehend one sinner, but he will storm at it, and bear us a deadly malice. We can prevail with very few to make a public profession of true repentance. If we proceed to excommunicate them, they will be raging mad against us. If we should deal as God requireth us, with all the obstinate sinners in the parish, there would be no living among them; we should be so hated of all, that, as our lives would be uncomfortable, so our labours would become unprofitable; for men would not hear us when they are possessed with a hatred of us: therefore duty ceaseth to be duty to us, because the hurt that would follow would be greater than the good.'

These are the great reasons for the non-execution of discipline, together with the great labour that private admonition of each offender would cost us. Now, to all this I answer:

[a] Are not these reasons as valid against Christianity itself, especially in some times and places, as they are against discipline? Christ came not to send peace on earth: We shall have his peace, but not the world's; for he hath told us that it will hate us. Might not Bradford, or Hooper, or any that were burned in Queen Mary's days, have alleged more than all this against the duty of owning the Reformation? Might they not have said, 'It will make us hated, and it will expose our very lives to the flames?' He is concluded by Christ to be no Christian, who hateth not all that he hath, and his own life, for him; and yet we can take the hazard of worldly loss as a reason against his work! What is it but hypocrisy to shrink from sufferings, and to take up none but safe and easy works,

and make ourselves believe that the rest are no duties? Indeed this is the common way of escaping suffering, to neglect the duty that would expose us to it. If we did our duty faithfully, ministers would find the same lot among professed Christians as their predecessors have done among Pagans and other infidels. But if you cannot suffer for Christ, why did you put your hand to his plough? Why did you not first sit down and count the cost? This makes the ministerial work so unfaithfully executed, because it is so carnally undertaken; men enter upon it as a life of ease, and honour, and respectability, and they resolve to attain their ends, and have what they expected by right or wrong. They looked not for hatred and suffering, and they will avoid it, though by the avoiding of their work.

[b] As for the making yourselves incapable of doing them good, I answer, That reason is as valid against plain preaching, reproof, or any other duty which wicked men will hate us for. God will bless his own ordinances to do good, or else he would not have appointed them. If you publicly admonish and rebuke the scandalous, and call them to repentance, and cast out the obstinate, you may do good to many whom you reprove, and possibly to the excommunicated themselves. I am at least sure it is God's means; and it is his last means when reproofs will do no good. It is therefore perverse to neglect the last means, lest we frustrate the foregoing means, when the last are not to be used but upon supposition that the former were all frustrated before. However, those within and those without may receive good by it, if the offender should receive none; and God will have the honour, when his Church is manifestly distinguished from the world, and the heirs of heaven and hell are not totally confounded, nor the world made to think that Christ and Satan do but contend for superiority, and that they have the like inclination to holiness or to sin.

[c] But yet let me tell you, that there are not such difficulties in the way, nor is discipline such a useless thing as you imagine. I bless God upon the small and too late trial which I have made of it myself. I can speak by experience, that it is

not in vain; nor are the hazards of it such as may excuse our neglect.

I confess, if I had my will, that man should be ejected as a negligent pastor, that will not rule his people by discipline, as well as he is ejected as a negligent preacher that will not preach; for ruling I am sure is as essential a part of the pastor's office as preaching.

I shall proceed no further in these confessions. And now, brethren, what remaineth, but that we all cry guilty of these fore-mentioned sins, and humble our souls for our miscarriages before the Lord? Is this 'taking heed to ourselves and to all the flock?' Is this like the pattern that is given us in the text? If we should now prove stout-hearted and un-humbled, how sad a symptom would it be to ourselves, and to the Church! The ministry hath oft been threatened and maligned by many sorts of adversaries; and though this may show their impious malice, yet may it also intimate to us God's just indignation. Believe it, brethren, the ministry of England are not the least nor the last in the sins of the land. It is time, therefore, for us to take our part of that humiliation to which we have been so long calling our people. If we have our wits about us, we may perceive that God hath been offended with us, and that the voice that called this nation to repentance, did speak to us as well others. 'He that hath ears to hear, let him hear' the precepts of repentance proclaimed in so many admirable deliverances and preservations; he that hath eyes to see, let him see them written in so many lines of blood. By fire and sword hath God been calling us to humiliation; and as 'judgment hath begun at the house of God,' so, if humiliation begin not there too, it will be a sad prognostication to us and to the land.

What! shall we deny or extenuate our sins while we call our people to free and full confession? Is it not better to give glory to God by humble confession, than, in tenderness to ourselves, to seek for fig-leaves to cover our nakedness; and to put God to it to build his glory, which we denied him, upon the ruins of our own, which we preferred before him; and to distrain for that by yet sorer judgments which we refused voluntarily to surrender to him? Alas! if you put God to get his honour as he can, he may get it, to your everlasting sorrow and dishonour. Sins openly committed, are more dishonourable to us when we hide them, than when we confess them. It is the sin, and not the confession, that is our dishonour. We have committed them before the sun, so that they cannot be hid; and attempts to cloak them do but increase our guilt and shame. There is no way to repair the breaches in our honour, which our sin hath made, but by free confession and humiliation. I durst not but make confession of my own sins: and if any be offended that I have confessed theirs, let them know, that I do but what I have done by myself. And if they dare disown the confession of their sin, let them do it at their peril. But as for all the truly humble ministers of Christ, I doubt not but they will rather be provoked to lament their sins more solemnly in the face of their several congregations, and to promise reformation.

Section 2

The duty of personal catechizing and instructing the flock particularly recommended

Having disclosed and lamented our miscarriages and neglects, our duty for the future lies plain before us. God forbid that we should now go on in the sins which we have confessed, as carelessly as we did before. Leaving these things, therefore, I shall now proceed to exhort you to the faithful discharge of the great duty which you have undertaken, namely, personal catechizing and instructing every one in your parishes or congregations that will submit thereto.

First, I shall state to you some motives to persuade you to this duty.

Secondly, I shall answer some objections which may be made to this duty.

Lastly, I shall give you some directions for performing this duty.

PART I
Motives to this duty

Agreeably to this plan, I shall proceed to state to you some motives to persuade you to this duty. The first reasons by which I shall persuade you to this duty, are taken from the benefits of it: The second, from its difficulty: And the third, from its necessity, and the many obligations that are upon us for the performance of it.

ARTICLE I
Motives from the benefits of the work

When I look before me, and consider what, through the blessing of God, this work, if well managed, is like to effect, it makes my heart leap for joy. Truly, brethren, you have begun a most blessed work, and such as your own consciences may rejoice in, and your parishes rejoice in, and the nation rejoice in, and the child that is yet unborn rejoice in. Yea, thousands and millions, for aught we know, may have cause to bless God for it, when we shall have finished our course. And though it is our business this day to humble ourselves for the neglect of it so long, as we have very great cause to do, yet the hopes of a blessed success are so great in me, that they are ready to turn it into a day of rejoicing.

I bless the Lord that I have lived to see such a day as this, and to be present at so solemn an engagement of so many servants of Christ to such a work. I bless the Lord, that hath honoured you of this county to be the beginners and awakeners of the nation to this duty. It is not a controverted point, as

to which the exasperated minds of men might pick quarrels
with us, nor is it a new invention, as to which envy might
charge you as innovators, or pride might scorn to follow,
because you had led the way. No; it is a well-known duty.
It is but the more diligent and effectual management of the
ministerial work. It is not a new invention, but simply the
restoration of the ancient ministerial work. And because it is
so pregnant with advantages to the Church, I will enumerate
some of the particular benefits which we may hope to result
from it, that when you see the excellency of it, you may be
the more set upon it, and the more loath, by any negligence or
failing of yours, to frustrate or destroy it. For certainly he
who hath the true intentions of a minister of Christ will
rejoice in the appearance of any further hope of attaining the
ends of his ministry; and nothing will be more welcome to
him than that which will further the very business of his life.
That this work is calculated to accomplish this, I shall now
show you more particularly.

1. It will be a most hopeful mean of the conversion of souls;
for it unites those great things which most further such an
end.

(1) As to the matter of it; it is about the most necessary things,
the principles or essentials of the Christian faith.

(2) As to the manner of it: it will be by private conference,
when we may have an opportunity to set all home to the
conscience and the heart.

The work of conversion consisteth of two parts: First, the
informing of the judgment in the essential principles of
religion; Second, The change of the will by the efficacy of the
truth. Now in this work we have the most excellent advantages for both. For the informing of their understandings, it
must needs be an excellent help to have the sum of Christianity
fixed in their memory. And though bare words, not understood, will make no change, yet, when the words are plain
English, he that hath the words is far more likely to understand the meaning and matter than another. For what have
we by which to make known things which are themselves
invisible, but words or other signs? Those, therefore, who

deride all catechisms as unprofitable forms, may better deride themselves for talking and using the form of their own words to make known their minds to others. Why may not written words, which are constantly before their eyes, and in their memories, instruct them, as well as the transient words of a preacher? These 'forms of sound words' are, therefore, so far from being unprofitable, as some persons imagine, that they are of admirable use to all.

Besides, we shall have the opportunity, by personal conference, to try how far they understand the catechism, and to explain it to them as we go along; and to insist on those particulars which the persons we speak to have most need to hear. These two conjoined – a form of sound words, with a plain explication – may do more than either of them could do alone.

Moreover, we shall have the best opportunity to impress the truth upon their hearts, when we can speak to each individual's particular necessity, and say to the sinner, 'Thou art the man;' and plainly mention his particular case; and set home the truth with familiar importunity. If any thing in the world is likely to do them good, it is this. They will understand a familiar speech, who understand not a sermon; and they will have far greater help for the application of it to themselves. Besides, you will hear their objections, and know where it is that Satan hath most advantage of them, and so may be able to show them their errors, and confute their objections, and more effectually convince them. We can better bring them to the point, and urge them to discover their resolutions for the future, and to promise the use of means and reformation, than otherwise we could do. What more proof need we of this, than our own experience? I seldom deal with men purposely on this great business, in private, serious conference, but they go away with some seeming convictions, and promises of new obedience, if not some deeper remorse, and sense of their condition.

O brethren, what a blow may we give to the kingdom of darkness, by the faithful and skilful managing of this work! If, then, the saving of souls, of your neighbours' souls, of many souls, from everlasting misery, be worth your labour, up and be doing! If you would be the fathers of many that are born again, and would 'see of the travail of your souls,' and would be able to say at last, 'Here am I, and the children whom thou hast given me' – up and ply this blessed work! If it would do your heart good to see your converts among the saints in glory, and praising the Lamb before the throne; if it would rejoice you to present them blameless and spotless to Christ, prosecute with diligence and ardour this singular opportunity that is offered you. If you are ministers of Christ indeed, you will long for the perfecting of his body, and the gathering in of his elect; and you will 'travail as in birth' till Christ be formed in the souls of your people. You will embrace such opportunities as your harvest-time affords, and as the sunshine days in a rainy harvest, in which it is unreasonable and inexcusable to be idle. If you have a spark of Christian compassion in you, it will surely seem worth your utmost labour to save so many 'souls from death, and to cover' so great 'a multitude of sins.' If, then, you are indeed fellow-workers with Christ, set to his work, and neglect not the souls for whom he died. O remember, when you are talking with the unconverted, that now you have an opportunity to save a soul, and to rejoice the angels of heaven, and to rejoice Christ himself, to cast Satan out of a sinner, and to increase the family of God! And what is your 'hope, or joy, or crown of rejoicing?' Is it not your saved people 'in the presence of Christ Jesus at his coming?' Yes, doubtless 'they are your glory and your joy.'

2. It will essentially promote the orderly building up of those who are converted, and the establishment of them in the faith. It hazardeth our whole work, or at least much hindereth it, if we do it not in the proper order. How can you build, if you first not lay a good foundation? or how can you set on the top-stone, while the middle parts are neglected? 'Grace makes no leaps,' any more than nature. The second order of Christian truths have such a dependence upon the first, that they can never be well learned till the first are learned. This makes many labour so much in vain; they are 'ever learning,

but never come to the knowledge of the truth,' because they would read before they learn to spell, or to know their letters. This makes so many fall away: they are shaken with every wind of temptation, because they were not well settled in the fundamental principles of religion. It is these fundamentals that must lead men to further truths; it is these they must build all upon; it is these that must actuate all their graces, and animate all their duties; it is these that must fortify them against temptations. He that knows not these, knows nothing; he that knows them well, doth know so much as will make him happy; and he that knows them best, is the best and most understanding Christian. The most godly people, therefore, in your congregations, will find it worth their labour to learn the very words of a catechism. If, then, you would safely edify them, and firmly establish them, be diligent in this work.

3. It will make our public preaching better understood and regarded. When you have instructed them in the principles, they will the better understand all you say. They will perceive what you drive at, when they are once acquainted with the main points. This prepareth their minds, and openeth a way to their hearts; whereas, without this, you may lose the most of your labour; and the more pains you take in accurate preparation, the less good you may do. As you would not, therefore, lose your public labour, see that you be faithful in this private work.

4. By means of it, you will come to be familiar with your people, and may thereby win their affections. The want of this, with those who have very numerous congregations, is a great impediment to the success of our labours. By distance and unacquaintedness, abundance of mistakes between ministers and people are fomented; while, on the other hand, familiarity will tend to beget those affections which may open their ears to further instruction. Besides, when we are familiar with them, they will be encouraged to open their doubts to us and deal freely with us. But when a minister knows not his people, or is as strange to them as if he did not know them, it must be a great hindrance to his doing any good among them.

5. By means of it, we shall come to be better acquainted with each person's spiritual state, and so the better know how to watch over them. We shall know better how to preach to them, and carry ourselves to them, when we know their temper, and their chief objections, and so what they have most need to hear. We shall know better wherein to be 'jealous over them with a godly jealousy,' and what temptations to guard them most against. We shall know better how to lament for them, and to rejoice with them, and to pray for them. For as he that will pray rightly for himself must know his own wants, and the diseases of his own heart, so he that will pray rightly for others, should know theirs as far as possible.

6. By means of this trial and acquaintance with our people's state we shall be much assisted in the admission of them to the sacraments. Though I doubt not a minister may require his people to come to him at any convenient season, to give an account of their faith and proficiency, and to receive instruction, and therefore he may do it as a preparation for the Lord's supper, yet because ministers have laid the stress of that examination upon the mere necessity of fitness for that ordinance, and not upon their common duty to see the state and proficiency of each member of their flock at all fit seasons, and upon the people's duty to submit to the guidance and instruction of their pastors at all times, they have occasioned people ignorantly to quarrel with their examinations. Now, by this course we shall discover their fitness or unfitness, in a way that is unexceptionable; and in a way far more effectual than by some partial examination of them before they are admitted to the Lord's table.

7. It will show men the true nature of the ministerial office, and awaken them to the better consideration of it, than is now usual. It is too common for men to think that the work of the ministry is nothing but to preach, and to baptize, and to administer the Lord's supper, and to visit the sick. By this means the people will submit to no more; and too many ministers are such strangers to their own calling, that they will do no more. It hath oft grieved my heart to observe some

eminent able preachers, how little they do for the saving of souls, save only in the pulpit; and to how little purpose much of their labour is, by this neglect. They have hundreds of people that they never spoke a word to personally for their salvation; and if we may judge by their practice, they consider it not as their duty; and the principal thing that hardeneth men in this oversight is the common neglect of the private part of the work by others. There are so few that do much in it, and the omission hath grown so common among pious, able men, that the disgrace of it is abated by their ability; and a man may now be guilty of it without any particular notice or dishonour. Never doth sin so reign in a church or state, as when it hath gained reputation, or, at least, is no disgrace to the sinner, nor a matter of offence to beholders. But I make no doubt, through the mercy of God, that the restoring of the practice of personal oversight will convince many ministers, that this is as truly their work as that which they now do, and may awaken them to see that the ministry is another kind of business than too many excellent preachers take it to be.

Brethren, do but set yourselves closely to this work, and follow it diligently; and though you do it silently, without any words to them that are negligent, I am in hope that most of you who are present may live to see the day, when the neglect of private personal oversight of all the flock shall be taken for a scandalous and odious omission, and shall be as disgraceful to them that are guilty of it, as preaching but once a day was heretofore. A schoolmaster must take a personal account of his scholars, or else he is like to do little good. If physicians should only read a public lecture on physic, their patients would not be much the better of them; nor would a lawyer secure your estate by reading a lecture on law. Now, the charge of a pastor requireth personal dealing, as well as any of these. Let us show the world this by our practice; for most men are grown regardless of bare words.

The truth is, we have been led to wrong the Church exceedingly in this respect, by the contrary extreme of the Papists, who bring all their people to auricular confession; for, in overthrowing this error of theirs, we have run into the opposite extreme, and have led our people much further into it than we have gone ourselves. It troubled me much to read, in an orthodox historian, that licentiousness, and a desire to be from under the strict inquiries of the priests in confession, did much further the entertainment of the reformed religion in Germany. And yet it is like enough to be true, that they who were against reformation in other respects, might, on this account, join with better men in crying down the Romish clergy. I have no doubt that the Popish auricular confession is a sinful novelty, which the ancient Church was unacquainted with. But, perhaps, some will think it strange that I should say, that our common neglect of personal instruction is much worse, if we consider their confessions in themselves, and not as they respect their linked doctrines of satisfaction and purgatory. If any among us should be guilty of so gross a mistake, as to think that, when he hath preached, he hath done all his work, let us show him, by our practice of the rest, that there is much more to be done; and that 'taking heed to all the flock,' is another business than careless, lazy ministers imagine. If a man have an apprehension that duty, and the chiefest duty, is no duty, he is like to neglect it, and to be impenitent in the neglect.

8. It will help our people better to understand the nature of their duty toward their overseers, and, consequently, to discharge it better. This, indeed, were a matter of no consequence, if it were only for our sakes; but their own salvation is much concerned in it. I am convinced, by sad experience, that it is none of the least impediments to their salvation, and to a true reformation of the Church, that the people understand not what the work of a minister is, and what is their own duty towards him. They commonly think, that a minister hath no more to do with them, but to preach to them, and administer the sacraments to them, and visit them in sickness; and that, if they hear him, and receive the sacraments from him, they owe him no further obedience, nor can he require any more at their hands. Little do they know that the minister is in the church, as the schoolmaster in his school, to teach, and take an account of every one in particular; and that all

Christians, ordinarily, must be disciples or scholars in some such school. They think not that a minister is in the church, as a physican in a town, for all people to resort to, for personal advice for the curing of all their diseases; and that 'the priest's lips should keep knowledge, and the people should ask the law at his mouth, because he is the messenger of the Lord of hosts.' They consider not, that all souls in the congregation are bound, for their own safety, to have personal recourse to him, for the resolving of their doubts, and for help against their sins, and for direction in duty, and for increase of knowledge and all saving grace; and that ministers are purposely settled in congregations to this end, to be still ready to advise and help the flock.

If our people did but know their duty, they would readily come to us, when they are desired, to be instructed, and to give an account of their knowledge, faith, and life; and they would come of their own accord, without being sent for; and knock oftener at our doors; and call for advice and help for their souls; and ask, 'What shall we do to be saved?' Whereas now the matter is come to that sad pass, that they think a minister hath nothing to do with them: and if he admonish them, or if he call them to be catechized and instructed; or if he would take an account of their faith and profiting, they would ask him by what authority he doth these things? and think that he is a busy, pragmatical fellow, who loves to be meddling where he hath nothing to do; or a proud fellow, who would bear rule over their consciences; whereas they may as well ask, by what authority he preacheth, or prayeth, or giveth them the sacrament? They consider not, that all our authority is but for our work; even a power to do our duty; and that our work is for them: so that it is but an authority to do them good. They talk not more wisely, than if they should quarrel with a man who would help to quench a fire in their houses, and ask him, by what authority he doth it? Or that would give money to relieve the poor, and they should ask him, By what authority do you require us to take this money? Or as if I offered my hand to one that is fallen, to help him up, or to one that is in the water, to save him from drowning, and he should ask me by what authority I do it?

And what is it that hath brought our people to this ignorance of their duty, but custom? It is we, brethren, to speak truly and plainly, who are to blame, that have not accustomed them and ourselves to any more than common public work. We see how much custom doth with the people. Where it is the custom, as among the Papists, they hesitate not to confess all their sins to the priest; but, among us, they disdain to be catechized or instructed, because it is not the custom. They wonder at it, as a strange thing, and say, Such things were never done before. And if we can but prevail to make this duty as common as other duties, they will much more easily submit to it than now. What a happy thing would it be, if you might live to see the day, that it should be as ordinary for people of all ages to come in course to their ministers for personal advice and help for their salvation, as it is now usual for them to come to the church to hear a sermon, or receive the sacrament! Our diligence in this work, is the way to bring this about.

9. It will give the governors of the nation more correct views about the nature and burden of the ministry, and so may procure from them further assistance. It is a lamentable impediment to the reformation of the Church, and the saving of souls, that, in most populous towns, there are but one or two men to oversee many thousand souls, and so there are not labourers in any degree equal to the work; but it becomes an impossible thing for them to do any considerable measure of that personal duty which should be done by faithful pastors to all the flock. I have often said it, and still must say it, that this is a great part of England's misery, that a great degree of spiritual famine reigns in most cities and large towns throughout the land, even where they are insensible of it, and think themselves well provided. Alas! we see multitudes of ignorant, carnal, sensual sinners around us – here a family, and there a family, and there almost a whole street or village of them – and our hearts pity them, and we see that their necessities cry loud for our speedy and diligent relief, so that 'he that hath ears to hear' must needs hear. Yet if we were never

so fain, we cannot help them: and that not merely through their obstinacy, but also through our want of opportunity. We have found by experience, that if we could but have leisure to speak to them, and to open plainly to them their sin and danger, there were great hopes of doing good to many of them, that receive little by our public teaching. But we cannot come at them; more necessary work prohibits us: we cannot do both at once; and our public work must be preferred, because there we deal with many at once. And it is as much as we are able to do, to perform the public work, or some little more; and if we do take the time when we should eat or sleep, (besides the ruining of weakened bodies by it,) we shall not be able, after all, to speak to one of very many of them. So that we must stand by and see poor people perish, and can but be sorry for them, and cannot so much as speak to them to endeavour their recovery. Is not this a sad case in a nation that glorieth of the fulness of the gospel? An infidel will say, No: but, methinks, no man that believes an everlasting joy or torment should give such an answer.

I will give you the instance of my own case. We are together two ministers, and a third at a chapel, willing to spend every hour of our time in Christ's work. Before we undertook this work, our hands were full, and now we are engaged to set apart two days every week, from morning to night, for private catechizing and instruction; so that any man may see that we must leave undone all that other work that we were wont to do at that time: and we are necessitated to run upon the public work of preaching with small preparation, and so must deliver the message of God so rawly and confusedly, and unanswerably to its dignity and the need of men's souls, that it is a great trouble to our minds to consider it, and a greater trouble to us when we are doing it. And yet it must be so; there is no remedy: unless we will omit this personal instruction, we must needs run thus unpreparedly into the pulpit. And to omit this we dare not – it is so great and necessary a work. And when we have incurred all the forementioned inconveniences, and have set apart two whole days a week for this work, it will be as much as we shall be able to do, to go over the parish once in a year, (being about 800 families,) and which is worse than that, we shall be forced to cut it short, and do it less effectually to those that we do it, having above fifteen families a week to deal with. And, alas! how small a matter is it to speak to a man only once in a year, and that so cursorily as we must be forced to do, in comparison of what their necessities require. Yet are we in hope of some fruit of this much; but how much more might it be, if we could but speak to them once a quarter, and do the work more fully and deliberately, as you that are in smaller parishes may do. And many ministers in England have ten times the number of parishioners which I have: so that if they should undertake the work which we have undertaken, they can go over the parish but once in ten years. So that while we are hoping for opportunities to speak to them, we hear of one dying after another, and to the grief of our souls, are forced to go with them to their graves, before we could ever speak a word to them personally to prepare them for their change. And what is the cause of all this misery? Why, our rulers have not seen the necessity of any more than one or two ministers in such parishes; and so they have not allowed any maintenance to that end. Some have alienated much from the Church, (the Lord humble all them that consented to it, lest it prove the consumption of the nation at last,) while they have left this famine in the chief parts of the land. It is easy to separate from the multitude, and to gather distinct churches, and to let the rest sink or swim; and if they will not be saved by public preaching, to let them be damned: but whether this be the most charitable and Christian course, one would think should be no hard question.

But what is the matter that wise and godly rulers should be thus guilty of our misery, and that none of our cries will awaken them to compassion? What! are they so ignorant as not to know these things? Or are they grown cruel to the souls of men? Or are they false-hearted to the interest of Christ, and have a design to undermine his kingdom? No, I hope it is none of these; but, for aught I can find, it is we who are to blame, even we, the ministers of the gospel, whom they should thus maintain. For those ministers that have small parishes, and might do all this private part of the work, yet do it not, or at least few of them. And those in great towns and cities, that might do somewhat, though they cannot do all, will do just nothing but what accidentally falls in their way, or next to nothing; so that the magistrate is not awakened to the observance or consideration of the weight of our work. Or if they do apprehend the usefulness of it, yet if they see that ministers are so careless and lazy, that they will not do it, they think it in vain to provide them a maintenance for it – it would be but to cherish idle drones – and so they think, that if they maintain ministers enough to preach in the pulpit, they have done their part. And thus are they involved in heinous sin, and we are the occasion of it. Whereas, if we do but all heartily set ourselves to this work, and show the magistrate to his face, that it is a most weighty and necessary part of our business; and that we would do it thoroughly if we could; and that if there were hands enough, the work might go on: and, withal, when he shall see the happy success of our labours, then, no doubt, if the fear of God be in them, and they have any love to his truth and men's souls, they will set to their helping hand, and not let men perish because there is no man to speak to them to prevent it. They will one way or other raise maintenance in such populous places for labourers, proportioned to the number of souls, and greatness of the work. Let them but see us fall to the work, and behold it prosper in our hands; as, if it be well managed, there is no doubt it will, through God's blessing, and then their hearts will be drawn out to the promoting of it: and, instead of laying parishes together to diminish the number of teachers, they will either divide them, or allow more teachers to a parish. But when they see that many carnal ministers do make a greater stir to have more maintenance to themselves, than to have more help in the work of God, they are tempted by such worldlings to wrong the Church, that particular ministers may have ease and fulness.

10. It will exceedingly facilitate the ministerial work in succeeding generations. Custom, as I said before, is the thing

that sways much with the multitude; and they who first break a destructive custom, must bear the brunt of their indignation. Now, somebody must do this. If we do it not, it will lie upon our successors; and how can we expect that they will be more hardy, and resolute, and faithful than we? It is we that have seen the heavy judgments of the Lord, and heard him pleading by fire and sword with the land. It is we that have been ourselves in the furnace, and should be the most refined. It is we that are most deeply obliged by oaths and covenants, by wonderful deliverances, experiences, and mercies of all sorts. And if we yet flinch and turn our backs, and prove false-hearted, why should we expect better from them, that have not been driven by such scourges as we, nor drawn by such cords? But, if they do prove better than we, the same odium and opposition must befall them which we avoid, and that with some increase, because of our neglect; for the people will tell them that we, their predecessors did no such things. But if we would now break the ice for them that follow us, their souls will bless us, and our names will be dear to them, and they will feel the happy fruits of our labour every day of their ministry; when the people shall willingly submit to their private instructions and examinations, yea, and to discipline too, because we have acquainted them with it, and removed the prejudice, and broken the evil custom which our predecessors had been the cause of. Thus we may do much to the saving of many thousand souls, in all ages to come, as well as in the present age in which we live.

11. It will much conduce to the better ordering of families, and the better spending of the Sabbath. When we have once got the masters of families to undertake that they will, every Lord's day, examine their children and servants, and make them repeat some catechism and passages of Scripture, this will find them most profitable employment; whereas many of them would otherwise be idle or ill-employed. Many masters, who know little themselves, may yet be brought to do this for others, and in this way they may even teach themselves.

12. It will do good to many ministers, who are too apt to be idle, and to mis-spend their time in unnecessary discourse,

business, journeys, or recreations. It will let them see that they have no time to spare for such things; and thus, when they are engaged in so much pressing employment of so high a nature, it will be the best cure for all that idleness, and loss of time. Besides, it will cut off that scandal, which usually followeth thereupon; for people are apt to say, Such a minister can spend his time at bowls, or other sports, or vain discourse; and why may not we do so as well as he? Let us all set diligently to this part of our work, and then see what time we can find to spare to live idly, or in a way of voluptuousness, or worldliness, if we can.

13. It will be productive of many personal benefits to ourselves. It will do much to subdue our own corruptions, and to exercise and increase our own graces. It will afford much peace to our consciences, and comfort us when our past lives come to be reviewed.

To be much in provoking others to repentance and heavenly-mindedness may do much to excite them in ourselves. To cry down the sin of others, and engage them against it, and direct them to overcome it, will do much to shame us out of our own; and conscience will scarcely suffer us to live in that which we make so much ado to draw others from. Even our constant employment for God, and busying our minds and tongues against sin, and for Christ and holiness, will do much to overcome our fleshly inclinations, both by direct mortification, and by diversion, leaving our fancies no room nor time for their old employment. All the austerities of monks and hermits, who addict themselves to unprofitable solitude, and who think to save themselves by neglecting to show compassion to others, will not do near so much in the true work of mortification, as this fruitful diligence for Christ.

14. It will be some benefit, that by this means we shall take off ourselves and our people from vain controversies, and from expending our care and zeal on the lesser matters of religion, which least tend to their spiritual edification. While we are taken up in teaching, and they in learning the fundamental truths of the gospel, we shall divert our minds and tongues,

and have less room for lower things; and so it will cure much wranglings and contentions between ministers and people. For we do that which we need not and should not, because we will not fall diligently to do that which we need and should.

15. And then for the extent of the aforesaid benefits: The design of this work is, the reforming and saving of all the people in our several parishes. For we shall not leave out any man that will submit to be instructed; and though we can scarcely hope that every individual will be reformed and saved by it, yet have we reason to hope, that as the attempt is universal, so the success will be more general and extensive than we have hitherto seen of our other labours. Sure I am, it is most like to the spirit, and precept, and offers of the gospel, which requireth us to preach Christ to every creature, and promiseth life to every man, if he will accept it by believing. If God would have all men to be saved, and to come to the knowledge of the truth, (that is, as Rector and Benefactor of the world, he hath manifested himself willing to save all men, if they be willing themselves, though his elect he will also make willing,) then surely it beseems us to offer salvation unto all men, and to endeavour to bring them to the knowledge of the truth. And, if Christ 'tasted death for every man,' it is meet we should preach his death to every man. This work hath a more excellent design, than our accidental conferences with now and then a particular person. And I have observed, that in such occasional discourses men satisfy themselves with having spoken some good words, but seldom set plainly and closely home the matter, to convince men of sin and misery and mercy; as in this purposely appointed work we are more like to do.

16. It is like to be a work that will reach over the whole land, and not stop with us that have now engaged in it. For though it be at present neglected, I suppose the cause is the same with our brethren as it hath been with us, namely, that inconsiderateness and laziness, which we are here bewailing this day, but especially, despair of the submission of the people to it. But when they shall be reminded of so clear and great a

duty, and shall see the practicability of it, in a good measure, when it is done by common consent, they will, no doubt, universally take it up, and gladly concur with us in so blessed a work; for they are the servants of the same God, as sensible of the interests of Christ, and as compassionate to men's souls; as conscientious, and as self-denying, and ready to do or suffer for such excellent ends as we are. Seeing, therefore, they have the same spirit, rule, and Lord, I will not be so uncharitable as to doubt, whether all that are godly throughout the land (or at least the generality of them,) will gladly join with us. And oh, what a happy thing it will be to see such a general combination for Christ; and to see all England so seriously called upon, and importuned for Christ, and set in so fair a way to heaven! Methinks the consideration of it should make our hearts rejoice within us, to see so many faithful servants of Christ all over the land, addressing every particular sinner with such importunity, as men that will hardly take a denial. Methinks I even see all the godly ministers of England commencing the work already, and resolving to embrace the present opportunity, that unanimity may facilitate it.

17. Lastly, Of so great weight and excellency is the duty which we are now recommending, that the chief part of Church reformation that is behind as to *means* consisteth in it; and it must be the chief means to answer the judgments, the mercies, the prayers, the promises, the cost, the endeavours, and the blood of the nation; and without this it will not be done; the ends of all these will never be well attained; a reformation to purpose will never be wrought; the Church will be still low; the interest of Christ will be much neglected; and God will still have a controversy with the land, and, above all, with the ministry that have been deepest in the guilt.

How long have we talked of reformation, how much have we said and done for it in general, and how deeply and devoutly have we vowed it for our own parts; and, after all this, how shamefully have we neglected it, and neglect it to this day! We carry ourselves as if we had not known or considered what that reformation was which we vowed. As carnal men will take on them to be Christians, and profess with confidence that they believe in Christ, and accept of his salvation, and may contend for Christ, and fight for him, and yet, for all this, will have none of him, but perish for refusing him, who little dreamed that ever they had been refusers of him; and all because they understood not what his salvation is, and how it is carried on, but dream of a salvation without flesh-displeasing, and without self-denial and renouncing the world, and parting with their sins, and without any holiness, or any great pains and labour of their own in subserviency to Christ and the Spirit: even so did too many ministers and private men talk and write, and pray, and fight, and long for reformation, and would little have believed that man who should have presumed to tell them, that, notwithstanding all this, their very hearts were against reformation; and that they who were praying for it, and fasting for it, and wading through blood for it, would never accept it, but would themselves be the rejectors and destroyers of it. And yet so it is, and so it hath too plainly proved: and whence is all this strange deceit of heart, that good men should no better know themselves? Why, the case is plain; they thought of a re-formation to be given by God, but not of a reformation to be wrought on and by themselves. They considered the blessing, but never thought of the means of accomplishing it. But as if they had expected that all things besides themselves should be mended without them, or that the Holy Ghost should again descend miraculously, or every sermon should convert its thousands, or that some angel from heaven or some Elias should be sent to restore all things, or that the law of the parliament, and the sword of the magistrate, would have converted or constrained all, and have done the deed; and little did they think of a reformation that must be wrought by their own diligence and unwearied labours, by earnest preaching and catechizing, and personal instructions, and taking heed to all the flock, whatever pains or reproaches it should cost them. They thought not that a thorough reformation would multiply their own work; but we had all of us too carnal thoughts, that when we had ungodly men at our mercy, all would be done, and conquering them was converting them, or such a means as would have frightened them to heaven. But the business is far otherwise, and had we then known how a reformation must be attained, perhaps some would have been colder in the prosecution of it. And yet I know that even foreseen labours seem small matters at a distance, while we do but hear and talk of them; but when we come nearer them, and must lay our hands to the work, and put on our armour, and charge through the thickest of opposing difficulties, then is the sincerity and the strength of men's hearts brought to trial, and it will appear how they purposed and promised before.

Reformation is to many of us, as the Messiah was to the Jews. Before he came, they looked and longed for him, and boasted of him, and rejoiced in hope of him; but when he came they could not abide him, but hated him, and would not believe that he was indeed the person, and therefore persecuted and put him to death, to the curse and confusion of the main body of their nation. 'The Lord, whom ye seek, shall suddenly come to his temple, even the Messenger of the covenant, whom ye delight in. But who may abide the day of his coming? and who shall stand when he appeareth? For he is like a refiner's fire, and like fuller's soap: and he shall sit as a refiner and purifier of silver: and he shall purify the sons of Levi, and purge them as gold and silver, that they may offer unto the Lord an offering in righteousness.' And the reason was, because it was another manner of Christ that the Jews expected; it was one who would bring them riches and liberty, and to this day they profess that they will never believe in any but such. So it is with too many about reformation. They hoped for a reformation, that would bring them more wealth and honour with the people, and power to force men to do what they would have them: and now they see a reformation, that must put them to more condescension and pains than they were ever at before. They thought of having the opposers of godliness under their feet, but now they see they must go to them with humble entreaties, and put their hands under their feet, if they would do them good, and meekly beseech even those that sometime sought their lives, and make it now their daily business to overcome them by kindness, and win them with love. O how many carnal expectations are here crossed!

Motives from the difficulties of the work

Having stated to you the first class of reasons, drawn from the benefits of the work, I come to the second sort, which are taken from the difficulties. If these, indeed, were taken alone, I confess they might be rather discouragements than motives; but taking them with those that go before and follow, the case is far otherwise: for difficulties must excite to greater diligence in a necessary work.

And difficulties we shall find many, both in ourselves and in our people; but because they are things so obvious, that your experience will leave you no room to doubt of them, I shall pass them over in a few words.

1. Let me notice the difficulties in ourselves.

(1) In ourselves there is much dulness and laziness, so that it will not be easy to get us to be faithful in so hard a work. Like a sluggard in bed, that knows he should rise, and yet delayeth and would lie as long as he can, so do we by duties to which our corrupt natures are averse. This will put us to the use of all our powers. Mere sloth will tie the hands of many.

(2) We have a base man-pleasing disposition, which will make us let men perish lest we lose their love, and let them go quietly to hell, lest we should make them angry with us for seeking their salvation: and we are ready to venture on the displeasure of God, and risk the everlasting misery of our people, rather than draw on ourselves their ill-will. This distemper must be diligently resisted.

(3) Many of us have also a foolish bashfulness, which makes us backward to begin with them, and to speak plainly to them. We are so modest, forsooth, that we blush to speak for

Christ, or to contradict the devil, or to save a soul, while, at the same time, we are less ashamed of shameful works.

(4) We are so carnal that we are drawn by our fleshly interests to be unfaithful in the work of Christ, lest we should lessen our income, or bring trouble upon ourselves, or set people against us, or such like. All these things require diligence in order to resist them.

(5) We are so weak in the faith, that this is the greatest impediment of all. Hence it is, that when we should set upon a man for his conversion with all our might, if there be not the stirrings of unbelief within us, whether there be a heaven and a hell, yet at least the belief of them is so feeble, that it will hardly excite in us a kindly, resolute, constant zeal, so that our whole motion will be but weak, because the spring of faith is so weak. O what need, therefore, have ministers for themselves and their work, to look well to their faith, especially that their assent to the truth of Scripture, about the joys and torments of the life to come, be sound and lively.

(6) Lastly, We have commonly a great deal of unskilfulness and unfitness for this work. Alas! how few know how to deal with an ignorant, worldly man, for his conversion! To get within him and win upon him; to suit our speech to his condition and temper; to choose the meetest subjects, and follow them with a holy mixture of seriousness, and terror, and love, and meekness, and evangelical allurements – oh! who is fit for such a thing? I profess seriously, it seems to me, by experience, as hard a matter to confer aright with such a carnal person, in order to his change, as to preach such sermons as ordinarily we do, if not much more. All these difficulties in ourselves should awaken us to holy resolution, preparation, and diligence, that we may not be overcome by them, and hindered from or in the work.

2. Having noticed these difficulties in ourselves, I shall now mention some which we shall meet with in our people.

(1) Many of them will be obstinately unwilling to be taught; and scorn to come to us, as being too good to be catechized, or too old to learn, unless we deal wisely with them in public

and private, and study, by the force of reason, and the power of love, to conquer their perverseness.

(2) Many that are willing are so dull, that they can scarcely learn a leaf of a catechism in a long time, and therefore they will keep away, as ashamed of their ignorance, unless we are wise and diligent to encourage them.

(3) And when they do come, so great is the ignorance and unapprehensiveness of many, that you will find it a very hard matter to get them to understand you; so that if you have not the happy art of making things plain, you will leave them as ignorant as before.

(4) And yet harder will you find it to work things upon their hearts, and to set them so home to their consciences, as to produce that saving change, which is our grand aim, and without which our labour is lost. Oh what a block, what a rock, is a hardened, carnal heart! How strongly will it resist the most powerful persuasions, and hear of everlasting life or death, as a thing of nought! If, therefore, you have not great seriousness, and fervency, and powerful matter, and fitness of expression, what good can you expect? And when you have done all, the Spirit of grace must do the work. But as God and men usually choose instruments suitable to the nature of the work or end, so the Spirit of wisdom, life, and holiness doth not usually work by foolish, dead, carnal instruments, but by such persuasions of light and life and purity as are likest to itself, and to the work that is to be wrought thereby.

(5) Lastly, When you have made some desirable impressions on their hearts, if you look not after them, and have a special care of them, their hearts will soon return to their former hardness, and their old companions and temptations will destroy all again. In short, all the difficulties of the work of conversion, which you use to acquaint your people with, are before us in our present work.

Motives from the necessity of the work

The third sort of motives are drawn from the necessity of the work. For if it were not necessary, the slothful might be discouraged rather than excited by the difficulties now mentioned. But because I have already been longer than I intended, I shall give you only a brief hint of some of the general grounds of this necessity.

1. This duty is necessary for the glory of God. As every Christian liveth to the glory of God, as his end, so will he gladly take that course which will most effectually promote it. For what man would not attain his ends? O brethren, if we could set this work on foot in all the parishes of England, and get our people to submit to it, and then prosecute it skilfully and zealously ourselves, what a glory would it put upon the face of the nation, and what glory would, by means of it, redound to God! If our common ignorance were thus banished, and our vanity and idleness turned into the study of the way of life, and every shop and every house were busied in learning the Scriptures and catechisms, and speaking of the Word and works of God, what pleasure would God take in our cities and country! He would even dwell in our habitations, and make them his delight. It is the glory of Christ that shineth in his saints, and all their glory is his glory. That, therefore, which honoureth them, in number or excellency, honoureth him. Will not the glory of Christ be wonderfully displayed in the New Jerusalem, when it shall descend from heaven in all that splendour and magnificence with which it is described in the Book of Revelation? If, therefore, we can increase the number or strength of the saints, we shall thereby increase the glory of the King of saints; for he will have service and praise where before he had disobedience and dishonour. Christ will also be honoured in the fruits of his blood shed, and the Spirit of grace in the fruit of his operations. And do not such important ends as these require that we use the means with diligence?

Every Christian is obliged to do all he can for the salvation of others; but every minister is doubly obliged, because he is separated to the gospel of Christ, and is to give up himself wholly to that work. It is needless to make any further question of our obligation, when we know that this work is needful to our people's conversion and salvation, and that we are in general commanded to do all that is needful to these ends, as far as we are able. Whether the unconverted have need of conversion, I hope is not doubted among us. And whether this be a means, and a most needful means, experience may put beyond a doubt, if we had no more. Let them that have taken most pains in public, examine their people, and try whether many of them are not nearly as ignorant and careless as if they had never heard the gospel. For my part, I study to speak as plainly and movingly as I can, (and next to my study to speak truly, these are my chief studies,) and yet I frequently meet with those that have been my hearers eight or ten years, who know not whether Christ be God or man, and wonder when I tell them the history of his birth and life and death, as if they had never heard it before. And of those who know the history of the gospel, how few are there who know the nature of that faith, repentance, and holiness which it requireth, or, at least, who know their own hearts? But most of them have an ungrounded trust in Christ, hoping that he will pardon, justify, and save them, while the world hath their hearts, and they live to the flesh. And this trust they take for justifying faith. I have found by experience, that some ignorant persons, who have been so long unprofitable hearers, have got more knowledge and remorse of conscience in half an hour's close discourse, than they did from ten years' public preaching.

I know that preaching the gospel publicly is the most excellent means, because we speak to many at once. But it is usually far more effectual to preach it privately to a particular sinner, as to himself: for the plainest man that is, can scarcely speak plain enough in public for them to understand; but in private we may do it much more. In public we may not use such homely expressions, or repetitions, as their dulness requires, but in private we may. In public our speeches are long, and we quite over-run their understandings and memories, and they are confounded and at a loss, and not able to follow us, and one thing drives out another, and so they know not what we said. But in private we can take our work *gradatim*, and take our hearers along with us; and, by our questions, and their answers, we can see how far they understand us, and what we have next to do. In public, by length and speaking alone we lose their attention; but when they are interlocutors, we can easily cause them to attend. Besides, we can better answer their objections, and engage them by promises before we leave them, which in public we cannot do. I conclude, therefore, that public preaching will not be sufficient: for though it may be an effectual means to convert many, yet not so many, as experience, and God's appointment of further means, may assure us. Long may you study and preach to little purpose, if you neglect this duty.

2. This duty is necessary to the welfare of our people.

Brethren, can you look believingly on your miserable people, and not perceive them calling to you for help? There is not a sinner whose case you should not so far compassionate, as to be willing to relieve them at a much dearer rate than this comes to. Can you see them, as the wounded man by the way, and unmercifully pass by? Can you hear them cry to you, as the man of Macedonia to Paul, in vision, 'Come and help us;' and yet refuse your help? Are you intrusted with the charge of an hospital, where one languisheth in one corner, and another groaneth in another, and crieth out, 'Oh, help me, pity me for the Lord's sake!' and where a third is raging mad, and would destroy himself and you; and yet will you sit idle and refuse your help? If it may be said of him that relieveth not men's bodies, how much more of him that relieveth not men's souls, 'If he see his brother have need, and shut up his bowels of compassion from him, how dwelleth the love of God in him?' You are not such monsters, such hard-hearted men, but you will pity a leper; you will pity the naked, the imprisoned, or the desolate; you will pity him that is tormented with grievous pain or sickness; and will you not pity an ignorant, hard-hearted sinner? will you not pity one that must be shut out from the presence of the Lord, and lie under his remediless wrath, if thorough repentance speedily prevent it not? Oh what a heart is it that will not pity such a one! What shall I call the heart of such a man? A heart of stone, a very rock or adamant; the heart of a tiger; or rather the heart of an infidel: for surely if he believed the misery of the impenitent, it is not possible but he should take pity on him. Can you tell men in the pulpit that they shall certainly be damned, except they repent, and yet have no pity on them when you have proclaimed to them such a danger? And if you pity them, will you not do this much for their salvation?

How many around you are blindly hastening to perdition, while your voice is appointed to be the means of arousing and reclaiming them! The physician hath no excuse who is doubly bound to relieve the sick, when even every neighbour is bound to help them. Brethren, what if you heard sinners cry after you in the streets, 'O sir, have pity on me, and afford me your advice! I am afraid of the everlasting wrath of God. I know I must shortly leave this world, and I am afraid lest I shall be miserable in the next.' Could you deny your help to such poor sinners? What if they came to your study-door, and cried for help, and would not go away till you had told them how to escape the wrath of God? Could you find in your hearts to drive them away without advice? I am confident you could not. Why, alas! such persons are less miserable than they who will not cry for help. It is the hardened sinner who cares not for your help, that most needs it: and he that hath not so much life as to feel that he is dead, nor so much light as to see his danger, nor so much sense left as to pity himself – this is the man that is most to be pitied.

Look upon your neighbours around you, and think how many of them need your help in no less a case than the apparent danger of damnation. Suppose that you heard every impenitent person whom you see and know about you, crying to you for help, 'As ever you pitied poor wretches, pity us, lest we should be tormented in the flames of hell: if you have the hearts of men, pity us.' Now, do that for them that you would do if they followed you with such expostulations. Oh how can you walk, and talk, and be merry with such people, when you know their case? Methinks, when you look them in the face, and think how they must suffer everlasting misery, you should break forth into tears (as the prophet did when he looked upon Hazael), and then fall on with the most importunate exhortations. When you visit them in their sickness, will it not wound your hearts to see them ready to depart into misery, before you have ever dealt seriously with them for their conversion? Oh, then, for the Lord's sake, and for the sake of poor souls, have pity on them, and bestir yourselves, and spare no pains that may conduce to their salvation.

3. This duty is necessary to your own welfare, as well as to your people's. This is your work, according to which, among others, you shall be judged. You can no more be saved without ministerial diligence and fidelity, than they or you can be saved without Christian diligence and fidelity. If, therefore, you care not for others, care at least for yourselves. Oh what a dreadful thing is it to answer for the neglect of such a charge! and what sin more heinous than the betraying of souls? Doth not that threatening make you tremble –'If thou dost not speak to warn the wicked from his way, that wicked man shall die in his iniquity; but HIS BLOOD WILL I REQUIRE AT THY HAND?' I am afraid, nay, I have no doubt, that the day is near when unfaithful ministers will wish that they had never known the charge of souls; but that they had rather been colliers, or sweeps, or tinkers, than pastors of Christ's flock; when, besides all the rest of their sins, they shall have the blood of so many souls to answer for. O brethren, our death, as well as our people's, is at hand, and it is as terrible to an unfaithful pastor as to any. When we see that die we must, and that there is no remedy; that no wit, nor learning, nor popular applause, can avert the stroke, or delay the time; but, willing or unwilling, our souls must be gone, and that into a world which we never saw, where our persons and our worldly interest will not be respected; oh, then for a

clear conscience, that can say, 'I lived not to myself but to Christ; I spared not my pains; I hid not my talents; I concealed not men's misery, nor the way of their recovery.' O sirs, let us therefore take time while we have it, and work while it is day; 'for the night cometh, when no man can work.' This is our day too; and by doing good to others, we must do good to ourselves. If you would prepare for a comfortable death, and a great and glorious reward, the harvest is before you. Gird up the loins of your minds, and quit yourselves like men, that you may end your days with these triumphant words: 'I have fought a good fight, I have finished my course, I have kept the faith: henceforth there is laid up for me a crown of righteousness, which the Lord, the righteous Judge, shall give unto me in that day.' If you would be blessed with those that die in the Lord, labour now, that you may rest from your labours then, and do such works as you would wish should follow you, and not such as will prove your terror in the review.

ARTICLE 4
Application of these motives

Having found so many and so powerful reasons to move us to this work, I shall now apply them further for our humiliation and excitation.

1. What cause have we to bleed before the Lord this day, that we have neglected so great and good a work so long; that we have been ministers of the gospel so many years, and done so little by personal instruction and conference for the saving of men's souls! If we had but set about this business sooner, who knows how many souls might have been brought to Christ, and how much happier our congregations might have been? And why might we not have done it sooner as well as now? I confess, there were many impediments in our way, and so there are still, and will be while there is a devil to tempt, and a corrupt heart in man to resist the light: but if

the greatest impediment had not been in ourselves, even in our own darkness, and dulness, and indisposedness to duty, and our dividedness and unaptness to close for the work of God, I see not but much might have been done before this. We had the same God to command us, and the same miserable objects of compassion, and the same liberty from governors as now we have. We have sinned, and have no just excuse for our sin; and the sin is so great, because the duty is so great, that we should be afraid of pleading any excuse. The God of mercy forgive us, and all the ministry of England, and lay not this or any of our ministerial negligences to our charge! Oh that he would cover all our unfaithfulness, and, by the blood of the everlasting covenant, wash away our guilt of the blood of souls; that when the chief Shepherd shall appear, we may stand before him in peace, and may not be condemned for the scattering of his flock. And oh that he would put up his controversy which he hath against the pastors of his Church, and not deal the worse with them for our sakes, nor suffer underminers or persecutors to scatter them, as they have suffered his sheep to be scattered; and that he will not care as little for us, as we have done for the souls of men; nor think his salvation too good for us, as we have thought our labour and sufferings too much for men's salvation!

As we have had many days of humiliation in England for the sins of the land, and the judgments that have befallen us, I hope we shall hear that God will more thoroughly humble the ministry, and cause them to bewail their own neglects, and to set apart some days through the land to that end, that they may not think it enough to lament the sins of others, while they overlook their own; and that God may not abhor our solemn national humiliations, because they are managed by unhumbled guides; and that we may first prevail with him for a pardon for ourselves, that we may be the fitter to beg for the pardon of others.

And oh that we may cast out the dung of our pride, contention, self-seeking, and idleness; lest God should cast our sacrifices as dung in our faces, and should cast us out as the dung of the earth, as of late he hath done many others for a warning to us; and that we may presently resolve in concord to mend our pace, before we feel a sharper spur than hitherto we have felt.

2. And now, brethren, what have we to do for the time to come, but to deny our lazy flesh, and rouse up ourselves to the work before us. The harvest is great, the labourers are few; the loiterers and hinderers are many, the souls of men are precious, the misery of sinners is great, and the everlasting misery to which they are near is greater, the joys of heaven are inconceivable, the comfort of a faithful minister is not small, the joy of extensive success will be a full reward. To be fellow-workers with God and his Spirit is no little honour; to subserve the blood-shedding of Christ for men's salvation is not a light thing. To lead on the armies of Christ through the thickest of the enemy; to guide them safely through a dangerous wilderness; to steer the vessels through such storms and rocks and sands and shelves, and bring it safe to the harbour of rest, requireth no small skill and diligence. The fields now seem even white unto harvest; the preparations that have been made for us are very great; the season of working is more calm than most ages before us have ever seen. We have carelessly loitered too long already; the present time is posting away; while we are trifling, men are dying; oh how fast are they passing into another world! And is there nothing in all this to awaken us to our duty, nothing to resolve us to speedy and unwearied diligence? Can we think that a man can be too careful and painful under all these motives and engagements? Or can that man be a fit instrument for other men's illumination, who is himself so blind? or for the quickening of others, who is himself so senseless? What, sirs! are ye, who are men of wisdom, as dull as the common people? and do we need to heap up a multitude of words to persuade you to a known and weighty duty? One would think it should be enough to set you on work, to show a line in the Book of God; to prove it to be his will; or to prove to you that the work hath a tendency to promote men's salvation. One would think that the very sight of

your miserable neighbours would be motive sufficient to draw out your most compassionate endeavours for their relief. If a cripple do but unlap his sores, and show you his disabled limbs, it will move you without words; and will not the case of souls, that are near to damnation, move you? O happy church, if the physicians were but healed themselves; and if we had not too much of that infidelity and stupidity against which we daily preach in others; and were more soundly persuaded of that of which we persuade others; and were more deeply affected with the wonderful things wherewith we would affect them!

Were there but such clear and deep impressions upon our own souls of those glorious things which we daily preach, oh what a change would it make in our sermons, and in our private course of life! Oh what a miserable thing it is to the Church and to themselves, that men must preach of heaven and hell, before they soundly believe that there are such things, or have felt the weight of the doctrines which they preach! It would amaze a sensible man to think what matters we preach and talk of; what it is for the soul to pass out of this flesh, and appear before a righteous God, and enter upon unchangeable joy or unchangeable torment! Oh, with what amazing thoughts do dying men apprehend these things! How should such matters be preached and discoursed of! Oh the gravity, the seriousness, the incessant diligence, which these things require! I know not what others think of them; but for my part, I am ashamed of my stupidity, and wonder at myself that I deal not with my own and others' souls, as one that looks for the great day of the Lord; and that I can have room for almost any other thoughts or words; and that such astonishing matters do not wholly absorb my mind. I marvel how I can preach of them slightly and coldly, and how I can let men alone in their sins, and that I do not go to them, and beseech them, for the Lord's sake, to repent, however they may take it, and whatever pains or trouble it may cost me! I seldom come out of the pulpit, but my conscience smiteth me that I have been no more serious and fervent in such a case. It accuseth me not so much for want of ornaments or elegancy, nor for letting fall an unhandsome word; but it asketh me, 'How couldst thou speak of life and death with such a heart? How couldst thou preach of heaven and hell in such a careless, sleepy manner? Dost thou believe what thou sayest? Art thou in earnest or in jest? How canst thou tell people that sin is such a thing, and that so much misery is upon them and before them, and be no more affected with it? Shouldst thou not weep over such a people, and should not thy tears interrupt thy words? Shouldst not thou cry aloud, and show them their transgressions, and entreat and beseech them as for life and death?' Truly, this is the peal that conscience doth ring in my ears, and yet my drowsy soul will not be awakened.

Oh what a thing is a senseless, hardened heart! O Lord, save us from the plague of infidelity and hard-heartedness ourselves, or else how shall we be fit instruments of saving others from it? Oh, do that on our own souls, which thou wouldst use us to do on the souls of others! I am even confounded to think what a difference there is between my sick-bed apprehensions, and my pulpit apprehensions, of the life to come; that ever that can seem so light a matter to me now, which seemed so great and astonishing a matter then, and I know will do so again when death looks me in the face, when yet I daily know and think of that approaching hour; and yet these forethoughts will not recover such working apprehensions! O sirs, surely if you had all conversed with neighbour Death as oft as I have done, and as often received the sentence in yourselves, you would have an unquiet conscience, if not a reformed life, as to your ministerial diligence and fidelity; and you would have something within you that would frequently ask you such questions as these: 'Is this all thy compassion for lost sinners? Wilt thou do no more to seek and to save them? Is there not such and such – oh how many round about thee! – that are yet the visible sons of death? What hast thou said to them, or done for their conversion? Shall they die and be in hell before thou wilt speak to them one serious word to prevent it? shall they there curse thee for ever that didst no more in time to save them?'

Such cries of conscience are daily ringing in mine ears, though, the Lord knows, I have too little obeyed them. The God of mercy pardon me, and awaken me, with the rest of his servants that have been thus sinfully negligent. I confess to my shame that I seldom hear the bell toll for one that is dead, but conscience asketh me, 'What hast thou done for the saving of that soul before it left the body? There is one more gone to judgment; what didst thou to prepare him for judgment?' and yet I have been slothful and backward to help them that survive. How can you choose, when you are laying a corpse in the grave, but think with yourselves, 'Here lieth the body; but where is the soul? and what have I done for it, before it departed? It was part of my charge; what account can I give of it?'

O sirs, is it a small matter to you to answer such questions as these? It may seem so now, but the hour is coming when it will not seem so. 'If our hearts condemn us, God is greater than our hearts,' and will condemn us much more, even with another kind of condemnation than conscience doth. The voice of conscience is a still voice, and the sentence of conscience is a gentle sentence, in comparison of the voice and the sentence of God. Alas! conscience seeth but a very little of our sin and misery, in comparison of what God seeth. What mountains would these things appear to your souls, which now seem molehills? What beams would these be in your eyes, that now seem motes, if you did but see them with a clearer light? (I dare not say, As God seeth them.) We can easily make shift to plead the cause with conscience, and either bribe it, or bear its sentence; but God is not so easily dealt with, nor his sentence so easily borne. 'Wherefore we receiving,' and preaching, 'a kingdom that cannot be moved, let us have grace whereby we may serve God acceptably, with reverence, and godly fear; for our God is a consuming fire.' But because you shall not say that I affright you with bugbears, and tell you of dangers and terrors when there are none, I will here show you the certainty and sureness of that condemnation that is like to befall negligent pastors, particularly how many will be ready to rise up against us and condemn us, if we shall hereafter be wilful neglecters of this great work.

(1) Our parents, that destined us to the ministry, will condemn us, and say, 'Lord, we devoted them to thy service, and they made light of it, and served themselves.'

(2) Our masters that taught us, our tutors that instructed us, the schools and universities where we lived, and all the years that we spent in study, will rise up in judgment against us, and condemn us; for why was all this, but for the work of God?

(3) Our learning and knowledge and ministerial gifts will condemn us; for to what end were we made partakers of these, but for the work of God?

(4) Our voluntary undertaking the charge of souls will condemn us; for all men should be faithful to the trust which they have undertaken.

(5) All the care of God for his Church, and all that Christ hath done and suffered for it, will rise up in judgment against us, if we be negligent and unfaithful, and condemn us; because by our neglect we destroyed them for whom Christ died.

(6) All the precepts and charges of Holy Scripture, all the promises of assistance and reward, all the threatenings of punishment, will rise up against us and condemn us; for God did not speak all this in vain.

(7) All the examples of the prophets and apostles, and other preachers recorded in Scripture, and all the examples of the faithful and diligent servants of Christ in these latter times, and in the places around us, will rise up in judgment and condemn us; for all these were for our imitation, and to provoke us to a holy emulation in fidelity and ministerial diligence.

(8) The Holy Bible that lies open before us, and all the books in our studies that tell us of our duty, directly or indirectly, will condemn the lazy and unprofitable servant; for we have not all these helps and furniture in vain.

(9) All the sermons that we preach to persuade our people to work out their salvation with fear and trembling, to lay violent hands upon the crown of life, and take the kingdom by force, to strive to enter in at the strait gate, and so to run as

to obtain, will rise up against the unfaithful and condemn them; for if it so nearly concern them to labour for their salvation, doth it not concern us who have the charge of them to be also violent, laborious, and unwearied in striving to help on their salvation? Is it worth their labour, and patience, and is it not also worth ours?

(10) All the sermons that we preach to them to set forth the evil of sin, the danger of a natural state, the need of a Saviour, the joys of heaven, and the torments of hell, yea, and the truth of the Christian religion, will rise up in judgment against the unfaithful, and condemn them. And a sad review it will be to themselves, when they shall be forced to think, 'Did I tell them of such great dangers and hopes in public, and would I do no more, in private, to help them? What? tell them daily of damnation, and yet let them run into it so easily? Tell them of such a glory, and scarcely speak a word to them personally, to help them to it? Were these such great matters with me at church, and so small matters when I came home?' Ah! this will be dreadful self-condemnation.

(11) All the sermons that we have preached to persuade other men to such duties – as neighbours to exhort one another daily, and parents and masters to teach their children and servants the way to heaven – will rise up in judgment against the unfaithful, and condemn them; for will you persuade others to that which you will not do, as far as you can, yourselves? When you threaten them for neglecting their duty, how much more do you threaten your own souls!

(12) All the maintenance which we take for our service, if we be unfaithful, will condemn us; for who is it that will pay a servant to take his pleasure, or sit idle, or work for himself? If we have the fleece, surely it is that we may look after the flock; and, by taking the wages, we oblige ourselves to the work.

(13) All the witness that we have borne against the scandalous, negligent ministers of this age, and all the endeavours that we have used for their removal, will condemn the unfaithful; for God is no respecter of persons. If we succeed them in their sins, we have spoken all that against ourselves; and, as we

condemned them, God and others will condemn us, if we imitate them. And, though we should not be so bad as they, it will prove sad if we are even like them.

(14) All the judgments that God hath, in this age, executed on negligent ministers, before our eyes, will condemn us, if we be unfaithful. Hath he made the idle shepherds and sensual drones to stink in the nostrils of the people? And will he honour us, if we be idle and sensual? Hath he sequestrated them, and cast them out of their habitations, and out of their pulpits, and laid them by as dead, while they are yet alive, and made them a hissing and a by-word in the land? And yet dare we imitate them? Are not their sufferings our warnings? and did not all this befall them as an example to us? If any thing in the world would awaken ministers to self-denial and diligence, methinks we have seen enough to do it. Would you have imitated the old world if you had seen the flood that drowned it? Would you have indulged in the sins of Sodom – idleness, pride, fulness of bread – if you had stood by, and seen the flames which consumed it ascending up to heaven? Who would have been a Judas, that had seen him hanged and burst asunder? And who would have been a lying, sacrilegious hypocrite, that had seen Ananias and Sapphira die? And who would not have been afraid to contradict the gospel, that had seen Elymas smitten with blindness? And shall we prove idle, self-seeking ministers, when we have seen God scourging such out of his temple, and sweeping them away as dirt into the channels? God forbid! For then how great and how manifold will our condemnation be![1]

(15) Lastly, All the days of fasting and prayer, which have, of late years, been kept in England for a reformation, will rise up in judgment against the unreformed, who will not be persuaded to the painful part of the work. This, I confess, is so

[1] Though we are persuaded that England was never blessed with so able, so faithful, so diligent, and so pious a ministry, as about the period when Baxter wrote this work, yet it is worthy of notice, that the apprehensions which he here expressed were, in a short time, realized in a very melancholy manner. By the Act of Uniformity, passed soon after the restoration of Charles II, about two thousand of these excellent men were cast out of their churches, and, among others, himself. If it was thus 'in the green tree, what shall it be in the dry?' *Editor*

heavy an aggravation of our sin, that it makes me ready to tremble to think of it. Was there ever a nation on the face of the earth, which so long and so solemnly followed God with fasting and prayer, as we have done? Before the parliament began, how frequent and fervent were we in secret! After that, for many years together, we had a monthly fast commanded by the parliament, besides frequent private and public fasts on other occasions. And what was all this for? Whatever was, for some time, the means we looked at, yet still the end of all our prayers was Church-reformation, and, therein, especially these two things, a faithful ministry, and the exercise of discipline in the Church. And did it once enter then into the hearts of the people, or even into our own hearts, to imagine, that when we had all we would have, and the matter was put into our own hands, to be as painful as we could, and to exercise what discipline we would, that then we would do nothing but publicly preach? that we would not be at the pains of catechizing and instructing our people personally, nor exercise any considerable part of discipline at all? It astonisheth me to think of it. What a depth of deceit is the heart of man! What? are good men's hearts so deceitful? Are all men's hearts so deceitful? I confess, I then told many soldiers, and other sensual men, that though they had fought for a reformation, I was confident they would abhor it, and be enemies to it, when they saw and felt it; thinking that the yoke of discipline would have pinched their necks, and that, when they were catechized and personally dealt with, and reproved for their sin, in private and public, and brought to public confession and repentance, or avoided as impenitent, they would scorn and spurn at all this, and take the yoke of Christ for tyranny; but little did I think that the ministers would let all fall, and put almost none of this upon them; but let them alone for fear of displeasing them, and let all run on as it did before.

Oh the earnest prayers which I have heard for a painful ministry, and for discipline! It was as if they had even wrestled for salvation itself. Yea, they commonly called discipline, 'the kingdom of Christ, or the exercise of his kingly office in his church;' and so preached and prayed for it, as if the setting up of discipline had been the setting up of the kingdom of Christ. And did I then think that they would refuse to set it up when they might? What! is the kingdom of Christ now reckoned among things indifferent?

If the God of heaven, who knew our hearts, had, in the midst of our prayers and cries, on one of our public monthly fasts, returned us this answer, with his dreadful voice, in the audience of the assembly: 'You deceitful-hearted sinners! What hypocrisy is this, to weary me with your cries for that which you will not have, if I would give it to you; and thus to lift up your voices for that which your souls abhor! What is reformation, but the instructing and importunate persuading of sinners to entertain my Christ and grace, as offered to them, and the governing of my Church according to my word? Yet these, which are your work, you will not be persuaded to, when you come to find it troublesome and ungrateful. When I have delivered you, it is not me, but yourselves, that you will serve; and I must be as earnest to persuade you to reform the Church, in doing your own duty, as you are earnest with me to grant you liberty for reformation. And, when all is done, you will leave it undone, and will be long before you will be persuaded to my work.' If the Lord, or any messenger of his, had given us such an answer, would it not have amazed us? Would it not have seemed incredible to us, that our hearts should be such as now they prove? And would we not have said, as Hazael, 'Is thy servant a dog, that he should do this thing?' or as Peter, 'Though all men forsake thee, yet will not I?' Well, brethren, sad experience hath showed us our frailty. We have refused the troublesome and costly part of the reformation that we prayed for; but Christ yet turneth back, and looketh with a merciful eye upon us. Oh that we had yet the hearts immediately to go out and weep bitterly, and to do no more as we have done, lest a worse thing come upon us; and now to follow Christ, whom we have so far forsaken, through labour and suffering, even though it were to death!

I have thus showed you what will come of it, if you will not set yourselves faithfully to this work, to which you are under so many obligations and engagements; and what an inexcusable thing our neglect will be, and how great and manifold a condemnation it will expose us to. Truly, brethren, if I did not apprehend the work to be of exceeding great moment to yourselves, to the people, and to the honour of God, I would not have troubled you with so many words about it, nor have presumed to speak so sharply as I have done. But when the question is about life and death, men are apt to forget their reverence and courtesy and compliments and good manners. For my own part I apprehend this is one of the best and greatest works I ever in my life put my hand to; and I verily think, that if your thoughts of it are as mine, you will not think my words too many or too keen. I can well remember the time when I was earnest for the reformation of matters of ceremony; and, if I should be cold in such substantial matter as this, how disorderly and disproportionable would my zeal appear! Alas! can we think that the reformation is wrought, when we cast out a few ceremonies, and changed some vestures, and gestures, and forms! Oh no, sirs! it is the converting and saving of souls that is our business. That is the chiefest part of reformation, that doth most good, and tendeth most to the salvation of the people.

And now, brethren, the work is before you. In these personal instructions of all the flock, as well as in public preaching, doth it consist. Others have done their part, and borne their burden, and now comes in yours. You may easily see how great a matter lies upon your hands, and how many will be wronged by your failing of your duty, and how much will be lost by the sparing of your labour. If your labour be more worth than the souls of men, and than the blood of Christ, then sit still, and look not after the ignorant or the ungodly; follow your own pleasure or worldly business, or take your ease; displease not sinners, nor your own flesh, but let your neighbours sink or swim; and, if public preaching will not save them, let them perish. But, if the case be far otherwise, you had best look about you.

PART II
Objections to this duty

I shall next answer some of those objections, which may be made to the practice I have been recommending.

OBJECTION 1: We teach our people in public; and how then are we bound to teach them, man by man, besides?

ANSWER: You pray for them in public: must you not also pray for them in private? Paul taught every man, and exhorted every man, and that both publicly, and from house to house, night and day, with tears. But what need we say more, when experience speaks so loudly on this subject? I am daily forced to wonder how lamentably ignorant many of our people are, who have seemed diligent hearers of me these ten or twelve years, while I spoke as plainly as I was able to speak. Some know not that each person in the Trinity is God; nor that Christ is God and man; nor that he took his human nature to heaven; nor what they must trust to for pardon and salvation; nor many similar important principles of our faith. Nay, some who come constantly to private meetings are grossly ignorant: whereas, in one hour's familiar instruction of them in private, they seem to understand more, and better entertain it than they did in all their lives before.

OBJECTION 2: All the parish are not the church, nor do I take the pastoral charge of them, and therefore I am not satisfied that I am bound to take these pains with them.

ANSWER: I will pass by the question, Whether all the parish are to be taken for your church, because in some places it is so, and in others not. [a] The common maintenance which most receive is for teaching the whole parish, though you be not obliged to take them all for a church. [b] What need we look for a stronger obligation than the common bond that lieth on all Christians, to further the work of men's salvation and the good of the Church, and the honour of God, to the utmost of their power; together with the common bond that is on all ministers, to further these ends by ministerial teaching to the utmost of their power? Is it a work so good, and apparently conducing to so great benefits to the souls of men, and yet can you perceive no obligation to the doing of it?

OBJECTION 3: This course will take up so much time, that a man will have no opportunity to follow his studies. Most of us are young and inexperienced, and have need of much time to improve our own abilities, and to increase our own knowledge, which this course will entirely prevent.

ANSWER (1): We suppose those whom we persuade to this work, to understand the substance of the Christian religion, and to be able to teach it to others; and the addition of lower and less necessary things, is not to be preferred before this needful communication of the fundamental principles of religion. I highly value common knowledge, and would not encourage any to set light by it; but I value the saving of souls more. That work which is our great end must be done, whatever be left undone. It is a very desirable thing for a physician to be thoroughly studied in his art; and to be able to see the reason of his practice, and to resolve such difficult controversies as are before him. But if he had the charge of a hospital, or lived in a city where the pestilence was raging, if he would be studying fermentation, the circulation of the blood, blisters, and the like, and such like excellent points, when he should be visiting his patients, and saving men's lives; if he should even turn them away, and let them perish, and tell them that he has not time to give them advice, because he must follow his own studies, I would consider that man as a most preposterous student, who preferred the remote means before the end itself of his studies: indeed, I would think him but a civil kind of murderer. Men's souls may be saved without knowing whether God did predetermine the creature in all its acts; whether the understanding necessarily determines the will; whether God works grace in a physical or in a moral way of causation; what freewill is; whether God have *scientiam mediam*,[1] or positive decrees concerning the blame for

---

[1] 'mediate knowledge': a term used by Molina, a Jesuit theologian, to harmonize human 'free-will' and Divine foreknowledge.

evil deeds; and a hundred similar questions, which are probably the things you would be studying when you should be saving souls. Get well to heaven, and help your people thither, and you shall know all these things in a moment, and a thousand more, which now, by all your studies, you can never know; and is not this the most expeditious and certain way to knowledge?

(2) If you grow not extensively in knowledge, you will by this way of diligent practice obtain the intensive more excellent growth. If you know not so many things as others, you will know the great things better than they; for this serious dealing with sinners for their salvation, will help you to far deeper apprehensions of the saving principles of religion than you will get by any other means; and a little more knowledge of these is worth all the other knowledge in the world. Oh, when I am looking heavenward, and gazing towards the inaccessible light, and aspiring after the knowledge of God, and find my soul so dark and distant, that I am ready to say, 'I know not God – he is above me – quite out of my reach,' methinks I could willingly exchange all the other knowledge I have, for one glimpse more of the knowledge of God and of the life to come. Oh that I had never known a word in logic or metaphysics, nor known whatever schoolmen said, so I had but one spark more of that light which would show me the things that I must shortly see. For my part, I conceive, that by serious talking of everlasting things, and teaching the creed, or some short catechism, you may grow more in knowledge, (though not in the knowledge of more things,) and prove much wiser men, than if you spent that time in studying common or curious, yet less necessary things.

And perhaps it will be found, before we have done, that this employment tends to make men much abler pastors for the Church, than private studies alone. He will be the ablest physician, lawyer, and divine too, that addeth practice and experience to his studies: while that man shall prove a useless drone, that refuseth God's service all his life, under pretence of preparing for it, and lets men's souls pass on to perdition, while he pretendeth to be studying how to recover them, or to get more ability to help and save them.

(3) Yet let me add, that though I count this the chief, I would have you to have more, because these subservient sciences are very useful; and, therefore, I say, that you may have competent time for both, lose no time upon vain recreations and employments; consume it not in needless sleep; trifle not away a minute. Do what you do with all your might; and then see whether you have not competent time for these other pursuits. If you set apart but two days in a week to this great work, you may find some time for common studies out of the other four.

Indeed, are not four days in the week, (after so many years spent in the university,) a fair proportion for men to study controversies and sermons? Though my weakness deprive me of abundance of time, and extraordinary works take up six, if not eight parts of my time, yet I bless God I can find time to provide for preaching two days a week, notwithstanding the two days for personal instruction. Now, for those that are not troubled with any extraordinary work, (I mean writings, and vocations of several sorts, besides the ordinary work of the ministry,) I cannot believe, but, if they are willing, they may find two half days a week at least for this work.

(4) Duties are to be taken together: the greatest is to be preferred, but none are to be neglected that can be performed; no one is to be pleaded against another, but each is to know its proper place. But if there were such a case of necessity, that we could not carry on further studies, and instruct the ignorant too, I would throw aside all the libraries in the world, rather than be guilty of the perdition of one soul; or at least, I know that this would be my duty.

OBJECTION 4: But this course will destroy the health of our bodies, by continual spending our spirits, and allowing us no time for necessary recreations; and it will wholly lock us up from friendly intercourse with others, so that we must never stir from home, nor enjoy ourselves a day with our friends, for the relaxation of our minds; but, as we shall seem uncourteous and morose to others, so we shall tire ourselves, and the bow that is always bent will be in danger of breaking at last.

ANSWER (1): This is the plea of the flesh for its own interest. The sluggard saith, 'There is a lion in the way;' nor will he plough because of the cold. There is no duty of moment and self-denial, but, if you consult with flesh and blood, it will give you as wise reasons as these against it. Who would ever have been burned at a stake for Christ, if this reasoning had been good? Yea, or who would ever have been a Christian?

(2) We may take time for necessary recreation, and yet attend to this work. An hour, or half an hour's walk before meat, is as much recreation as is necessary for the health of most of the weaker sort of students. I have reason to know somewhat of this by long experience. Though I have a body that hath languished under great weaknesses for many years, and my diseases have been such as require as much exercise as almost any in the world, and I have found exercise the principal means of my preservation till now, and, therefore, have as great reason to plead for it as any man that I know, yet I have found that the foresaid proportion hath been blessed to my preservation, though I know that much more had been like to have tended to my greater health. Indeed, I do not know one minister in a hundred that needeth so much exercise as myself. Yea, I know abundance of ministers, that scarce ever use any exercise at all, though I commend them not in this. I doubt not but it is our duty to use so much exercise as is necessary for the preservation of our health, so far as our work requireth; otherwise, we should, for one day's work, lose the opportunity of many. But this may be done, and yet the work that we are engaged in, be done too. On those two days a week that you set apart for this work, what hinders but you may take an hour or two to walk for the exercise of your bodies? Much more on other days.

But as for those men, who limit not their recreations to stated hours, but must have them for the pleasing of their voluptuous humour, and not merely to fit them for their work, such sensualists have need to study better the nature of

Christianity, and to learn the danger of living after the flesh, and to get more mortification and self-denial before they preach these things to others. If you must needs have your pleasures, you should not have put yourselves into a calling that requireth you to make God and his service your pleasure, and restraineth you so much from fleshly pleasures. Is it not your baptismal engagement to fight against the flesh? and do you not know that much of the Christian warfare consisteth in the combat between the flesh and the spirit? and that this is the difference between a true Christian and an unconverted man, that the one liveth after the spirit, and mortifieth the deeds and desires of the body, and the other liveth after the flesh? And do you make it your calling to preach all this to others; and, notwithstanding this, must you needs have your pleasures? If you must, then, for shame, give over the preaching of the gospel, and the profession of Christianity, and profess yourselves to be what you are; and as 'you sow to the flesh, so of the flesh you shall reap corruption.' Doth even Paul say: 'I therefore so run, not as uncertainly; so fight I, not as one that beateth the air: but I keep under my body, and bring it into subjection; lest that by any means, when I have preached to others, I myself should be a castaway?' And have not such sinners as we still more need to do so? What? shall we pamper our bodies and give them their desires in unnecessary pleasure, when Paul must keep under his body, and bring it into subjection? Must Paul do this, lest, after all his preaching, he should be a castaway? and have not we much more cause to fear it of ourselves? I know that some pleasure is lawful; that is, when it is of use to fit us for our work. But for a man to be so far in love with his pleasures, as for the sake of them to waste unnecessarily his precious time, and to neglect the great work of men's salvation, yea, and to plead for this, as if it must or might be done, and so to justify himself in such a course, is a wickedness inconsistent with the common fidelity of a Christian, much more with the fidelity of a minister of Christ. Such wretches as are 'lovers of pleasure more than lovers of God,' must look to be loved of him accordingly, and are fitter to be cast out of Christian communion, than to be the chief in the Church; for we are commanded 'from such to turn away.' Recreations for a student must be specially for the exercise of his body, he having before him such variety of delights to his mind. And they must be used as whetting is by the mower, that is, only so far as is necessary to his work. We must be careful that they rob us not of our precious time, but be kept within the narrowest possible bounds.

(3) The labour in which we are engaged is not likely much to impair our health. It is true, it must be serious; but that will but excite and revive our spirits, and not so much spend them. Men can talk all day long about other matters without any abatement of their health; and why may we not talk with men about their salvation without such great abatement of ours?

(4) What have we our time and strength for, but to lay them out for God? What is a candle made for, but to burn? Burned and wasted we must be; and is it not fitter it should be in lighting men to heaven, and in working for God, than in living to the flesh? How little difference is there between the pleasure of a long and of a short life, when they are both at an end! What comfort will it be to you at death, that you lengthened your life by shortening your work? He that worketh much, liveth much. Our life is to be esteemed according to the ends and works of it, and not according to the mere duration. As Seneca says of a drone, 'There he lies, not there he lives; and long he abode, not long he lived.' Will it not comfort us more at death, to review a short time faithfully spent, than a long life spent unfaithfully?

(5) As for visits and civilities, if they be of greater use than our ministerial employments, you may break the Sabbath for them; you may forbear preaching for them, and you may also forbear this private work. But if it be otherwise, how dare you make them a pretence for neglecting so great a duty? Must God wait on your friends? What though they be lords, or knights, or gentlemen; must they be served before God? Or is their displeasure or censure a greater hurt to you than God's displeasure or censure? Or dare you think, when

God will question you for your neglects, to put him off with this excuse: 'Lord, I would have spent more of my time in seeking men's salvation; but such a gentleman, or such a friend, would have taken it ill, if I had not waited on them?' If you yet 'seek to please men,' you are no longer the servants of Christ. He that dare spend his life in flesh-pleasing, and man-pleasing, is bolder than I am. And he that dare waste his time in compliments, doth little consider what he hath to do with it. Oh that I could but improve my time, according to my convictions of the necessity of improving it! He that hath looked death in the face as oft as I have done, I will not thank him if he value his time. I profess I wonder at those ministers who have time to spare; who can hunt or shoot or bowl, or use the like recreations two or three hours, yea, whole days together; that can sit an hour together in vain discourse, and spend whole days in complimental visits, and journeys to such ends. Good Lord! What do these men think on, when so many souls around them cry for help, and death gives us no respite, and they know not how short a time their people and they may be together; when the smallest parish hath so much work that may employ all their diligence, night and day?

Brethren, I hope you are content to be plainly dealt with. If you have no sense of the worth of souls, and of the preciousness of that blood which was shed for them, and of the glory to which they are going, and of the misery of which they are in danger, you are not Christians, and consequently are very unfit to be ministers. And if you have, how can you find time for needless recreations, visits or discourses? Dare you, like idle gossips, chat and trifle away your time, when you have such works as these to do, and so many of them? O precious time! How swiftly doth it pass away! How soon will it be gone! What are the forty years of my life that are past? Were every day as long as a month, methinks it were too short for the work of a day. Have we not already lost time enough, in the days of our vanity? Never do I come to a dying man that is not utterly stupid, but he better sees the worth of time. O then, if they could call time back again, how loud would they call! If they could but buy it, what would they not give for it? And yet we can afford to trifle it away; yea, and to allow ourselves in this, and wilfully to cast off the greatest works of God. O what a befooling thing is sin, that can thus distract men that seem so wise! Is it possible that a man of any compassion and honesty, or any concern about his ministerial duty, or any sense of the strictness of his account, should have time to spare for idleness and vanity?

And I must tell you further, brethren, that, if another might take some time for mere delight, which is not necessary, yet so cannot you; for your undertaking binds you to stricter attendance than other men are bound to. May a physician, when the plague is raging, take any more relaxation or recreation than is necessary for his life, when so many are expecting his help in a case of life and death? As his pleasure is not worth men's lives, still less is yours worth men's souls. Suppose a city were besieged, and the enemy watching, on one side, all advantages to surprise it, and, on the other, seeking to fire it with grenadoes,[1] which they are throwing in continually, I pray you, tell me, if certain men undertake, as their office, to watch the ports, and others to quench the fire that may be kindled in the houses, what time will you allow these men for recreation or relaxation when the city is in danger, and the fire will burn on and prevail, if they intermit their diligence? Or would you excuse one of these men, if he come off his work, and say, I am but flesh and blood, I must have some relaxation and pleasure? Surely, at the utmost, you would allow him none but what was absolutely necessary.

Do not grudge at this, and say, 'This is a hard saying; who can hear it?' For it is your mercy; and you are well, if you know when you are well, as I shall show you in answering the next objection.

OBJECTION 5: I do not think that it is required of ministers that they make drudges of themselves. If they preach diligently, and visit the sick, and perform other ministerial duties, and occasionally do good to those they converse with, I do not think that God doth require that we should thus tie

[1] Small, explosive charge.

ourselves to instruct every person distinctly, and to make our
lives a burden and a slavery.

ANSWER: Of what use and weight the duty is, I have showed
before, and how plainly it is commanded. And do you think
God doth not require you to do all the good you can? Will
you stand by, and see sinners gasping under the pangs of
death, and say, 'God doth not require me to make myself a
drudge to save them?' Is this the voice of Christian or
ministerial compassion? Or rather is it not the voice of
sensual laziness and diabolical cruelty? Doth God set you
work to do, and will you not believe that he would have you
do it? Is this the voice of obedience, or of rebellion? It is all
one whether your flesh prevail with you to deny obedience
to acknowledged duty, and say plainly, I will obey no further
than it pleaseth me; or whether it may make you wilfully
reject the evidence that should convince you that it is a duty,
and say, I will not believe it to be my duty, unless it please
me. It is the character of a hypocrite, to make a religion to
himself of the cheapest part of God's service which will stand
with his fleshly ends and felicity, and to reject the rest, which
is inconsistent therewith. And to the words of hypocrisy,
this objection superaddeth the words of gross impiety. For
what a wretched calumny is this against the most high God,
to call his service a slavery and drudgery! What thoughts have
such men of their Master, their work, and their wages? the
thoughts of a believer, or of an infidel? Are these men
like to honour God, and promote his service, that have such
base thoughts of it themselves? Do these men delight in
holiness, that account it a slavish work? Do they believe indeed the misery of sinners, that account it such a drudgery
to be diligent to save them? Christ saith, that 'he that denieth
not himself, and forsaketh not all, and taketh not up his cross,
and followeth him, cannot be his disciple.' But these men
count it a slavery to labour hard in his vineyard, and to deny
their ease, at a time when they have all accommodations and
encouragements. How far is this from forsaking all! And how
can these men be fit for the ministry, who are such enemies to
self-denial, and so to true Christianity?

I am, therefore, forced to say, that hence arises the chief misery of the Church, THAT SO MANY ARE MADE MINISTERS BEFORE THEY ARE CHRISTIANS. If these men had seen the diligence of Christ in doing good, when he neglected his meat to talk with one woman, and when he had no time to eat bread, would they not have been of the mind of his carnal friends, who went to lay hold on him, and said, 'He is beside himself?' They would have told Christ he made a drudge or a slave of himself, and God did not require all this ado. If they had seen him all day in preaching, and all night in prayer, it seems he would have had this censure from them for his labour. I cannot but advise these men to search their own hearts, whether they unfeignedly believe that Word which they preach. Do you indeed believe that such glory awaiteth those who die in the Lord, and such torment those that die unconverted? If you do, how can you think any labour too much for such weighty ends? If you do not, say so, and get you out of the vineyard, and go with the prodigal to keep swine, and undertake not to feed the flock of Christ.

Do you not know, brethren, that it is your own benefit which you grudge at? The more you do, the more you will receive: the more you lay out, the more you will have coming in. If you are strangers to these Christian paradoxes, you should not have undertaken to teach them to others. At present, our incomes of spiritual life and peace are commonly in the way of duty; so that he who is most in duty hath most of God. Exercise of grace increaseth it. And is it a slavery to be more with God, and to receive more from him, than other men? It is the chief solace of a gracious soul to be doing good, and receiving by doing; and to be much exercised about those Divine things which have his heart. Besides, we prepare for fuller receivings hereafter; we put out our talents to usury, and, by improving them, we shall make five become ten, and so be made rulers of ten cities. Is it a drudgery to send to the most distant parts of the world, to exchange our trifles for gold and jewels? Do not these men seek to justify the profane, who make all diligent godliness a drudgery, and reproach it as a precise and tedious life, and say they will never believe but a man may be saved without all this ado? Even so say these in respect to the work of the ministry. They take this diligence for ungrateful tediousness, and will not believe but a man may be a faithful minister without all this ado!

It is a heinous sin to be negligent in so great a business; but to approve of that negligence, and so to be impenitent, and to plead against duty as if it were none, and when they should lay out themselves for the saving of souls, to say, I do not believe that God requireth it – this is so great an aggravation of the sin, that, where the Church's necessity doth not force us to make use of such men for want of better, I cannot but think them worthy to be cast out as rubbish, and as 'salt that hath lost its savour, that is neither fit for the land, nor yet for the dunghill.' 'He that hath ears to hear,' adds Christ, 'let him hear.' And if such ministers become a by-word and a reproach, let them thank themselves; for it is their own sin that maketh them vile. And while they thus debase the service of Christ, they do but debase themselves, and prepare for a greater debasement at the last.

OBJECTION 6: The times that Paul lived in required more diligence than ours. The churches were but in the planting, the enemies many, and persecution great. But now it is not so.

ANSWER: This argument savours of a man locked up in a study and unacquainted with the world. Good Lord! Are there such multitudes round about us that know not whether Christ be God or man, whether he have taken his body to heaven or left it on earth, nor what he hath done for their salvation, nor what they must trust to for pardon and ever-lasting life? Are there so many thousands round about us who are drowned in presumption, security, and sensuality, and, when we have done all we can in the pulpit, will neither feel us nor understand us? Are there so many wilful drunkards, worldlings, self-seekers, railers, haters of a holy life, that want nothing but death to make them remediless? Are there so many ignorant, dull, and scandalous professors, so many dividers, seducers, and troublers of the Church? And yet is the happiness of our times so great, that we may excuse ourselves from personal instruction, because of the less necessity of the times? What needs there but faith and experience to answer this objection? Believe better within and look more without among the miserable, and I warrant you, you will not see cause to spare your pains for want of work, or of necessities to invite you. What conscientious minister finds not work enough to do from one end of the year to another, if he have not even an hundred souls to care for? Are ungodly men the less miserable, because they make profession of Christianity, or the more?

OBJECTION 7: But if you make such severe laws for ministers, the Church will be left without them. For what man will choose such a toilsome life for himself? or what parents will impose such a burden on their children? Men will avoid it both for the bodily toil, and the danger to their consciences, if they should not well discharge it.

ANSWER (1): It is not we, but Christ, who hath made and imposed these laws which you call severe: and if I should silence them or misinterpret them, that would not relax them, nor excuse you. He that made them, knew why he did it, and will expect obedience to them. Is infinite goodness to be questioned or suspected by us, as making bad or unmerciful laws? Nay, it is pure mercy in him to impose this great duty upon us. If physicians were required to be as diligent as possible in hospitals, or pest-houses, or with other patients in order to save their lives, would there not be more of mercy than of rigour in this law? What! must God let the souls of your neighbours perish, to save you a little labour and suffering; and this in mercy to you? Oh, what a miserable world should we have, if blind, self-conceited man had the ruling of it!

(2) As to a supply of pastors, Christ will take care of that. He who imposeth duty hath the fulness of the Spirit, and can give men hearts to obey his laws. Do you think Christ will suffer all men to be as cruel, unmerciful, fleshly, and self-seeking as you? He who himself undertook the work of our redemption, and bore our transgressions, and hath been

faithful as the chief Shepherd of the Church, will not lose all his labour and suffering for want of instruments to carry on his work, nor will he come down again to do all himself, because no other will do it; but he will provide men to be his servants and ushers in his school, who shall willingly take the labour on them, and rejoice to be so employed, and account that the happiest life in the world which you account so great a toil, and would not exchange it for all your ease and carnal pleasure; but for the saving of souls, and the propagating of the gospel of Christ, will be content to bear the burden and heat of the day; and to fill up the measure of the sufferings of Christ in their bodies; and to work while it is day; and to do what they do with all their might; and to be the servants of all, and not to please themselves, but others, for their edification; and to become all things to all men, that they may save some; and to endure all things for the elect's sake; and to spend and be spent for their fellow-creatures; though the more they love, the less they should be beloved, and should be accounted their enemies for telling them the truth. Such pastors will Christ provide his people, after his own heart, who will 'feed them with knowledge and understanding;' as men that 'seek not theirs, but them.' What? do you think Christ will have no servants, if such as you shall, with Demas, turn to the present world, and forsake him?

If you dislike his service, you may seek a better where you can find it, and boast of your gain in the end; but do not threaten him with the loss of your service. He hath made such laws as you will call severe, for all who will be saved, as well as for his ministers; for all who will be his disciples must 'deny themselves, and mortify the flesh, and be crucified to the world, and take up their cross, and follow him.' And yet Christ will not be without disciples, nor will he conceal his seeming hard terms from men to entice them to his service; but he will tell them of the worst, and then let them come or not, as they choose. He will call to them beforehand to count the cost, and will tell them, that 'the foxes have holes, and the birds of the air have nests; but the Son of man hath not where to lay his head;' that he comes not to give them worldly peace and prosperity, but to call them to 'suffer with him, that they may reign with him,' and 'in patience to possess their souls;' to conquer, that they may be crowned and 'sit down with him on his throne.' And all this he will cause his chosen to perform. If you be come to that pass with Christ, as the Israelites were once with David, and say, 'Will the son of Jesse give you fields and vineyards? Every man to your tents, O Israel!' And if you say 'Now look to thy own house, thou Son of David;' you shall see that Christ will look to his own house; and do you look to yours as well as you can, and tell me, at the hour of death and judgment, which is the better bargain, and whether Christ had more need of you, or you of him.

As to scruples of conscience, for fear of failing, let it be remarked: First, It is not involuntary imperfections that Christ will take so heinously; it is unfaithfulness and wilful negligence. Second, It will not serve your turn to run out of the vineyard, on pretence of scruples that you cannot do the work as you ought. He can follow you, and overtake you, as he did Jonah, with such a storm as shall lay you 'in the belly of hell.' To cast off a duty because you cannot be faithful in the performance of it will prove but a poor excuse at last. If men had but reckoned well at first the difference between things temporal and things eternal, and what they shall lose or get by Christ, and had possessed that faith which is 'the evidence of things not seen,' and had lived by faith, and not by sense, all these objections would be easily resolved by us; and all the pleas of flesh and blood for its interest would appear as the reasoning of children, or rather of men who had lost their senses.

OBJECTION 8: But to what purpose is all this, when most of the people will not submit? They will not come to us to be catechized, and will tell us that they are now too old to go to school. And therefore it is better to let them alone, as trouble them and ourselves to no purpose.

ANSWER (1): It is not to be denied that too many people are obstinate in their wickedness, that the 'simple ones love simplicity, and the scorners delight in scorning, and fools hate knowledge.' But the worse they are, the sadder is their case, and the more to be pitied, and the more diligent should we be for their recovery.

(2) I would it were not the blame of ministers, that a great part of the people are so obstinate and contemptuous. If we did but burn and shine before them as we ought; had we convincing sermons and convincing lives; did we set ourselves to do all the good we could, whatever it might cost us; were we more meek and humble, more loving and charitable, and let them see that we set light by all worldly things, in comparison of their salvation; much more might be done by us than is done, and the mouths of many would be stopped; and though the wicked will still do wickedly, yet more would be tractable, and the wicked would be fewer and calmer than they are. If you say that some of the ablest and godliest ministers in the country have had as untractable and scornful parishioners as others, I answer, that some able godly men have been too lordly, and strange, and some of them too uncharitable and worldly, and backward to costly though necessary good works, and some of them have done but little in private, when they have done excellently in public, and so have hindered the fruit of their labours. But where there are not these impediments, experience telleth us that the success is much greater, at least as to the bowing of people to more calmness and teachableness; yet we cannot expect they all will be brought to so much reason.

(3) The wilfulness of the people will not excuse us from our duty. If we offer them not our help, how do we know who will refuse it? Offering it is our part, and accepting it is theirs. If we offer it not, we leave them excusable, for then they refuse it not; but then we are left without excuse. But if they refuse our help when it is offered, we have done our part, and delivered our own souls.

(4) If some refuse our help, others will accept it; and the success with them may be so much as may reward all our labour, were it even greater. All our people are not wrought on by our public preaching, and yet we must not, on this account, give it over as unprofitable.

OBJECTION 9: But what likelihood is there that men will be converted by this means, who are not converted by the preaching of the Word, when that is God's chief ordinance for that end? 'Faith cometh by hearing, and hearing by the preaching of the word.'

ANSWER (1): The advantages of this course I have showed you before, and therefore I will not now repeat them; only, lest any think that this will hinder them from preaching, I may add, to the many benefits before mentioned, that it will be an excellent means of helping you in preaching. For as the physician's work is half done when he understands the disease, so, when you are well acquainted with your people's case, you will know what to preach on; and it will furnish you with useful matter for your sermons, to talk an hour with an ignorant or obstinate sinner, as much as an hour's study will do, for you will learn what you have need to insist on, and what objections of theirs to repel.

(2) I hope there are none so silly as to think this conference is not preaching. What? doth the number we speak to make it preaching? Or doth interlocution make it none? Surely a man may as truly preach to one, as to a thousand. And, as we have already said, if you examine, you will find that most of the preaching recorded in the New Testament, was by conference, and frequently interlocutory, and that with one or two, fewer or more, as opportunity served. Thus Christ himself did most commonly preach. Besides, we must take account of our people's learning, if we regard the success of our work.

There is, therefore, nothing from God, from the Scriptures, or from right reason, to cause us to make any question of our work, or to be unwilling to it. But from the world, from the flesh, and from the devil, we shall have much, and more, perhaps, than we anticipate. But against all temptations, if we have recourse to God, and look, on the one hand, to our great obligations, and to the hopeful effects, and the blessed reward, on the other, we shall see that we have little cause to draw back, or to faint.

Let us set before us the pattern in our text, and learn thence our duty. O what a lesson is here before us! But how ill is it learned by those who still question whether these things be their duty! I confess, some of these words of Paul have been so often presented before my eyes, and impressed upon my conscience, that I have been much convinced by them of my duty and my neglect. And I think this one speech better deserveth a twelvemonth's study, than most things that young students spend their time upon. O brethren! write it on your study doors – set it in capital letters as your copy, that it may be ever before your eyes. Could we but well learn two or three lines of it, what preachers should we be!

[a] Our general business – SERVING THE LORD WITH ALL HUMILITY OF MIND, AND WITH MANY TEARS.

[b] Our special work – TAKE HEED TO YOURSELVES, AND TO ALL THE FLOCK.

[c] Our doctrine – REPENTANCE TOWARD GOD, AND FAITH TOWARD OUR LORD JESUS CHRIST.

[d] The place and manner of teaching – I HAVE TAUGHT YOU PUBLICLY, AND FROM HOUSE TO HOUSE.

[e] His diligence, earnestness, and affection – I CEASED NOT TO WARN EVERY ONE NIGHT AND DAY WITH TEARS. This is that which must win souls, and preserve them.

[f] His faithfulness – I KEPT BACK NOTHING THAT WAS PROFITABLE UNTO YOU, AND HAVE NOT SHUNNED TO DECLARE UNTO YOU ALL THE COUNSEL OF GOD.

[g] His disinterestedness and self-denial for the sake of the gospel – I HAVE COVETED NO MAN'S SILVER OR GOLD OR APPAREL: YEA, THESE HANDS HAVE MINISTERED UNTO MY NECESSITIES, AND TO THEM THAT WERE WITH ME, REMEMBERING THE WORDS OF THE LORD JESUS, HOW HE SAID, IT IS MORE BLESSED TO GIVE THAN TO RECEIVE.

[h] His patience and perseverance – NONE OF THESE THINGS MOVE ME, NEITHER COUNT I MY LIFE DEAR UNTO ME, SO THAT I MIGHT FINISH MY COURSE WITH JOY, AND THE MINISTRY WHICH I HAVE RECEIVED OF THE LORD JESUS.

[i] His prayerfulness – I COMMEND YOU TO GOD AND TO

THE WORD OF HIS GRACE, WHICH IS ABLE TO BUILD
YOU UP, AND TO GIVE YOU AN INHERITANCE AMONG
ALL THEM WHICH ARE SANCTIFIED.
[j] His purity of conscience – WHEREFORE I TAKE YOU
TO RECORD THIS DAY, THAT I AM PURE FROM THE
BLOOD OF ALL MEN.

Write all this upon your hearts, and it will do yourselves
and the Church more good than twenty years' study of those
lower things, which, though they may get you greater
applause in the world, yet, if separated from these, they will
make you but as 'sounding brass and a tinkling cymbal.'

The great advantage of ministers having a sincere heart, is
this, that the glory of God and the salvation of souls are their
very *end*; and where that end is truly intended, no labour or
suffering will stop them, or turn them back; for a man must
have his end, whatever it cost him. Whatever he forgets, he
will still retain this lesson: ONE THING IS NEEDFUL; SEEK
YE FIRST THE KINGDOM OF GOD AND HIS RIGHTEOUS-
NESS. Hence he says, 'Necessity is laid upon me, yea, woe is
unto me if I preach not the gospel.' This is it that will most
effectually make easy all our labours, and make light all our
burdens, and make tolerable all our sufferings, and cause us
to venture on any hazards, if we may only win souls to
Christ. That which I once made the motto of my colours in
another warfare, I desire may be still before my eyes in this;
which yet, according to my intentions, is not altogether
another. On one side, 'He that saveth his life shall lose it:' –
on the other, 'Ruin not the cause for the sake of keeping one's
life.' He who knoweth that he serveth a God that will never
suffer any man to be a loser by him, need not fear what
hazards he runs in his cause: and he who knows that he seeks
a prize, which, if obtained, will infinitely overbalance his cost,
may boldly engage his whole estate on it, and sell all to purchase so rich a pearl. Well, brethren, I will spend no more
words in exhorting wise merchants to such a bargain, nor telling teachers themselves such common truths; and if I have
already said more than is needful, I shall be glad. I hope I

may now take it for granted, that you are resolved on the
utmost diligence and fidelity in the work; and, on this supposition, I shall now proceed to give you some directions
for the right management of it.

PART III
Directions for this duty

It is so great a work which we have before us, that it is a
thousand pities it should be destroyed in the birth, and perish
in our hands. And though I know that we have a knotty
generation to deal with, and that it is past the power of any
of us to change a carnal heart without the effectual operation
of the Holy Ghost; yet it is so usual with God to work by
means, and to bless the right endeavours of his servants, that
I cannot fear but great things will be accomplished, and a
wonderful blow will be given to the kingdom of darkness
by this work, if it do not miscarry through the fault of the
ministers themselves. The main danger arises from the want
either of diligence, or of skill. Of the former, I have spoken
much already. As to the latter, I am so conscious of my own
unskilfulness, that I am far from imagining that I am fit to
give directions to any but the younger and more inexperienced of the ministry; and, therefore, I expect so much justice
in your interpretation of what I say, as that you will suppose
me now to speak to none but such. But yet something I shall
say, and not pass over this part in silence, because the number of such is so great; and I am apprehensive that the welfare
of the Church and nation doth so much depend on the right
management of this work.

The points as to which you need to be solicitous, are these
two:
1. To bring your people to submit to this course of private
catechizing or instruction; for, if they will not come to you,
or allow you to come to them, what good can they receive?
2. To do the work in such a way as will most tend to the success of it.

ARTICLE I

I am *first* to give you some directions for bringing your people to submit to this course of catechizing and instruction. 1. The chief means of all is this, for a minister so to conduct himself in the general course of his life and ministry, as to convince his people of his ability, sincerity, and unfeigned love to them. For if they take him to be ignorant, they will despise his teaching, and think themselves as wise as he; and if they think him self-seeking, or hypocritical, and one that doth not mean as he saith, they will suspect all he says and does for them, and will not regard him. Whereas, if they are convinced that he understandeth what he doth, and have high thoughts of his abilities, they will reverence him, and the more easily stoop to his advice; and when they are persuaded of his uprightness, they will the less suspect his motions; and when they perceive that he intendeth no private ends of his own, but merely their good, they will the more readily be persuaded by him. And because those to whom I write are supposed to be none of the ablest ministers, and may therefore despair of being reverenced for their parts, I would say to them, you have the more need to study and labour for their increase; and that which you want in ability, must be made up in other qualifications, and then your advice may be as successful as others.

If ministers were content to purchase an interest in the affections of their people at the dearest rates to their own flesh, and would condescend to them, and be familiar, and affectionate, and prudent in their carriage, and abound, according to their ability, in good works, they might do much more with their people than ordinarily they do; not that we should much regard an interest in them for our own sakes, but that we may be more capable of promoting the interest of Christ, and of furthering their salvation. Were it not for their own sakes, it were no great matter whether they love or hate us; but what commander can do any great service with an army that hates him? And how can we think that they will much regard our counsel, while they abhor or disregard the persons that give it them? Labour, therefore, for some competent interest in the estimation and affection of your people, and then you may the better prevail with them.

But perhaps some will say, What should a minister do who finds he hath lost the affections of his people? To this I answer, If they be so vile a people, that they hate him not for any weakness, or misconduct of his, but merely for endeavouring their good, and would hate any other that should do his duty; then must he with patience and meekness continue to 'instruct those that oppose themselves, if God peradventure will give them repentance to the acknowledgment of the truth.' But if it be on account of any weakness of his, or difference about lesser opinions, or prejudice against his own person, let him first try to rèmove the prejudice by all lawful means; and if he cannot, let him say to them, 'It is not for myself, but for you that I labour; and therefore, seeing that you will not obey the Word from me, I desire that you will agree to accept of some other that may do you that good which I cannot;' and so leave them, and try whether another man may not be fitter for them, and he fitter for another people. For an ingenuous man can hardly stay with a people against their wills; and a sincere man can still more hardly, for any benefit of his own, remain in a place where he is like to be unprofitable, and to hinder the good which they might receive from another man, who hath the advantage of a greater interest in their affection and esteem.

2. Supposing this general preparation, the next thing to be done is, to use the most effectual means to convince them of the benefit and necessity of this course to their own souls. The way to win the consent of people to anything that you propose, is to prove that it is good and profitable for them. You must therefore preach to them some powerful convincing sermons to this purpose before hand, and show them the benefit and necessity of the knowledge of divine truths in general, and of knowing the first principles in particular; and that the aged have the same duty and need as others, and in some respects much more: e.g. from Heb. 5.12: 'For

when for the time ye ought to be teachers, ye have need that one teach you again which be the first principles of the oracles of God; and are become such as have need of milk and not of strong meat,' which affordeth us many observations suitable to our present object:

As, (1) That God's oracles must be a man's lessons.

(2) Ministers must teach these, and people must learn them from them.

(3) The oracles of God have some fundamental principles, which all must know who wish to be saved.

(4) These principles must be first learned: that is the right order.

(5) It may be reasonably expected that people should thrive in knowledge, according to the means of instruction which they possess; and if they do not, it is their great sin.

(6) If any have lived long in the church, under the means of knowledge, and yet are ignorant of these first principles, they have need to be yet taught them, how old soever they may be.

All this is plain from the text; whence we have a fair opportunity, by many clear convincing reasons, to show them: First, The necessity of knowing God's oracles. Secondly, And more especially of knowing the fundamental principles. Thirdly, And particularly for the aged, who have sinfully lost so much time already, and have so long promised to repent when they were old; who should be teachers of the young, and whose ignorance is a double sin and shame; who have now so little time in which to learn, and are so near to death and judgment; and who have souls to save or lose as well as others. Convince them how impossible it is to go the way to heaven without knowing it, when there are so many difficulties and enemies in the way; and when men cannot do their worldly business without knowledge, nor learn a trade without an apprenticeship. Convince them what a contradiction it is to be a Christian, and yet to refuse to learn; for what is a Christian but a disciple of Christ? And how can he be a disciple of Christ, that refuseth to be taught by him? And he that refuseth to be taught by his ministers, refuseth to be taught by him; for Christ will not come down from heaven again to teach them by his own mouth, but hath appointed his ministers to keep school and teach them under him. To say, therefore, that they will not be taught by his ministers, is to say, they will not be taught by Christ; and that is to say, they will not be his disciples, or no Christians.

Make them understand that it is not an arbitrary business of our own devising and imposing; but that necessity is laid upon us, and that if we look not to every member of the flock according to our ability, they may perish in their iniquity; but their blood will be required at our hand. Show them that it is God, and not we, who is the contriver and imposer of the work; and that therefore they blame God more than us in accusing it. Ask them, would they be so cruel to their minister as to wish him to cast away his own soul, knowingly and wilfully, for fear of troubling them by trying to hinder their damnation? Acquaint them fully with the nature of the ministerial office, and the Church's need of it; how it consisteth in teaching and guiding all the flock; and that, as they must come to the congregation, as scholars to school, so must they be content to give an account of what they have learned, and to be further instructed, man by man. Let them know what a tendency this hath to their salvation, what a profitable improvement it will be of their time, and how much vanity and evil it will prevent. And when they once find that it is for their own good, they will the more easily yield to it.

3. When this is done, it will be very necessary that we give one of the catechisms to every family in the parish, whether rich or poor, that so they may be without excuse: for if you leave it to themselves to buy them, perhaps the half of them will not get them; whereas, when they have copies put into their hands, the receiving of them will be a kind of engagement to learn them; and if they do but read the exhortation (as it is likely they will), it will perhaps convince them and incite them to submit. As to the delivery of them, the best way is for the minister first to give notice in the congregation, that they shall be brought to their houses, and then to go himself from house to house and deliver them, and take the

opportunity of persuading them to the work; and, as he goes round, to take a list of all the persons who have come to years of discretion in the several families, that he may know whom he has to take care of and instruct, and whom he has to expect when it cometh to their turn. I have formerly, in distributing some other books among my people, desired every family to call for them; but I found more confusion and uncertainty in that way, and now adopt this as the better method. But in small congregations, either way may do.

As to the expense of the catechisms, if the minister be able, it will be well for him to bear it: if not, the best affected of his people of the richer sort should bear it among them. Or, on a day of humiliation, in preparation for the work, let the collection that is made for the poor be employed in buying catechisms, and the people be desired to be more liberal than ordinary; and what is wanting, the well-affected to the work may make up.

As to the order of proceeding, it will be necessary that we take the people in order, family by family, beginning a month or six weeks after the delivery of the catechisms, that they may have time to learn them. And thus, taking them together in common, they will be the more willing to come, and the backward will be the more ashamed to keep off.

4. Be sure that you deal gently with them, and take off all discouragements as effectually as you can.

(1) Tell them publicly, that if they have learned any other catechism already, you will not urge them to learn this, unless they desire it themselves: for the substance of all catechisms that are orthodox is the same; only that your reason for offering them this was its brevity and fulness, that you might give them as much as possible in few words, and so make their work more easy. Or, if any of them would rather learn some other catechism, let them have their choice.

(2) As for the old people who are of weak memories, and not likely to live long in the world, and who complain that they cannot remember the words; tell them that you do not expect them to perplex their minds overmuch about it, but to hear it often read over, and to see that they understand it, and to get

the matter into their minds and hearts; and then they may be borne with, though they remember not the words.

(3) Let your dealing with those you begin with be so gentle, convincing, and winning, that the report of it may be an encouragement to others to come.

5. Lastly, If all this will not serve to bring any particular persons to submit, do not cast them off; but go to them and expostulate with them, and learn what their reasons are, and convince them of the sinfulness and danger of their neglect of the help that is offered them. A soul is so precious that we should not lose one for want of labour, but follow them while there is any hope, and not give them up as desperate, till there be no remedy. Before we give them over, let us try the utmost, that we may have the experience of their obstinate contempt, to warrant our forsaking them. Charity beareth and waiteth long.

ARTICLE 2

Having used these means to procure them to come and submit to your instructions, we are next to consider how you may deal most effectually with them in the work. And again I must say, that I think it an easier matter by far to compose and preach a good sermon, than to deal rightly with an ignorant man for his instruction in the more essential principles of religion. As much as this work is contemned by some, I doubt not it will try the gifts and spirit of ministers, and show you the difference between one man and another, more fully than preaching will do. And here I shall, as fitting my purpose, transcribe the words of a most learned, orthodox, and godly man, Archbishop Ussher,[1] in his sermon before King James at Wanstead on Ephesians 4.13: 'Your Majesty's care can never be sufficiently commended, in taking order that the chief heads of the catechism should, in the ordinary ministry,

---

[1] The sermon was preached in June 1624, when Ussher was Bishop of Meath. He became Archbishop of Armagh in 1625. James I gave orders for the sermon to be published.

be diligently propounded and explained unto the people throughout the land; which I wish were as duly executed every where, as it was piously by you intended.

'Great scholars possibly may think, that it standeth not so well with their credit to stoop thus low, and to spend so much of their time in teaching these rudiments and first principles of the doctrine of Christ; but they should consider, that the laying of the foundation skilfully, as it is the matter of greatest importance in the whole building, so is it the very master-piece of the wisest-building. "According to the grace of God which is given unto me, as a wise master-builder, I have laid the foundation," saith the great apostle. And let the most learned of us all try it whenever we please, we shall find, that to lay this groundwork rightly, (that is, to apply ourselves to the capacity of the common auditory, and to make an ignorant man to understand these mysteries in some good measure) will put us to the trial of our skill, and trouble us a great deal more, than if we were to discuss a controversy, or handle a subtle point of learning in the schools. Yet Christ did give as well his apostles, and prophets, and evangelists, as his ordinary pastors and teachers, to bring us all, both learned and unlearned, unto the unity of this faith and knowledge; AND THE NEGLECTING OF THIS, IS THE FRUSTRAT-ING OF THE WHOLE WORK OF THE MINISTRY. For, let us preach never so many sermons to the people, our labour is but lost, as long as the foundation is unlaid, and the first principles untaught, upon which all other doctrine must be builded.'

The directions which I think it necessary to give for the right managing of the work, are the following:

1. When your people come to you, one family or more, begin with a brief preface, to mollify their minds and to take off all offence, unwillingness, or discouragement, and to prepare them for receiving your instructions. 'My friends,' you may say, 'it may perhaps seem to some of you an unusual and a troublesome business that I put you upon; but I hope you will not think it needless: for if I had thought so, I would have spared both you and myself this labour. But my con-

science hath told me, yea, God hath told me in his Word, so solemnly, what it is to have the charge of souls, and how the blood of them that perish will be required at the hands of a minister that neglecteth them, that I dare not be guilty of it as I have hitherto been. Alas! all our business in this world is to get well to heaven; and God hath appointed us to be guides to his people, to help them safe thither. If this be well done, all is done; and if this be not done, we are for ever undone. The Lord knows how short a time you and I may be together; and therefore it concerns us to do what we can for our own and your salvation before we leave you, or you leave the world. All other business in the world is but as toys and dreams in comparison of this. The labours of your calling are but to prop up a cottage of clay, while your souls are hastening to death and judgment, which may even now be near at hand. I hope, therefore, you will be glad of help in so needful a work, and not think it much that I put you to this trouble, when the trifles of the world cannot be got without much greater trouble.' This, or something to this purpose, may tend to make them more willing to hear you, and receive instruction, and to give you some account of their knowledge and practice.

2. When you have spoken thus to them all, take them one by one, and deal with them as far as you can in private, out of the hearing of the rest; for some cannot speak freely before others, and some will not endure to be questioned before others, because they think that it will tend to their shame to have others hear their answers; and some persons that can make better answers themselves, will be ready, when they are gone, to talk of what they heard, and to disgrace those that speak not so well as themselves; and so people will be discouraged, and persons who are backward to the exercise, will have pretences to forbear and forsake it, and to say, 'They will not come to be made a scorn and a laughing-stock.' You must, therefore, be very careful to prevent all these inconveniences. But the main reason is, as I find by experience, people will better take plain close dealing about their sin, and misery, and duty, when you have them alone,

than they will before others; and, if you have not an opportunity to set home the truth, and to deal freely with their
consciences, you will frustrate all. If, therefore, you have a
convenient place, let the rest stay in one room, while you
confer with each person by himself in another room; only,
in order to avoid scandal, we must speak to the women only
in presence of some others; and, if we lose some advantage
by this there is no remedy. It is better to do so, than, by giving
occasion of reproach to the malicious, to destroy all the work.
Yet we may so contrive it, that, though some others be in the
room, yet what things are less fit for their observance may be
spoken in a low voice that they may not hear it; and therefore
they may be placed at the remotest part of the room; or, at
least, let none be present but the members of the same family,
who are more familiar with each other, and not so likely to
reproach one another. And then, in your most rousing
examinations and reproofs, deal most with the ignorant,
secure, and vicious, that you may have the clearer ground for
your close dealing, and the hearing of it may awaken the by-
standers, to whom you seem not so directly to apply it. These
small things deserve attention, because they are in order to a
work that is not small; and small errors may hinder a great
deal of good.

3. Begin your work by taking an account of what they have
learned of the words of the catechism, and receiving their
answer to each question; and, if they are able to repeat but
little or none of it, try whether they can rehearse the creed
and the decalogue.

4. Then choose out some of the weightiest points, and try,
by further questions, how far they understand them. And
therein be careful of the following things:

(1) That you do not begin with less necessary points, but
with those which they themselves may perceive most nearly
concern them. For example: 'What do you think becomes of
men when they die? What shall become of us after the end
of the world? Do you believe that you have any sin; or that
you were born with sin? What doth every sin deserve? What
remedy hath God provided for the saving of sinful, miserable

souls? Hath any one suffered for our sins in our stead; or must we suffer for them ourselves? Who are they that God will pardon; and who shall be saved by the blood of Christ? What change must be made on all who shall be saved; and how is this change effected? Wherein lies our chief happiness? And what is it that our hearts must be most set upon?' And such like other questions.

(2) Beware of asking them nice, or needless, or doubtful, or very difficult questions, though about those matters that are of greatest weight in themselves. Some self-conceited persons will be as busy with such questions which they cannot answer themselves, and as censorious of the poor people that cannot answer them, as if life and death depended on them.

You will ask them perhaps, 'What is God?': and how defective an answer must you make yourselves! You may tell what he is not sooner than what he is. If you ask, 'What is *repentance*, what *faith*, or what is *forgiveness of sin*'?, how many ministers may you ask before you have a right answer, or else they would not be so disagreed in the point! Likewise if you ask them what *regeneration* is, what *sanctification* is. But you will perhaps say, 'If men know not what God is, what repentance, faith, conversion, justification, and sanctification are, how can they be true Christians and be saved?'. I answer, It is one thing to know exactly what they are, and another thing to know them in their nature and effects, though with a more general and indistinct knowledge; and it is one thing to *know*, and another thing to *tell* what this or that is. The very name as commonly used doth signify to them, and express from them the thing without a definition; and they partly understand what that name signifieth, when they cannot tell it you in other words; as they know what it is to repent, to believe, to be forgiven. By custom of speech they know what these mean, and yet cannot define them, but perhaps put you off with the country answer: 'To repent is to repent; and to be forgiven is to be forgiven'; or if they can say, 'It is to be pardoned,' it is fair. Yet do I not absolutely dissuade you from the use of such questions; but do it cautiously, in case you suspect some gross ignorance in the point; especially about God himself.

(3) So contrive your questions, that they may perceive what you mean, and that it is not a nice definition, but simply a solution, that you expect; and look not after words, but things, and even leave them to a bare Yes, or No, or the mere election of one of the two descriptions which you yourself may have propounded. For example: 'What is God? Is he made of flesh and blood, as we are; or is he an invisible Spirit? Is he a man, or is he not? Had he any beginning? Can he die? What is faith? Is it a believing all the Word of God? What is it to believe in Christ? Is it all one as to become a true Christian? or to believe that Christ is the Saviour of sinners, and to trust in him, as your Saviour, to pardon, sanctify, govern, and glorify you? What is repentance? Is it only to be sorry for sin? or is it the change of the mind from sin to God, and a forsaking of it? or does it include both?'

(4) When you perceive that they do not understand the meaning of your question, you must draw out their answer by an equivalent, or expository question; or, if that will not do, you must frame the answer into your question, and require in reply, but Yes, or No. I have often asked some very ignorant people, 'How do you think that your sins, which are so many and so great, can be pardoned?' And they tell me, 'By their repenting, and amending their lives;' and never mention Jesus Christ. I ask them further, 'But do you think that your amendment can make God any amends or satisfaction for the sin that is past?' They will answer, 'We hope so, or else we know not what will?' One would now think that these men had no knowledge of Christ at all, since they make no mention of him; and some I indeed find have no knowledge of him; and when I tell them the history of Christ, and what he is, and did, and suffered, they stand wondering at it as a strange thing; and some say, They never heard this much before, nor knew it, though they came to church every Lord's day. But some, I perceive, give such answers, because they understand not the scope of my question; but suppose that I take Christ's death for granted, and that I only ask

them, 'What shall make God satisfaction, as their part under Christ?' – though in this, also, they reveal sad ignorance. And when I ask them, 'Whether their good deeds can merit any thing from God?' they answer, 'No; but they hope God will accept them.' And if I ask further, 'Can you be saved without the death of Christ?' they say, 'No.' And if I ask, still further, 'What hath he done or suffered for you?' they will say, 'He died for us; or he shed his blood for us;' and will profess that they place their confidence in that for salvation.

Many men have that in their minds which is not ripe for utterance; and, through an imperfect education and disuse, they are strangers to the expression of those things of which they yet have some conception. And, by the way, you may here see reason why you should deal very tenderly with the common people for matter of knowledge and defect of expression, if they are teachable and tractable, and willing to use the means; for many, even ancient godly persons, cannot express themselves with any tolerable propriety, nor yet learn when expressions are put into their mouths. Some of the most pious, experienced, approved Christians that I know (aged people), complain to me, with tears, that they cannot learn the words of the catechism; and when I consider their advantages – that they have enjoyed the most excellent helps, in constant duty, and in the best company, for forty, fifty, or sixty years together – it teacheth me what to expect from poor ignorant people, who never had such company and converse for one year or week; and not to reject them so hastily as some hot and too high professors would have us do.

(5) If you find them at a loss, and unable to answer your questions, do not drive them too hard, or too long, with question after question, lest they conceive you intend only to puzzle them, and disgrace them; but when you perceive that they cannot answer, step in yourself, and take the burden off them, and answer the question yourselves; and do it thoroughly and plainly, and give a full explanation of the whole truth to them, that, by your teaching, they may be brought to understand it before you leave them. And herein it is commonly necessary that you fetch up the matter from

the beginning, and take it in order, till you come to the point
in question.

5. When you have done what you see cause in the trial of
their knowledge, proceed next to instruct them yourselves,
and this must be according to their several capacities. If it be a
professor that understandeth the fundamental principles of
religion, fall upon somewhat which you perceive that he most
needeth, either explaining further some of the mysteries of
the gospel, or laying the grounds of some duty which he may
doubt of, or showing the necessity of what he neglecteth, or
pointing out his sins or mistakes, as may be most convincing
and edifying to him. If, on the other hand, it be one who is
grossly ignorant, give him a plain, familiar recital of the sum
of the Christian religion in a few words; for though it be in
the catechism already, yet a more familiar way may better
help him to understand it. Thus: 'You must know, that from
everlasting there was one God, who had no beginning, and
will have no end, who is not a body as we are, but a most pure,
spiritual Being, that knoweth all things, and can do all things;
and hath all goodness and blessedness in himself. This God
is but one, but yet Three Persons, the Father, the Son, and
Holy Ghost, in a manner that is above our understanding.
And you must know, that this one God did make all the
world by his Word; the heavens he made to be the place of
his glory, and a multitude of holy angels to serve him. But
some of these did, by pride or some other sin, fall from their
high estate, and are become devils, and shall be miserable for
ever. When he had created the earth, he made man, as his
noblest creature here below, even one man and one woman,
Adam and Eve; and he made them perfect, without any sin,
and put them into the garden of Eden, and forbade them to
eat of one tree in the garden, and told them that if they ate of it
they should die. But the devil, who had first fallen himself,
did tempt them to sin, and they yielded to his temptation,
and thus fell under the curse of God's law. But God, of his
infinite wisdom and mercy, did send his own Son, Jesus
Christ, to be their Redeemer, who, in the fulness of time, was
made man, being born of a virgin, by the power of the Holy

Ghost, and lived on earth, among the Jews, about thirty-three years, during which time he preached the gospel himself, and wrought many miracles to prove his doctrine, healing the lame, the blind, the sick, and raising the dead by his Divine power; and in the end he was offered upon the cross as a sacrifice for our sins to bear that curse which we should have borne.

'And now, if sinners will but believe in him, and repent of their sins, he will freely pardon all that is past, and will sanctify their corrupted nature, and will at length bring them to his heavenly kingdom and glory. But if they make light of their sins and of his mercy, he will condemn them to everlasting misery in hell. This gospel, Christ, having risen from the dead on the third day, appointed his ministers to preach to all the world; and when he had given this in charge to all his apostles, he ascended up into heaven, before their faces, where he is now in glory, with God the Father, in our nature. And at the end of this world, he will come again in our nature, and will raise the dead to life again, and bring them all before him, that they may "give an account of all the deeds done in the body, whether they be good, or whether they be evil." If, therefore, you mean to be saved, you must believe in Christ, as the only Saviour from the wrath to come; you must repent of your sins; you must, in short, be wholly new creatures, or there will be no salvation for you.' Some such short rehearsal of the principles of religion, in the most familiar manner that you can devise, with a brief touch of application in the end, will be necessary when you deal with the grossly ignorant. And if you perceive they understand you not, go over it again, and ask them whether they understand it, and try to fix it in their memories.

6. Whether they be grossly ignorant or not, if you suspect them to be unconverted, endeavour next to make some prudent inquiry into their state. The best and least offensive way of doing this will be to prepare them for the inquiry by saying something that may mollify their minds, and convince them of the necessity of the inquiry, and then to take occasion from some article in the catechism to touch their consciences.

For example: 'You see that the Holy Ghost doth, by the Word, enlighten men's minds, and soften and open their hearts, and turn them from the power of Satan unto God, through faith in Christ, and "purifies them unto himself a peculiar people;" and that none but these shall be made partakers of everlasting life. Now, though I have no desire, needlessly, to pry into any man's secrets, yet, because it is the office of ministers to give advice to their people in matters of salvation, and because it is so dangerous a thing to be mistaken as to points which involve everlasting life or everlasting death, I would entreat you to deal honestly, and tell me, Whether or not you ever found this great change upon your own heart? Did you ever find the Spirit of God, by the Word, come in upon your understanding, with a new and heavenly life, which hath made you a new creature? The Lord, who seeth your heart, doth know whether it be so or not; I pray you, therefore, see that you speak the truth.'

If he tell you that he hopes he is converted – all are sinners – but he is sorry for his sins, or the like; then tell him more particularly, in a few words, of some of the plainest marks of true conversion, and so renew and enforce the inquiry, thus: 'Because your salvation or damnation is involved in this, I would fain help you a little in regard to it, that you may not be mistaken in a matter of such moment, but may find out the truth before it be too late; for as God will judge us impartially, so we have his Word before us, by which we may judge ourselves; for this Word tells us most certainly who they are that shall go to heaven, and who to hell. Now the Scripture tells us that the state of an unconverted man is this: he seeth no great felicity in the love and communion of God in the life to come, which may draw his heart thither from this present world; but he liveth to his carnal self, or to the flesh; and the main bent of his life is, that it may go well with him on earth; and that religion which he hath is but a little by the by, lest he should be damned when he can keep the world no longer; so that the world and the flesh are highest in his esteem, and nearest to his heart, and God and glory stand below them, and all their service of God is but a giving him that which the world and flesh can spare. This is the case of every unconverted man; and all who are in this case are in a state of misery. But he that is truly converted, hath had a light shining into his soul from God, which hath showed him the greatness of his sin and misery, and made it a heavy load upon his soul; and showed him what Christ is, and what he hath done for sinners, and made him admire the riches of God's grace in him.

'Oh, what glad news it is to him, that yet there is hope for such lost sinners as he; that so many and so great sins may be pardoned; and that pardon is offered to all who will accept of it! How gladly doth he entertain this message and offer! And for the time to come, he resigneth himself and all that he hath to Christ, to be wholly his, and to be disposed of by him, in order to the everlasting glory which he hath promised. He hath now such a sight of the blessed state of the saints in glory, that he despiseth all this world as dross and dung, in comparison of it; and there he layeth up his happiness and his hopes, and takes all the affairs of this life but as so many helps or hindrances in the way to that; so that the main care and business of his life is to be happy in the life to come. This is the case of all who are truly converted and who shall be saved. Now, is this the case with you, or is it not? Have you experienced such a change as this upon your soul?'

If he say, he hopes he hath, descend to some particulars, thus: 'I pray you then answer me these two or three questions. (1) Can you truly say, that all the known sins of your past life are the grief of your heart, and that you have felt that everlasting misery is due to you for them; and that, under a sense of this heavy burden, you have felt yourself a lost man, and have gladly entertained the news of a Saviour, and cast your soul upon Christ alone, for pardon by his blood?

(2) Can you truly say, that your heart is so far turned from sin, that you hate the sins which you once have loved, and love that holy life which you had no mind to before; and that you do not now live in the wilful practice of any known sin? Is there no sin which you are not heartily willing to forsake,

whatever it cost you; and no duty which you are not willing to perform?

(3) Can you truly say, that you have so far taken the ever-lasting enjoyment of God for your happiness, that it hath the most of your heart, of your love, desire, and care; and that you are resolved, by the strength of Divine grace, to let go all that you have in the world, rather than hazard it; and that it is your daily, and your principal business to seek it? Can you truly say, that though you have your failings and sins, yet your main care, and the bent of your whole life, is to please God, and to enjoy him for ever; and that you give the world God's leavings, as it were, and not God the world's leavings; and that your worldly business is but as a traveller's seeking for provision in his journey, and heaven is the place that you take for your home?'

If he answer in the affirmative to these questions, tell him how great a thing it is for a man's heart to abhor his sin, and to lay up his happiness unfeignedly in another world; and to live in this world for another that is out of sight; and, therefore, desire him to see that it be so indeed. Then turn to some of the articles in the catechism, which treat of those duties which you most suspect him to omit, and ask him, whether he performs such or such a duty; as for instance, prayer in his family, or in private, and the holy spending of the Lord's day.

I would, however, advise you to be very cautious how you pass too hasty or absolute censures on any you have to do with; because, it is not so easy a matter to discern a man to be certainly graceless, as many imagine it to be; and you may do the work in hand as well without such an absolute conclusion as with it.

7. If, however, you have, either by former discovery of gross ignorance, or by these later inquiries into his spiritual state, discerned an apparent probability that the person is yet in an unconverted state, your next business is, to employ all your skill to bring his heart to a sense of his condition. For example: 'Truly, my friends, I have no mind, the Lord knows, to make your condition worse than it is, nor to occasion you

any causeless fear or trouble; but, I suppose, you would account me a treacherous enemy, and not a faithful minister, if I should flatter you, and not tell you the truth. If you seek a physician in your sickness, you would have him tell you the truth, though it were the worst. Much more here! For there the knowledge of your disease may, by your fears, increase it; but here you must know it, or else you can never be recovered from it. I much fear that you are yet a stranger to the Christian life. For if you were a Christian indeed, and truly converted, your very heart would be set on God and the life to come, and you would make it your chief business to prepare for everlasting happiness; and you durst not, you would not, live in any wilful sin, nor in the neglect of any known duty.

'Alas! what have you done? how have you spent your time till now? Did you not know that you had a soul to be saved or lost; and that you must live in heaven or in hell for ever; and that you had your life and time in this world chiefly for the purpose of preparing for another? Alas! what have you been doing all your days that you are so ignorant, or so unprepared for death, if it should now find you? If you had but as much mind of heaven as of earth, you would have known more of it, and done more for it, and inquired more diligently after it, than you have done. You can learn how to do your business in the world; and why could you not learn more of the will of God, if you had but attended to it? You have neighbours that could learn more, that have had as much to do in the world as you, and who have had as little time. Do you think that heaven is not worth your labour? or that it can be had without any care or pains, when you cannot have the trifles of this world without them, and when God hath bid you seek first his kingdom and the righteousness thereof? Alas! my friends, what if you had died before this hour in an unconverted state? what then had become of you, and where had you now been? Alas! that you were so cruel to yourselves as to venture your everlasting state so desperately as you have done! What did you think of? Did you not all this while know that you must shortly die, and be judged as you were then found? Had you any greater work to do, or any greater business to mind, than your everlasting salvation? Do you think that all that you can get in this world will comfort you in a dying hour, or purchase your salvation, or ease the pains of hell?'

Set these things home with a peculiar earnestness; for if you get not to the heart, you do little or nothing; and that which affecteth not is soon forgotten.

8. Conclude the whole with a practical exhortation, which must contain two parts; first, the duty of believing in Christ; and secondly, of using the external means of grace for the time to come, and the avoiding of former sins. For example: 'My friend, I am heartily sorry to find you in so sad a case, but I should be more sorry to leave you in it, and therefore let me entreat you, for the Lord's sake, and for your own sake, to regard what I shall say to you, as to the time to come. It is of the Lord's great mercy that he did not cut you off in your unconverted state, and that you have yet life and time, and that there is a remedy provided for you in the blood of Christ, and that pardon and sanctification and everlasting life are offered to you as well as to others. God hath not left sinful man to utter destruction, as he hath done the devils; nor hath he made any exception in the offer of pardon and eternal life against you any more than against any other.

'If you had yet but a bleeding heart for sin, and could come to Christ believingly for recovery, and resign yourself to him as your Saviour and Lord, and would be a new man for the time to come, the Lord would have mercy on you in the pardon of your sins, and the everlasting salvation of your soul. And I must tell you that, as it must be the great work of God's grace to give you such a heart, so if ever he mean to pardon and save you, he will make this change upon you; he will make you feel your sin as the heaviest burden in the world, as that which is most odious in itself, and hath rendered you liable to his wrath and curse; he will make you see that you are a lost man, and that there is nothing for you but everlasting damnation, unless you are pardoned by the blood of Christ, and sanctified by his Spirit; he will make you see the need you have of Christ, and how all your hope and life is in him; he will make you see the vanity of this world and all that it can afford you, and that all your happiness is with God, in that everlasting life in heaven, where you may, with the saints and angels, behold his glory, and live in his love, and be employed in his praises. Let me tell you that, till this work be done upon you, you are a miserable man; and if you die before it is done, you are lost for ever. Now you have hope and help before you, but then there will be none.

'Let me therefore entreat you, as you love your soul, First, That you will not rest in the condition in which you at present are. Be not quiet in your mind till a saving change is wrought in your heart. Think, when you rise in the morning, Oh, what if this day should be my last, and death should find me in an unrenewed state? Think, when you are about your labour, Oh, how much greater a work have I yet to do, to get my soul reconciled to God, and sanctified by his Spirit! Think, when you are eating, or drinking, or looking on anything that you possess in the world, What good will all this do me, if I live and die an enemy to God, and a stranger to Christ and his Spirit, and so perish for ever? Let these thoughts be day and night upon your mind till your soul be changed. Secondly, I entreat you to bethink yourself seriously what a vain world this is, and how shortly it will leave you to a cold grave, and to everlasting misery, if you have not a better treasure than it. And consider what it is to live in the presence of God, and to reign with Christ, and be like the angels; and that this is the life that Christ hath procured you, and is preparing for you, and offereth you, if you will only accept of it; and oh think, whether it be not madness to slight such an endless glory, and to prefer these fleshly dreams and earthly shadows before it. Accustom yourself to such considerations as these when you are alone, and let them dwell upon your mind. Thirdly, I entreat, that you will presently, without any more delay, accept of this felicity, and this Saviour. Close with the Lord Jesus that offereth you this eternal life: joyfully and thankfully accept his offer as the only way to make you happy: and then you may believe that all your sins will be done away by him. Fourthly, Resolve presently against your former sins; find out what hath defiled your heart and life, and cast it from you, as you would do poison out of your stomach, and abhor the thought of taking it again.

'My last request to you is, that you will set yourself to the diligent use of the means of grace till this change be wrought, and then continue the use of these means till you are confirmed, and at last perfected. (1) As you cannot of yourself effect this change upon your heart and life, betake yourself daily to God in prayer, and beg earnestly, as for your life, that he will pardon all your sins, and change your heart, and show you the riches of his grace in Christ, and the glory of his king-dom. Follow God day and night with these requests. (2) Fly from temptations and occasions of sin, and forsake your former evil company, and betake yourself to the company of those that fear God, and will help you in the way to heaven. (3) Be specially careful to spend the Lord's day in holy exercises, both public and private, and lose not one quarter of an hour of any of your time; but especially of that most precious time which God hath given you purposely, that you may set your mind upon him, and be instructed by him, and prepare yourself for your latter end. What say you to these things? Will you do this presently, or at least so much of it as you can? Will you give me a promise to this effect, and study henceforth to keep that promise?'

And here be sure, if you can, to get their promise, and engage them to amendment, especially to use the means of grace, and to change their company, and to forsake their sins, because these are more within their reach; and in this way they may wait for the accomplishing of that change that is not yet wrought. And do this solemnly, reminding them of the presence of God who heareth their promises, and who will expect the performance of them; and when you afterward have opportunity, you may remind them of their promise.

9. At the dismissing of them, do these two things:

(1) Mollify their minds again by a few words, deprecating anything like offence. For example: 'I pray you, take it not

ill that I have put you to this trouble, or dealt thus freely
with you. It is as little pleasure to me as to you. If I did not
know these things to be true and necessary, I would have
spared this labour to myself and you; but I know that we
shall be here together but a little while: We are almost at the
world to come already; and therefore it is time for us all to
look about us, and see that we be ready when God shall call
us.'

(2) As you may not soon have an opportunity to speak with
the same persons, set them in the way of perfecting what you
have begun. Engage the master of each family to call all his
family to repeat, every Lord's day, what they have learned of
the catechism; and to continue this practice till they have all
learned it perfectly: and when they have done so, still to
continue to hear them regularly recite it, that they may not
forget it; for, even to the most judicious, it will be an excellent
help to have in memory a Sum of the Christian Religion, as
to matter, method, and words.

As to the rulers of families themselves, or those that are
under such masters as will not help them, if they have learned
some part of the catechism only, engage them either to come
again to you (though before their course) when they have
learned the rest, or else to go to some able experienced neighbour, and repeat it to him; and do you take the assistance of
such persons, when you cannot have time yourself.

10. Have the names of all your parishioners by you in a book;
and when they come and repeat the catechism, note in your
book who come, and who do not; and who are so grossly
ignorant as to be unfit for the Lord's supper and other holy
communion, and who not: and as you perceive the necessities
of each, so deal with them for the future. But as to those that
are utterly obstinate, and will not come to you, nor be instructed by you, deal with them as the obstinate despisers of
instruction should be dealt with, in regard to sealing and
confirming ordinances; which is, to avoid them, and not to
hold holy or familiar communion with them in the Lord's
supper or other ordinances. And though some reverend
brethren are for admitting their children to baptism (and

offended with me for contradicting it), yet so cannot I, nor shall I dare to do it upon any pretences of their ancestors' faith, or of a dogmatical faith of these rebellious parents.

11. Through the whole course of your conference with them, see that the manner as well as the matter be suited to the end. And concerning the manner observe these particulars:

(1) That you make a difference according to the character of the persons whom you have to deal with. To the youthful, you must lay greater shame on sensual voluptuousness, and show them the nature and necessity of mortification. To the aged, you must do more to disgrace this present world, and make them apprehensive of the nearness of their change, and the aggravations of their sin, if they shall live and die in ignorance or impenitency. To inferiors and the young, you must be more free; to superiors and elders, more reverent. To the rich, you must show the vanity of this world; and the nature and necessity of self-denial; and the damnableness of preferring the present state to the next; together with the necessity of improving their talents in doing good to others. To the poor, you must show the great riches of glory which are offered to them in the gospel, and how well present comfort may be spared when everlasting joy may be got. Those sins must also be most insisted on which each one's age, or sex, or temperament, or calling and employment in the world, doth most incline them to; as in females, loquacity, evil speeches, passion, malice, pride; in males, drunkenness, ambition, &c.

(2) Be as condescending, familiar, and plain as possible, with those that are of weaker capacity.

(3) Give them Scripture proof of all you say, that they may see that it is not you only, but God by you that speaketh to them.

(4) Be as serious as you can in the whole exercise, but especially in the applicatory part. I scarce fear anything more, than that some careless ministers will slubber over the work, and do all superficially and without life, and destroy this as they do all other duties, by turning it into a mere formality; putting a few cold questions to their people, and giving them

two or three cold words of advice, without any life and feeling in themselves, and not likely to produce any feeling in the hearers. But surely he that valueth souls, and knoweth what an opportunity is before him, will go through the exercise with deep seriousness, and will be as earnest with them as for life or death.

(5) To this end, I should think it very necessary that, both before and in the work, we take special pains with our own hearts, to excite and strengthen our belief of the truth of the gospel, and of the invisible glory and misery that are to come. I am confident this work will exceedingly try the strength of our belief. For he that is but superficially a Christian, and not sound at bottom, will likely feel his zeal quite fail him, especially when the duty is grown common, for want of a belief of the things of which he is to treat. An affected hypocritical fervency will not hold out long in duties of this kind. A pulpit shall have more of it, than a conference with poor ignorant souls. For the pulpit is the hypocritical minister's stage: there, and in the press, and in other public acts, where there is room for ostentation, you shall have his best, perhaps his all. It is other kind of men that must effectually do the work now in hand.

(6) It is, therefore, very meet that we prepare ourselves for it by secret prayer; and, if time would permit, and there be many together, it were well if we began and ended with a short prayer with our people.

(7) Carry on all, even the most earnest passages, with clear demonstrations of love to their souls, and make them feel through the whole, that you aim at nothing but their salvation. Avoid all harsh, discouraging language.

(8) If you have not time to deal so fully with each individual as is here directed, then omit not the most necessary parts. Take several of them together who are friends, and who will not seek to divulge each other's weaknesses, and speak to them in common as much as concerneth all. Only the examinations of their knowledge and state, and of their convictions of sin and misery, and special directions to them, must be used to the individuals alone; but take heed of slubbering it over

with an unfaithful laziness, or by being too brief, without a real necessity.

12. Lastly, If God enable you, extend your charity to those of the poorest sort, before they part from you. Give them somewhat towards their relief and for the time that is thus taken from their labours, especially for the encouragement of them that do best. And to the rest, promise them so much when they have learned the catechism. I know you cannot give what you have not, but I speak to them that can.

And now, brethren, I have done with my advice, and leave you to the practice. Though the proud may receive it with scorn, and the selfish and slothful with distaste, or even indignation, I doubt not but God will use it, in despite of the opposition of sin and Satan, to the awakening of many of his servants to their duty, and the promoting of the work of a right reformation; and that his blessing will accompany the present undertaking, for the saving of many a soul, the peace of you that undertake and perform it, the exciting of his servants throughout the nation to second you, and the increase of the purity and the unity of his churches. *Amen*